T0214066

Communications in Computer and Information Science 1126

Commenced Publication in 2007
Founding and Former Series Editors:
Phoebe Chen, Alfredo Cuzzocrea, Xiaoyong Du, Orhun Kara, Ting Liu,
Krishna M. Sivalingam, Dominik Ślęzak, Takashi Washio, Xiaokang Yang,
and Junsong Yuan

More information about this series at http://www.springer.com/series/7899

Dana Simian · Laura Florentina Stoica (Eds.)

Modelling and Development of Intelligent Systems

6th International Conference, MDIS 2019
Sibiu, Romania, October 3–5, 2019
Revised Selected Papers

 Springer

Editors
Dana Simian
Lucian Blaga University of Sibiu
Sibiu, Romania

Laura Florentina Stoica
Lucian Blaga University of Sibiu
Sibiu, Romania

ISSN 1865-0929   ISSN 1865-0937 (electronic)
Communications in Computer and Information Science
ISBN 978-3-030-39236-9   ISBN 978-3-030-39237-6 (eBook)
https://doi.org/10.1007/978-3-030-39237-6

This Springer imprint is published by the registered company Springer Nature Switzerland AG
The registered company address is: Gewerbestrasse 11, 6330 Cham, Switzerland

Preface

This volume contains selected, refereed papers, presented at the 6th International Conference on Modelling and Development of Intelligent Systems (MDIS 2019), which was held during October 3–5, 2019, in Sibiu, Romania. The conference was organized by the Research Center in Informatics and Information Technology (ITI) and the Department of Mathematics and Informatics from the Faculty of Sciences, Lucian Blaga University of Sibiu (LBUS), Romania. This edition of the conference was partially supported by the HPI Knowledge Transfer Institute at LBUS.

The topic of the MDIS 2019 conference aligned with a research area that is currently of major interest. Intelligent systems development is an area that has developed and diversified significantly in recent years. The Recommendation on Artificial Intelligence (AI) – the first intergovernmental standard on AI – was adopted by the Organization for Economic Cooperation and Development (OECD) Council at Ministerial level on May 22, 2019, and Romania is in the process of elaborating the first AI strategy, according to this recommendation. In this context, the importance of international forums allowing the exchange of ideas in all problems concerning AI is increasing at global level.

The purpose of MDIS 2019 was to bring together scientists, researchers, academics, IT specialists, and students to present and discuss original results on current theoretical and practical problems in fields related to modelling and development of intelligent systems. Original contributions ranging from concepts and theoretical developments to advanced technologies and innovative applications were presented. Specific topics of interest included, but were not restricted to, evolutionary algorithms, evolutionary computing, genetic algorithms and their applications, data mining, machine learning, intelligent systems for decision support, robotics, knowledge based systems, computational and conceptual models, pattern recognition, e-learning, swarm intelligence, metaheuristics and applications, hybrid computation for artificial vision, modelling and optimization of dynamic systems, adaptive systems, multiagent systems, and mathematical models for development of intelligent systems.

The invited plenary speakers and their lectures were:

- Lyubomyr Demkiv, "Intelligent Real-Time Control of Ground Robots"
- George Eleftherakis, "Using Primitive Brains to Achieve Emergent Smart Solutions"
- Milan Tuba, "Swarm Intelligence Applied to Medical Image Analysis"

All submitted papers underwent a thorough double-blind peer review. Each paper was reviewed by at least three independent reviewers, chosen based on their qualifications and field of expertise.

This volume contains 13 selected papers submitted by authors from 12 countries.

We thank all the participants for their interesting talks and discussions. We also thank the Scientific Committee members and all the other reviewers for their help in reviewing the submitted papers and for their contributions to the scientific success of the conference and to the quality of this proceedings volume.

December 2019   Dana Simian
                                                      Laura Florentina Stoica

Organization

General Chair

Dana Simian   Lucian Blaga University of Sibiu, Romania

Scientific Committee

Kiril Alexiev	Bulgarian Academy of Sciences, Bulgaria
Alina Bărbulescu	Ovidius University of Constanţa, Romania
Lasse Berntzen	Buskerud and Vestfold University College, Norway
Charul Bhatnagar	Institute of Engineering and Technology - GLA University, India
Florian Boian	Babeş-Bolyai University, Romania
Peter Braun	University of Applied Sciences Würzburg-Schweinfurt, Germany
Manuel Campos Martinez	University of Murcia, Spain
Steve Cassidy	Macquarie University, Australia
Dan Cristea	Alexandru Ioan Cuza University, Romania
Gabriela Czibula	Babeş-Bolyai University, Romania
Daniela Dănciulescu	University of Craiova, Romania
Thierry Declerck	German Research Center for Artificial Intelligence, Germany
Lyubomyr Demkiv	Lviv National Polytechnic University, Ukraine
Alexiei Dingli	University of Malta, Malta
Oleksandr Dorokhov	Kharkiv National University of Economics, Ukraine
George Eleftherakis	International Faculty of the University of Sheffield, Greece
Ralf Fabian	Lucian Blaga University of Sibiu, Romania
Stefka Fidanova	Bulgarian Academy of Sciences, Bulgaria
Ulrich Fiedler	Bern University of Applied Science, Switzerland
Martin Fränzle	Carl von Ossietzky University of Oldenburg, Germany
Amir Gandomi	Michigan State University, USA
Dejan Gjorgjevikj	Ss. Cyril and Methodius University in Skopje, Republic of Macedonia
Andrina Granić	University of Split, Croatia
Katalina Grigorova	University of Ruse, Bulgaria
Masafumi Hagiwara	Keio University, Japan
Axel Hahn	Carl von Ossietzky University of Oldenburg, Germany
Raka Jovanovic	Hamad bin Khalifa University, Qatar
Saleema JS	Christ University, India
Adnan Khashman	European Centre for Research and Academic Affairs, Cyprus

Plenary Lecture 1

Intelligent Real-Time Control of Ground Robots

Lyubomyr Demkiv

Lviv Polytechnic National University, Robotics Lead at SoftServe Inc.,
Lviv, Ukraine
demkivl@gmail.com

Abstract. The motion strategy for a ground robot significantly depends on the type of the terrain. Response time for tire-terrain interaction is crucial factor for the mobility of the robot. However, agile control of the robot requires not only the fast-responding controller, but also a state observer that is capable to provide necessary information about sensor data to the controller. Application of hybrid control strategies are beneficial for the mobility of the robot and will be discussed during the presentation.

Brief Biography of the Speaker: Lyubomyr Demkiv received his PhD in 2006 in Numerical Mathematics and ScD in 2019 in Control Engineering. Since 2006, he is Associate Professor at Lviv Polytechnic National University. Since 2018, he is with SoftServe Inc. where he presently works as Robotics Lead. His research field is intelligent control of dynamical systems.

Plenary Lecture 2

Using Primitive Brains to Achieve Emergent Smart Solutions

George Eleftherakis

The University of Sheffield International Faculty, CITY College,
Thessaloniki, Greece
eleftherakis@city.academic.gr

Abstract. Either for or against the validity of Kurzweil's law, it is a fact that technology accelerates at an astonishing pace achieving breathtaking results in any kind of human activity. The Internet of Things, the Cloud, Fog and Edge computing, the daily increasing visions for smarter systems following the advancements in machine learning, and many more technological innovations lead to more demanding requirements than in previous decades for emergent applications of extreme complexity. A promising solution to deal with such complexity is to employ systems that exhibit self* properties, composed by simple agents that communicate and interact following simple protocols achieving desirable emergent properties that allow smart solutions in dynamic environments of extreme complexity. Nature, through millions of years of evolution, has many systems like that to exhibit. Studying systems of agents with primitive brains that demonstrate remarkable self* properties that emerge and are not explicitly engineered could prove of great value regardless of the required effort. Imitating similar behaviors in artificial systems could offer smart solutions to problems exhibiting high-level complexity that seemed unsolvable, or are solved under very restricting and concrete conditions. This presentation will present and discuss experiences studying ants, large-bodied animals, bees, hornets, focusing on the latest study of frogs and how their mating strategies could potentially lead to smart solutions in acoustic scene analysis field, disaster management, and many other complex dynamic systems.

Brief Biography of the Speaker: George Eleftherakis is an Associate Professor and the Director of the PhD program at the University of Sheffield International Faculty, CITY College, in Thessaloniki, Greece. He has authored more than 95 publications on the interface of computer science, biology, and engineering. His honors include receiving the Senate Award for Sustained Excellence in Learning and Teaching from the University of Sheffield. Eleftherakis is a Senior ACM member and has been a member of the administration board of the Greek Computer Society since 2002. Since 2013, he has been the Chair of ACM's Committee of European Chapter Leaders and a member of the Advisory Committee of ACM-W Europe Council, participating actively in all womENcourage conferences in Europe. He is also the Faculty Advisor for the City College ACM-W Student Chapter at the University of Sheffield International Faculty. His research is in the wider area of software engineering, and, more specifically, nature-inspired computing. His PhD in Formal Methods and Bachelor in Physics made him realize that computing has reached an extreme level of continuously increasing complexity following an extreme rate of technological advancement, and led him to investigate natural systems exhibiting emergence (the study of how collective properties arise from the properties of parts). This work tried to establish a well-defined, disciplined, scientific way to perform research on natural systems. It established a framework to study diverse biological systems, such as the herding behavior of large animals, as well as the characteristics of ants, bees, frogs, and other systems found in nature. All of these systems exhibited emergence and achieved some remarkable properties, such as self-adaptation, self-organization, etc., that would be desirable in artificial systems. His research investigates ways of modelling artificial solutions mimicking those behaviors inherent in natural systems to achieve artificial systems that were self-adaptive and self-organizing. An architecture for IoT solutions in dynamic environments, based on the initial abstract bio-inspired overlay network proposal called EDBO, and its implementation as middleware, was a concrete outcome of this work. Currently, he is applying these findings to health monitoring, with a focus on chronic diseases, and on acoustic scene analysis.

Plenary Lecture 3

Swarm Intelligence Applied to Medical Image Analysis

Milan Tuba[1,2]

[1] Vice-Rector for International Relations, Singidunum University,
Belgrade, Serbia
[2] Head of the Department for Mathematical Sciences,
State University of Novi Paza, Novi Pazar, Serbia
tuba@matf.bg.ac.rs

Abstract. Digital images introduced big changes in the world. It is significantly easier to make and process digital images than analog ones. Besides using digital images in everyday life, they are an irreplaceable part of numerous scientific areas such as medicine. Images have been used in medicine for over a century but transition from analog to digital images has brought a true revolution in the diagnostic process. Before digital images, medical image analysis depended on physicians' knowledge, experience but also on current psychophysical state of the experts, their visual acuity, concentration, etc. Digital images drastically simplified the process of medical image analysis since various digital image processing algorithms can significantly speed up and automatize analysis and diagnostics and moreover, computer-aided systems enable objective detection of small changes in digital images of body parts and tissues, even the ones that are not visible to the naked human eye. Applications of medical image processing include tasks such as image enhancement, segmentation, registration, anomaly detection, etc. These applications commonly contain hard optimization problems that need to be solved. Swarm intelligence algorithms, a class of nature-inspired algorithms, have been proved to be very efficient for tackling this class of problems. In the past decades, many different swarm intelligence algorithms have been proposed and applied to various real-world problems, especially to applications of computer-aided diagnostic systems and medical digital image analysis. Examples of successful applications of swarm intelligence algorithms to the medical image processing and analysis problems will be presented in this talk.

Brief Biography of the Speaker: Milan Tuba is the Vice-Rector for International Relations at Singidunum University, Belgrade, and Head of the Department for Mathematical Sciences at State University of Novi Pazar. He received B. S. in Mathematics, M. S. in Mathematics, M. S. in Computer Science, M. Ph. in Computer Science, Ph. D. in Computer Science from University of Belgrade and New York University. From 1983 to 1994 he was in the USA, first as a graduate student and teaching and research assistant at Vanderbilt University in Nashville and Courant Institute of Mathematical Sciences, New York University, and later as Assistant Professor of Electrical Engineering at Cooper Union School of Engineering, New York. During that time he was the founder and director of Microprocessor Lab and VLSI Lab, leader of scientific projects and theses supervisor. From 1994 he was

Assistant Professor of Computer Science and Director of Computer Center at University of Belgrade, from 2001 Associate Professor, Faculty of Mathematics, University of Belgrade, from 2004 a Professor of Computer Science and Dean of the College of Computer Science, Megatrend University Belgrade, and from 2014 Dean of the Graduate School of Computer Science at John Naisbitt University. He was teaching more than 20 graduate and undergraduate courses, from VLSI Design and Computer Architecture to Computer Networks, Operating Systems, Image Processing, Calculus, and Queuing Theory. His research interests include heuristic optimizations applied to computer networks, image processing, and combinatorial problems. Prof. Tuba is the author or co-author of more than 150 scientific papers and co-editor or member of the editorial board or scientific committee of number of scientific journals and conferences, as well as member of the ACM, IEEE, AMS, SIAM, and IFNA.

Contents

Machine Learning

Adaptive Systems

A Model of a Weighted Agent System for Personalised E-Learning Curriculum

Ufuoma Chima Apoki[1(✉)], Soukaina Ennouamani[2],
Humam K. Majeed Al-Chalabi[3], and Gloria Cerasela Crisan[1,4]

[1] Faculty of Computer Science, Alexandru Ioan Cuza University, Iasi, Romania
apoki.ufuoma@info.uaic.ro
[2] National School of Applied Sciences, Ibn Zohr University, Agadir, Morocco
soukaina.ennouamani@edu.uiz.ac.ma
[3] Faculty of Automatics, Computer Science and Electronics, University of Craiova,
Craiova, Romania
hemoomajeed@gmail.com
[4] Faculty of Sciences, Vasile Alecsandri University of Bacau, Bacau, Romania
ceraselacrisan@ub.ro

Abstract. Progressive developments in the world of Information and Communications Technology open up many frontiers in the educational sector. One of such is adaptive e-learning systems, which is currently attracting a lot of research and development. Several conceptualisations and implementations rely on single parameters, or at most three or four parameters. This is not sufficient to account for the wide range of factors which can affect the learning process in an unconventional learning environment such as the web. Being able to choose relevant parameters for personalisation in different learning scenarios is vital to accommodate a wide range of these factors. In this paper, we'll do a review of the basic concepts and components of an adaptive e-learning system. Afterwards, we'll present a model of an adaptive e-learning system which generates a specialised curriculum for a learner based on a multi-parameter approach, thereby allowing for more choices in the process of creating a personalised and learner-oriented experience for such user. This will involve assembling (and/or suggesting) learning resources encompassed in a general curriculum and adapting it to specific personalities and preferences of users. The degree of adaptation (of the curriculum) is dependent on a weighted algorithm matching user features (relevant in each learning scenario) to the corresponding features of available learning resources.

Keywords: Personalised online learning environments ·
Personalisation parameters · Personalised curriculum · Software agents

1 Introduction

As learning is an essential human process, it has attracted a lot of research interest for many decades. Having access to education, which is a process that

© Springer Nature Switzerland AG 2020
D. Simian and L. F. Stoica (Eds.): MDIS 2019, CCIS 1126, pp. 3–17, 2020.
https://doi.org/10.1007/978-3-030-39237-6_1

stimulates knowledge, is a very potent means of diminishing disadvantage, ending poverty, and lessening disparity according to a Global Education Monitoring (GEM) Report, 2016 [1]. Because of the importance of education, a lot of effort has been put into e-learning research and development in the last few decades. In this context, various proposals and systems have been developed and implemented. Also, many concepts and notions related to education have been introduced and spread.

Formal education and learning is usually achieved through a sequence of activities encompassed in a curriculum, and although there is no generally accepted definition of what a *curriculum of learning* is [2], it has evolved from the traditional sense of a sequence of learning resources, concepts, and syllabus given to a student to achieve a goal. The definition of a curriculum, which will be most applicable (from different thoughts) in this context, is the cumulative experiences a student goes through in an educational process to achieve a target [2]. This is a very dynamic definition that can be applied to both traditional and online learning environments and, most especially, considers *change* as part of the planning process in achieving effective learning.

For a long period, formal learning was classroom-based; however, as learning evolves and with the introduction of e-learning possibilities, the physical interactions between teachers and learners have the possibility of being much reduced. With continuous advances in the Information and Communications Technology (ICT) sector, and the availability of ubiquitous internet-enabled devices and systems, online education and distance learning are experiencing unprecedented reforms in a bid to provide education for all. However, being able to successfully transit from well-established traditional systems of learning to e-learning systems has its complexity and has brought up several and interesting challenges. According to Fischer [3], the process of modelling systems, which interact with users, has a fundamental need to make such systems (e-learning systems in this case) able to deliver experiences that are peculiar to the user's background learning experience and intended goals. He goes on to say that it involves conveying information to users in the most appropriate form and time, and at any time, place, or manner.

When discussing e-learning in recent times, a lot of focus is placed on the learner as each student/pupil has different skills, preferences, and needs. Several pedagogues and psychologists distinguish a part of these differences as individual learning styles [4] and recommend the possibility of learning to be adaptive to accommodate such individualities. In other words, a learning process should involve adaptive and personalised learning in a manner that suits the learner's preferences, characteristics, and intended goals. To achieve such personalisation, adaptive e-learning systems are created to present information in a peculiar way to each learner. The system interacts with the user and collects information statically or dynamically [5] and adapts the learning content or presentation to suit the user (based on selected parameters).

In an online learning environment, there are a multitude of factors that can affect the learning process and creating personalised learning paths based on one, two, or three parameters might not achieve true satisfaction for the learner. However, creating learning paths for all possible affecting parameters would result in an exponential number of possibilities as more parameters are included. A solution to this will be taking into account as many affecting parameters, but selecting the most important ones in each learning scenario, according to the user's needs and available learning resources.

In this context, this paper proposes a model of an adaptive learning system that can assemble learning resources (such as text, video, and audio files) in a learning platform, encompassed in a general curriculum, and adapt it to specific preferences and needs of learners as the learning scenario requires. The rest of this paper is structured as follows: Sect. 2 discusses the main aspects of adaptive e-learning systems; Sect. 3 presents a state-of-the-art of adaptive educational systems; Sect. 4 proposes a model of an adaptive learning system which creates personalised curricula for users based on their preferences, characteristics, and goals; finally, conclusions and future work come in Sect. 5.

2 Adaptive E-Learning Systems

Over the past few decades, there has been an increased interest in the possibilities of adaptive systems. In the early '90s, research ideas were centred around the use of hypertext and user-modelling to achieve adaptation [5] as a result of the degree of improvement such studies attained.

Currently, tremendous researches, works, and studies seek new improvements to adapt the behaviour of hypertext systems to users in a suitable and personalised way, using parameters such as student's learning performance, learning style, interest, previous knowledge level, etc. [6]. In [7], the authors listed 16 parameters, which are usually used for adaptation in e-learning systems. They include information-seeking task, preference of media resources, learning goals[1], learner's knowledge level, language, level of participation of students, level of motivation, pedagogical approach, cognitive traits, learning styles and cycles (Felder-Silverman, Honey-Mumford, Kolb, La Garanderie), etc. The ultimate aim of such different measures in adaptation is to enhance the quality of learning such that the learning process can be facilitated and individual student satisfaction can be achieved (as much as possible) [8].

By modelling learning environments based on students' specific needs and characteristics that are classified in various categories [9], adaptive learning systems attempt to enhance their experiences over the learning platforms as well as hypermedia systems. For this reason, many links are created between learner characteristics and available learning resources, taking into consideration the condition of making learning flexible and available using a dynamic design [10].

---

[1] *learning goals*, used in this context (and hereafter), represents Bloom's Taxonomy of educational objectives in the cognitive domain, which include knowledge, comprehension, application, analysis, and synthesis.

In the following subsections, the important components in the architecture of an adaptive system, the adaptation process, and the role of learning objects will be discussed.

2.1   Components of an Adaptive E-Learning System

To achieve personalisation in an e-learning system, it is pertinent to ask the following questions [11]: 1. "What is the cause for which personalisation is made?" 2. "What is going to be adapted?" 3. "What rules do we apply to achieve adaptation?" These questions specify the source of adaptation, the target of adaptation, and adaptation path, respectively. Although there are different approaches taken in designing adaptive systems, three main models are usually required [5]; they include the learner model, domain model, and adaptation model. Other components such as a pedagogical model and interface model can be added in a more robust architecture [12]. Figure 1 shows the architecture of an adaptive system (with a supportive software agent).

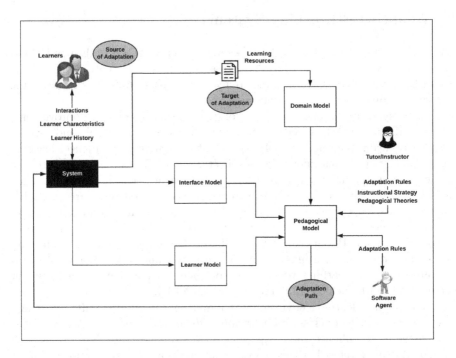

Fig. 1. Architecture of an adaptive e-learning system with software agents

Source of Adaptation. The source of adaptation seeks to answer the question of what the cause for personalisation is. The source of adaptation, as described in [11], could be from the characteristics of the learner, the interactivity between learner and learning environment, or a combination of both learner characteristics and interactivity. These are used in modelling the learner.

Learner Model. The learner model extracts and stores information (characteristics, history, and interactivity) which is specific to each user. The characteristics of learners have been widely considered as can be seen by the various parameters which have been used to adapt e-learning systems from the theoretical and empirical studies presented in Sect. 3. The characteristics which are chosen for adaptation are dependent on available content and design of the system. Thus, the goal will be to collect significant information which can be used to provide a different experience for each user, as not all features can be incorporated in each learning scenario [13].

When modelling learners, different approaches can be taken. A first approach is to create a static model of the user with characteristics which are considered to be stable [11]. These include information like educational history of learner, learning style, and cognitive style. Another approach is modelling the user with characteristics which are 'unstable' or change often with time (dynamic). These include information such as learner's level of knowledge, learning goals, and emotional states (as discussed in [14]). Learner models can also combine both static and dynamic characteristics. This creates a model which is dynamically updated as the learner interacts with the system and proceeds in a curriculum. Learner models can also be designed using machine learning approaches because of the complexities involved in the dynamic relationships between learner characteristics [15]. Some techniques usually employed include k-Nearest Neighbours (k-NN) [16], neural networks [6,17], decision network [17], and fuzzy logic [14].

Target of Adaptation. The target of adaptation seeks to answer the question of what is to be adapted, given the parameters derived from the source of adaptation. Adaptable targets could be the learning material, which is mostly applied in both theoretical and empirical models [11]. This can be in varying levels of difficulty of the content, according to specific learning goals, in different languages, or different multimedia formats. As regards content, its presentation could also be a target of adaptation. The same learning content could be presented in different colours, fonts, granularity, etc.

Adaptation could also be in the form of system support/feedback. Another target of adaptation could be in collaboration. Learners with similar features such as level of knowledge, geographical area, language, etc., can be put in the same group for collaborative learning as described in [15].

Finally, adaptation targets could be in navigation while interacting with the system. Different features of learners would prompt different options while navigating through the local learning system or when redirected to external learning sources outside the system.

Domain Model. The targets of adaptation usually form the domain model, which is a characterisation of the knowledge which is to be instructed, and the relationships between the knowledge elements in the domain.

Digital Learning Resources and Learning Objects. In the context of e-learning systems, the distinction between learning resources and learning objects (LO) is rather unclear. Generally speaking, a learning resource refers to materials that are included in the context of a course or curriculum to assist a learner in accomplishing educational goals. Being in digital or non-digital forms, they include text, video, games, graphics, audio, etc. A learning object, however, is a modular resource, in a digital form, offline or web-based, that can be used to support learning activities and objectives. Learning objects are usually expected to conform to some standard such as SCORM (Shareable Content Object Reference Model) [18] for reusability and portability between different learning platforms. SCORM defines standards and specifications for web-based educational technologies, also giving learning objects key characteristics of accessibility and durability. A learning object must be instructional, have intended learning outcomes, and should be interactive. Examples of learning objects include text, videos, webinars, simulation, interactive multimedia, discussions (synchronous and asynchronous), auto-graded objective tests, essays, peer assessments, etc.

A learning object can be further transformed based on given criteria (such as concepts, educational objectives, and learning styles), while adhering to given rules of adaptation that are set in its contextual relationship [19]. It can be broken down to smaller segments, which have increased granularity, or smaller LOs can be aggregated to form a composite LO, which has less granularity than its combining elements.

A segment of a LO is presented in Fig. 2, showing its features, and the relationship between digital learning resources and learning objects. It also shows the relationship between learning objects in the domain.

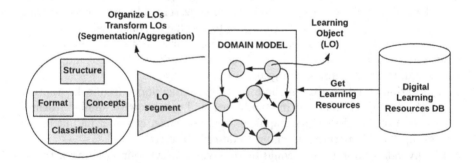

Fig. 2. An LO segment

Interface Model. The tasks of presenting learning materials to the learner in an optimal manner, ensuring proper interaction with the learner, and display configuration are controlled by the Interface model. The two aspects which are usually studied in interface modelling include multimedia content and learner exploration [12]. The interface model functions as an external rendition of the knowledge in the domain model, the rules, strategies, and theories of the peda-gogical model [9].

Adaptation Path. After the questions of what the cause of adaptation is and what is to be adapted are answered, the adaptation path provides the rules and methods for adapting the target to the preferences of the source. When develop-ing the rules of adaptation, content, time, or method are dimensions which are considered [11]. As regards content, attributes such as form, detail, semantic den-sity, display, support, etc., are explored. The factor of time determines whether adaptation is applied statically (at the beginning of the course) or dynamically (as the course progress and current information is retrieved from user). Finally, 'method' regulates who has control over adaptation, and to what level [11]; adap-tation could be controlled by the instructor/tutor, or by the learner, or there could be a form of shared control between instructor and learner.

Pedagogical Model. This model contains a combination of pedagogical the-ories, learning strategies, and adaptation rules which describe the source(s) of adaptation, target(s) of adaptation, and the adaptation path [11]. Sometimes, it is referred to as the adaptation model or tutor/instructional model. The learner model is inputted to the pedagogical model in three stages [12]: epistemic stage (which considers the level of learner's knowledge), behavioural stage (which con-siders the perceivable behaviour of the learner from interactions with the learn-ing system), and personal stage (which considers features such as learning style, learning goals, motivation, etc.). This ensures the solutions to adaptation made by the pedagogical model express the varying needs of each learner.

3   Literature Survey

The following ideas summarise the evolution of learning and its transition from traditional forms to adaptable e-learning systems.

- The traditional role of achieving an educational objective in an institution is through the attendance of classes, more often in a group, in the same geographical location, without individualities being optimally accounted for.
- Achieving a 'learning-for-all' paradigm involves the development of various e-learning systems.
- Personalised and adaptive systems would be effective in the transition between traditional learning and online systems of learning.
- There have been many features that have been sought to characterise person-alisation, which include learning styles, level of knowledge, language, learning goals, motivational level, etc., in modelling adaptive systems.
- Successfully integrating these individual features in an e-learning system is of major interest to recent studies in enhanced learning and system modelling.

There have been several systems and models described in the literature to achieve personalised content and curriculum in e-learning. Many of these models and systems are usually centred on just a single type of personalisation, with very rare considerations of interactions between more than 2 or 3 sources of personalisation [6]. Currently, most adaptation models have been centred around learning styles and learner's level of knowledge. However, to create a robust adaptive system, more features need to be taken into consideration to provide a more satisfying experience.

In the following paragraphs, we'll briefly analyse a few models and systems which achieve personalisation with multi-parameters and pedagogical agents.

A model is proposed in [6] which generates individual learning paths for students based on multiple parameters with machine learning algorithms. Users are modelled with static and dynamic information regarding personal details, user interests, performance results, and log data. The log data provides information to model users based on a self-directed or tutor-directed approach. Learning paths are generated through SPARQL queries. A Query Results Management (QRM) component which supports querying the RDF database, stores the results in a proper format for the machine learning algorithm. Successful learning paths are stored for future use by a Machine Learning Management (MLM) component. Users who have similar features and in similar learning scenarios can be suggested with successful learning paths.

In [7] an architecture of a two-layer adaptive system is described and implemented. The two layers ELP1 and ELP2 allow for the specification and combination of multiple parameters for personalisation. ELP2 (E-learning personalisation 2) is responsible for specifying strategies for personalisation according to user needs. Here, multiple parameters (such as level of knowledge, Felder-Silverman learning style classification, Honey-Mumford learning styles, media preferences, etc.) can be selected and combined from the set of possible factors that can affect learning. Each course is represented by different concepts, and learning objects which are connected to these concepts are grouped into categories according to divergent characteristics. The most influencing parameters for each course are subsequently chosen. ELP1 (E-learning Personalisation 1) is responsible for applying the combined parameters and strategies which were selected. ELP1 + ELP2 personalisation is achieved through web services.

A context-aware system for personalised learning is proposed in [10]. In addition to the learner, domain, and adaptation model, the system has a context module with sensors for getting the attributes of the learner's state and device. The system uses this information in addition to the user's level of knowledge, learning style (Felder-Silverman Model), history of interactions with the system, behaviour, and learning progress to provide personalised content. Learning content in the domain model is arranged in a hierarchical structure of disciplines, subjects, courses, chapters, and learning objects.

A multi-agent system (MAS) model is proposed in [20] capable of creating personalised learning paths according to learner preferences and needs, while monitoring and giving feedback to students in real-time. The architecture comprises of three levels: the first level represents an interaction multi-agent system, the second level is the interface multi-agent system, and the final level is the human agent system (representing the learner and tutor). The Interaction MAS includes agents such as the Profile Blackboard Agent which keeps a model of the learner's history and tracks the learner's performance and competences in the learning environment. The Learning Blackboard Agent tracks information used in adaptation during the learning process. A Course Generator Agent subsequently uses the information from the Profile Blackboard Agent and the Learning Blackboard Agent to present learning content suited to a learner's preferences. The system utilises object Petri nets and blackboard systems.

Another multi-agent system, AILS (Adaptive Intelligent Learning System), implemented with JADE (Java Agent Development Framework) agents is presented in [21]. The learner model comprises information about the student's learning style (Felder-Silverman Model), preferences, learning goals, and other information which can affect the learning process. Six agents provide intelligent support and feedback in AILS. They include an LMS interface manager (which manages communication between the learning platform and other agents), learner assistant agent (which keeps track of the student's learning progress), content adapter agent (applies the adaptive strategies to create personalised content for the learner), profile agent (responsible for managing information about the learner), researcher agent (which tracks concepts related to searches made by learners), and agent manager (responsible for managing agent activities). Strategies for personalisation include content adaptation, presentation adaptation, participation adaptation, and perspective adaptive.

4   Proposed Model

In the previous section, we described the basic components an adaptive system requires. Here, we give a brief description of the proposed system architecture, components, and adaptation process of the Weighted Agent System for Personalised E-Learning Curriculum (WASPEC).

4.1   System Architecture and Component Details

For prototyping the system model, the architecture is composed of (in addition to the basic components described in Sect. 2) an application module and a session monitor.

Learner Model. This stores information about the user, which includes personal information and other features which can be used for personalisation. The information would is stored using an RDF (Resource Description Framework) database [22] which makes it easy for updating user information, keeping track of learning process, and semantic reasoning between user data and the domain model. The initial profiling of the users would include language, learning goals, level of knowledge, learning style, and media preferences. The options of language will be determined by the available learning resources. Learning goals can knowledge, comprehension, or application. Level of knowledge will have the categories of beginner, intermediate, and advanced. For learning style classification, we adopt the Felder-Silverman Model [23] which has the dimensions of active/reflective, sensing/intuitive, visual/verbal, and sequential/global. Media preferences will be either text, image, video, audio, and multimedia.

Domain Model. This is a collection of all learning resources, tutorials, and assessment tests.

The learning resources in the knowledge base repository should have the potential to be characterised by specific features. A learning resource of type T (text, video, audio, presentation, etc.) is characterised by a set of features (metadata descriptions), which could include language, educational level, format, etc., culled from the Learning Object Metadata (LOM) standard [24]. Therefore, the features, F_T, can be represented as a finite vector of pairs, (f_i^T, w_i), in which f_i^T is the feature, and w_i is the relevance/weight.

$$F_T = <(f_1^T, w_1), ...(f_n^T, w_n)> \tag{1}$$

The primary properties of these selected features (which describe the learning object) should be of relevance with respect to the learning objectives, and have the potential to be automatically extracted from the learning resources. The learning objects created at the end of the transformation should, therefore, be characterised by a list of features for each type which also align with the corresponding features of the learning resource from which it was created.

The knowledge base can, hence, be organised in an ontology (a hierarchy of concepts and learning objectives). For upward extensibility of the ontology, a learning object representing a concept, C, can be added, which has features that characterise the concepts below it. Each learning object can then be segmented based on topics, concepts, or learning objectives. For each object O, of type T, there are a finite set of related segments S_i^O.

$$O_T = S_1^O, S_2^O, ...S_m^O \tag{2}$$

Each segment, S_i^O, should be characterised by the set of features F_T, of that particular object type.

Pedagogical Model. This model provides an instructional strategy by defining what learning content in the system can be adapted and how it is adapted [11], thereby generating an optimum learning object (from the domain model) and path for a learning scenario with the user data assembled from the learner model. An important addition to this model are pedagogical agents which will act as tutor assistants. Pedagogical agents have the characteristics of being semi-autonomous and can achieve goals which have not been explicitly predefined through programs. The pedagogical agents will be implemented with JADE

(Java Agent Development Framework) [25] which conforms to FIPA (Foundation for Intelligent Physical Agents) standards for intelligent agents.

Adaptive Module. This component is similar to the interface model described in Sect. 2. It contains the rules of adaptation from the pedagogical model. For implementation purposes, it is necessary to separate operations of the pedagogical model and adaptive module to ensure a straightforward addition of new adaptation functionalities [4].

Session Monitor. This component keeps track of the interactions between the learner and the system. This information is used to update the learner model after every learning session and also used (with the rules of adaptation and instructional strategy) to load the next session for the learner [4]. Log data about learner's actions, progress, and errors after assessment can be subsequently used to determine successful paths for other users with similar characteristics through machine learning techniques.

4.2   Adaptation Process

As shown in Fig. 3, the learning cycle begins with an interaction between the user and system to extract user details and preferences of the user. Such information can be obtained through tests, forms, or questionnaires. This stage in which the information collected is used to create the user model is regarded as the acquisition stage of adaptive learning process [26].

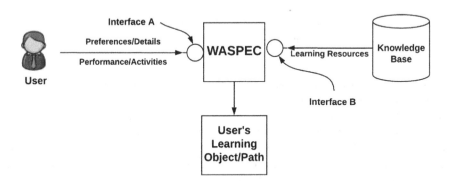

Fig. 3. Weighted Agent System for Personalised E-Learning Curriculums

The next step involves modelling extracted preferences and features of the learner model based on predetermined weights.

Therefore, a specific user, U, can be expressed by a finite set of paired elements, f and w, where f represents a user feature, and w the corresponding weight (salience) of the user feature in the configuration of that particular user, U.

If F_U represents the finite set, then,

$$F_U = (f_1, w_1), (f_2, w_2), ...(f_n, w_n) \qquad (3)$$

$$\sum_{i=1}^{n} w_i = 1 \qquad (4)$$

In the next step of the adaptation process, the digital learning resources are transformed to learning objects with semantic annotation. The transformation of the learning resources is necessary for reuse, easy handling by the system, and semantic mapping between user features and learning objects.

We are currently working with Moodle [27], which is an open-source learning management system. Moodle, by default, is not meant for personalised courses, but has several options for extendibility, and one of such is web services, which offers a robust solution for interoperability between different applications. Although Moodle stores its data in a relational database, a platform such as D2RQ [28] offers possibilities of assessing such databases as read-only RDF graphs. This technology, hence, allows for semantic queries to be written, tested, and executed using SPARQL [29], which is an RDF query language. Protégé [30], an open source ontology editor also provides a framework for integration of external components and declaration of semantic rules (Fig. 4).

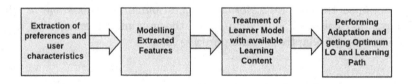

Fig. 4. Adaptation process

For a given learning path for a student, the learning objects which are characterised by features, F_T in (1), are ranked with respect to the features, F_U, obtained from the user. A selection (which forms the personalised curriculum) for the specific user, PC_U, is then made by the system of the most relevant objects required to achieve the learning objective. The selection, PC_U, should be organised and presented in an efficient way for the user to derive the best gain possible. For a user to successfully learn about a concept, C, it is imperative that he/she should know everything below C in the ontology.

As mentioned previously, learner features will be given predetermined weights as regards their importance in the personalisation process. We attribute language (L) a weight of 5, learning goal (LG) 4, level of knowledge (LoK) 3, learning style (LS) 2, and media preference (MP) 1.

Therefore, each user can be expressed according to (3) and (4) as:

$$F_U = (L, 0.33), (LG, 0.27), (LoK, 0.2), (LS, 0.13), (MP, 0.07) \qquad (5)$$

If we have a curriculum composed of 10 modular segments, with features which are relevant to providing personalisation of the user. Each segment is represented by features from the metadata description which are relevant to the learner model.

According to (1), we can assign weights to selected features of each segment as:

$F_T = ((language, 5), (purpose, 4), (keywords, 4), (typical\ learning\ time, 4),$
$(difficulty, 3), (semantic\ density, 3), (learning\ resource\ type, 2), (format, 1)).$

There will be two levels of selection in the personalisation process. The first level is compatibility selection and the next level is the priority selection. The first level determines if the segment is compatible with the user while the next level determines how important the segment is (if it has been selected) to the user preferences. If we have two learners, learner 1 can get a personalised curriculum of $(S_2^O, S_3^O, S_6^O, S_5^O)$ and learner 2 can get of $(S_1^O, S_4^O, S_3^O, S_5^O, S_6^O, S_9^O, S_10^O)$.

It should be noted that as much as there is a natural sequence in the order in which a curriculum should be followed, defined by prerequisite and competence relationships, there exists the possibility for an unnatural selection according to relevance. Therefore, in the sequence, it might be necessary to have S_2^O before S_3^O; however, a user can also have S_6^O before S_5^O. It becomes more interesting and more relevant to the process of personalisation when user parameters such as motivation, time, context, user platform are integrated to the set of user features. At such point, a user can have different number of features from another user.

5   Conclusion and Future Work

In this paper, we reviewed current approaches in the development of adaptive e-learning systems. We discussed the basic components and models required in the design of such systems. In the process of reviewing and analysing studies and models over the last two decades, it has been observed that most models specific to courses incorporating two or three parameters for personalisation. If online learning is to be effective in accommodating learner differences as traditional learning environments, different parameters should be chosen for different learning scenarios in the modelling process of the learner. This also requires that dynamic factors which could affect learning be taken into consideration such as time, user device, emotional state, etc.

To address some of these challenges, we propose a model which has the ability to incorporate multiple features, and weigh such features in the magnitude of impact in a learning scenario in the adaptation process. We also propose the inclusion of pedagogical agents which should serve as tutor assistants during the learning process.

Future work will describe the implementation of weighted algorithm for adaptation comprehensively and the role of agents in the learning process. Furthermore, the first stage of learner modelling was centred on static features of the user which do not change (or are fixed at learning time). We will incorporate more dynamic features in future which should make adaptivity real-time in the learning process.

References

1. UNESCO Global Education Monitoring Report: Education for people and planet: Creating Sustainable Futures for All, Paris, France (2016)
2. Wiles, J.: Leading Curriculum Development, p. 2. Corwin Press, Thousand Oaks (2008)
3. Fischer, G.: User modeling in human-computer interaction. User Model. User Adapt. Interact. **11**, 65–86 (2001). https://doi.org/10.1023/A:1011145532042
4. Klašnja-Milićević, A., Vesin, B., Ivanović, M., Budimac, Z., Jain, L.C.: E-Learning Systems: Intelligent Techniques for Personalization. Springer, Switzerland (2017). https://doi.org/10.1007/978-3-319-41163-7
5. Ennouamani, S., Mahani, Z.: An overview of adaptive e-learning systems. In: 2017 Eighth International Conference on Intelligent Computing and Information Systems (ICICIS), pp. 342–347. IEEE (2017). https://doi.org/10.1109/INTELCIS. 2017.8260060
6. Chrysoulas, C., Fasli, M.: Building an adaptive e-learning system. In: Proceedings of the 9th International Conference on Computer Supported Education, pp. 375–382. SCITEPRESS - Science and Technology Publications (2017). https://doi.org/ 10.5220/0006326103750382
7. Essalmi, F., Ayed, L.J.B., Jemni, M., Kinshuk, Graf, S.: A fully personalization strategy of E-learning scenarios. Comput. Hum. Behav. **26**, 581–591 (2010). https://doi.org/10.1016/j.chb.2009.12.010
8. Boticario, J.G., Santos, O.C., Van Rosmalen, P.M.: Issues in developing standard-based adaptive learning management systems. Science (80), 2–5 (2005)
9. Phobun, P., Vicheanpanya, J.: Adaptive intelligent tutoring systems for e-learning systems. Procedia Soc. Behav. Sci. **2**, 4064–4069 (2010). https://doi.org/10.1016/ j.sbspro.2010.03.641
10. Ennouamani, S., Mahani, Z.: Designing a practical learner model for adaptive and context-aware mobile learning systems. IJCSNS Int. J. Comput. Sci. Netw. Secur. **18**, 84–93 (2018)
11. Vandewaetere, M., Desmet, P., Clarebout, G.: The contribution of learner characteristics in the development of computer-based adaptive learning environments. Comput. Hum. Behav. **27**, 118–130 (2011). https://doi.org/10.1016/j.chb.2010.07. 038
12. Sampson, D., Karagiannidis, C., Kinshuk, C.: Personalised learning: educational, technological and standardisation perspective. Interact. Educ. Multimed. **4**, 24–39 (2002)
13. Brusilovsky, P., Millán, E.: User models for adaptive hypermedia and adaptive educational systems. In: Brusilovsky, P., Kobsa, A., Nejdl, W. (eds.) The Adaptive Web. LNCS, vol. 4321, pp. 3–53. Springer, Heidelberg (2007). https://doi.org/10. 1007/978-3-540-72079-9_1
14. Hamada, M., Hassan, M.: An enhanced learning style index: implementation and integration into an intelligent and adaptive e-learning system. Eurasia J. Math. Sci. Technol. Educ. **13**, 4449–4470 (2017). https://doi.org/10.12973/eurasia.2017. 00940a
15. Al-Hmouz, A., Shen, J., Yan, J., Al-Hmouz, R.: Enhanced learner model for adaptive mobile learning. In: Proceedings of the 12th International Conference on Information Integration and Web-based Applications and Services - iiWAS 2010, pp. 783–786. ACM Press, New York (2010). https://doi.org/10.1145/1967486.1967614

16. Chang, Y.C., Kao, W.Y., Chu, C.P., Chiu, C.H.: A learning style classification mechanism for e-learning. Comput. Educ. **53**, 273–285 (2009). https://doi.org/10.1016/j.compedu.2009.02.008

17. Red, E.R., Borlongan, H.G.S., Briagas, T.T., Mendoza, M.J.M.: Classification of Students Performance in a Learning Management System Using their eLearning Readiness Attributes. In: 2015 International Conference on e-Commerce, e-Administration, e-Society, e-Education, and e-Technology (e-CASE and e-Tech 2015), pp. 199–211 (2015)

18. Learning object standard - EduTech Wiki. http://edutechwiki.unige.ch/en/Learning_object_standard

19. Guevara, C., Aguilar, J., González-Eras, A.: The model of adaptive learning objects for virtual environments instanced by the competencies. Adv. Sci. Technol. Eng. Syst. J. **2**, 345–355 (2017). https://doi.org/10.25046/aj020344

20. Hammami, S., Mathkour, H.: Adaptive e-learning system based on agents and object Petri nets (AELS-A/OPN). Comput. Appl. Eng. Educ. **23**, 170–190 (2015). https://doi.org/10.1002/cae.21587

21. Serçe, F.C., Alpaslan, F.N., Jain, L.C.: Adaptive intelligent learning system for online learning environments. In: The Handbook on Reasoning-Based Intelligent Systems, pp. 353–387. World Scientific (2013). https://doi.org/10.1142/9789814329484_0014

22. Resource Description Framework (RDF) - W3C Semantic Web. https://www.w3.org/RDF/

23. Felder, R.M., Silverman, L.K.: Learning and teaching styles in engineering education. Eng. Educ. **78**, 674–681 (1988)

24. Institute of Electrical and Electronics Engineers, IEEE Computer Society. Learning Technology Standards Committee, IEEE-SA Standards Board: IEEE Standard for Learning Object Metadata. Institute of Electrical and Electronics Engineers (2002)

25. Bellifemine, F., Caire, G., Trucco, T., Rimassa, G.: JADE programmer's guide (2010)

26. Ennouamani, S., Akharraz, L., Mahani, Z.: Integrating ICT in education: an adaptive learning system based on users' context in mobile environments. In: Farhaoui, Y., Moussaid, L. (eds.) ICBDSDE 2018. SBD, vol. 53, pp. 15–19. Springer, Cham (2019). https://doi.org/10.1007/978-3-030-12048-1_3

27. Moodle. https://moodle.org/

28. D2RQ, Accessing Relational Databases as Virtual RDF Graphs. http://d2rq.org/

29. SPARQL Query Language for RDF, W3C. https://www.w3.org/TR/rdf-sparql-query/

30. Protege, Stanford University. https://protege.stanford.edu/

From Digital Learning Resources to Adaptive Learning Objects: An Overview

Ufuoma Chima Apoki[1(✉)], Humam K. Majeed Al-Chalabi[2],
and Gloria Cerasela Crisan[1,3]

[1] Faculty of Computer Science, Alexandru Ioan Cuza University, Iasi, Romania
`apoki.ufuoma@info.uaic.ro`
[2] Faculty of Automatics, Computer Science and Electronics, University of Craiova,
Craiova, Romania
`hemoomajeed@gmail.com`
[3] Faculty of Sciences, Vasile Alecsandri University of Bacau, Bacau, Romania
`ceraselacrisan@ub.ro`

Abstract. To successfully achieve the goal of providing global access to quality education, the Information and Communications Technology (ICT) sector has provided tremendous advances in virtual/online learning. One of such advances is the availability of digital learning resources. However, to successfully accommodate learner peculiarities and predispositions, traditional online learning is gradually being transformed from a one-size-fits-all paradigm towards personalised learning. This transformation requires that learning resources are treated not as static content, but dynamic entities, which are reusable, portable across different platforms, and ultimately adaptive to user needs. This article takes a review of how digital learning resources are modelled in adaptive hypermedia systems to achieve adaptive learning, and we highlight prospects of future work.

Keywords: Personalised learning · Learning objects · Adaptive learning systems · E-learning · Digital learning resources

1 Introduction

Over the last few decades, learning systems which are computer-based have become web-based to ensure a wider reach to users. As part of this evolution of global access to quality learning resources, a whole industry has been built around e-learning systems to enforce reusability, interchangeability of learning materials, and a path for proprietors to protect their intellectual properties.

However, to successfully achieve this aim of global reach to education, which, according to a United Nations Educational, Scientific, and Cultural Organization (UNESCO) Report, is key to reducing disadvantage, ending poverty, and lessening disparity [1], an educator has to consider factors beyond the features of the learning device [2]. This gives rise to the paradigm of personalised learning, which involves adapting the learning process/experience to suit user needs.

© Springer Nature Switzerland AG 2020
D. Simian and L. F. Stoica (Eds.): MDIS 2019, CCIS 1126, pp. 18–32, 2020.
https://doi.org/10.1007/978-3-030-39237-6_2

This is important as personalised learning is crucial in enabling learners to be motivated and assimilate knowledge more efficiently [3].

In personalised learning, the learning material is mostly used as a target of adaptation in both empirical and theoretical implementation of adaptive educational systems [4,5]. Therefore, the main goal of this paper is to study virtual learning objects (LOs) as they are used in adaptive systems, the standards that allow for interoperability, and to analyse systems that utilise this in the design and modelling process. To achieve this goal, the following questions can be asked: What are learning objects and how do they differ from traditional digital learning resources? How are they modelled in the quest for adaptation in Adaptive Hypermedia Systems (AHS)? What are the standards that should be considered during design?

To answer some of these questions, we studied various publications concerned with adaptive learning content from (but not exclusively limited to) the following online databases: *Google Scholar, Science Direct, IEEE Xplore, ResearchGate, SpringerLink*, and *ACM Portal*. As this concept is quite recent, most articles were from the last two decades. The publications included review articles, empirical models, theoretical proposals, etc. The search items included: "adaptive learning", "personalised e-learning", "adaptive educational systems", "adaptive hypermedia systems", "adaptive learning objects", "personalisation parameters". The publications and adaptive models and systems selected were those in which learning content was treated as dynamic and changing.

Furthermore, in reaction to the questions posed above, this article is structured as follows: Sect. 2 briefly describes AHS and the techniques used in adaptation, with more emphasis on the domain model; Sect. 3 answers the question of what makes a learning resource a learning object; Sect. 4 goes on to discuss Adaptive Learning Objects (ALO) as it is used in state-of-the-art AHS; Sect. 5 analyses related works in the development of ALOs and the paper concludes with Sect. 6 with future prospects and our developing studies and works as regards ALOs.

2 Adaptive Hypermedia Systems

2.1 Adaptivity in Online Learning Environments

The transition between a traditional and an online learning environment has been one area researchers and pedagogues have studied over a long period of time. In a traditional environment, a teacher can assess the factors which might affect learning positively or negatively and can choose the most effective method to proceed considering the background and perceivable features of the group [2]. Researchers have sought to replicate this in the creation of adaptive learning environments.

In [6], the authors describe an adaptive environment as a platform that incorporates soft and hard technologies with an aim of improving the learning experience of users through adaptation. Such environments include Adaptive

Hypermedia Environments, Collaborative Learning Environments, and Simulative/Immersive Environments. Adaptive Hypermedia Environments seek to present learning content in a way that suits a user's educational background, interests, and proclivities [7]. Collaborative Learning Environments provide a method of group learning where learners improve on knowledge by sharing complementary ideas, while Simulative/Immersive Environments (through a set of predefined rules) change according to user actions [6].

In recent times, adaptivity is also complemented by intelligence in online environments as implemented in Intelligent Tutoring Systems (ITS). Such intelligence is achieved through artificial intelligence to provide better support and instruction for learners. Classic examples include intelligent solution analysis (which provides a procedural analysis of solutions to tasks or problems as opposed to right or wrong results of solutions) and problem-solving support (which provides intelligent support to users during tasks). While there might be no clear-cut distinction between adaptive and intelligent learning environments, one difference is that adaptive systems behave differently according to user preferences and needs, while intelligent systems provide the same kind of intelligent tutoring for all users [8].

2.2   Adaptive Educational Hypermedia Systems

An important type of AHS—which will be our main focus—are Adaptive Educational Hypermedia Systems (AEHS). Brusilovsky described these platforms (which have been predominantly web-based since the early 1990s [9]) as systems that provide navigational support to learner-driven acquisition of knowledge in an educational hyperspace, considering the history and features of the user [10]. Another description, provided by [11], is a system which recommends learning content, and changes the presentation and display based on observations from user interactions with the system stored in a user model. The system also has a document space of connected hypermedia educational content.

From these descriptions, we can characterise AEHS as possessing the following basic components: a knowledge hyperspace, a learner model, and adaptive functions. Hence, an AEHS is usually modelled with a learner model (also referred to as student or user model), domain model (also referred to as expert model), and a pedagogical model (also referred to as tutoring, instructional, or adaptation model) [8].

The *learner model* comprises of information which is peculiar to each user through direct questionnaires, tests, or log information from user interaction with the system or other users. It is essential that such information can be used for some sort of personalisation because this model provides input for the pedagogical model of the system [12]. Furthermore, the learner can be modelled in static or dynamic manner regarding the features which are selected [8]. With a static approach, parameters which do not change frequently are used in learner modelling, while a dynamic approach utilises present states and features of learners which change frequently. The *domain model*, from a broad perspective, is a representation of the essential learning content present in the system–the structure and relationships between the elements [8, 13]. The *pedagogical model* receives the information from the learner model, which it uses for adaptation. It describes the instructional strategies, the pedagogical theories, and the rules of adaptation.

2.3   Approaches to Adaptive Technologies for AEHS

In developing AEHS, 3 main questions define the different paths researchers take to achieve adaptation: 'What is the source of adaptation?', 'What is to be adapted?' and 'How will it be adapted?'.

The source of adaptation can be from the learner (level of knowledge, learning style, cognitive ability, etc.), the interaction between the learner and the adaptive environment, or a combination of both [14].

The source of adaptation, constituting the learner variables, provides the output/target of adaptation (instructional variables) [6]. These targets are implemented as adaptive content, adaptive presentation, and adaptive navigation. Adaptive content could be achieved through curriculum sequencing, changing presentation, or organisation [6, 14, 32]. Adaptive presentation is usually achieved through interface modelling (layout, size, colour, etc.) [12, 34] and feedback (type and time) [6]. Adaptive navigation could be in the form of navigation of content or navigation of learning environment [35]. Studies observe that the most implemented target of adaptation in AEHS is the content [15].

There are three primary approaches of adaptation in the design of AEHS [8, 14, 16], which include: macro- and micro-adaptive instruction and aptitude treatment interaction. Macro-adaptive instruction is a fairly static approach which considers the fact that learners differ in their characteristics and this affects the rate of learning process; hence adaptation is based on these preferences [16]. Micro-adaptive instruction, on the other hand, is a more dynamic approach which updates the learner model based on the learner's interaction with the system and tasks to determine the optimal adaptation requirement in a given situation [8]. Aptitude treatment interaction provides different instructional strategies based on learner aptitudes by allowing different levels of control to the learning process [16]. Using these approaches, AEHS can be implemented utilising different methods and technologies which include concept mapping, constraint-based tutoring, unsupervised machine learning, decision theories, taking advantage of learning standards, studying pedagogical experts, and matching educational support to learners' abilities [6].

3   Digital Learning Resources and Learning Objects

3.1   Digital Learning Resources

Learning is, for the most part, an intricate process as it has to take a host of affecting factors into consideration, even for a particular individual, in different learning scenarios. However, adaptive e-learning strive to accomplish a singular purpose, which is the absorption of learning content to the maximum by the learner [17]. As stated previously, the learning content is one of the most targeted forms of adaptation. Hence, it is imperative for the success of AEHS that learning content is highly flexible in its presentation and ability to respond to user individualities and essential needs [18]. It is a bad solution to just copy learning materials that proved to be efficient for learning to a group of learners to another group in different contexts. For this reason, designers and creators of online content spend considerable time and effort in the design and transformation of learning content used in e-learning systems.

We will refer to all digital learning content, either raw or processed, elementary or aggregated, which provide information to a learner as digital learning resources. Although, there is no standard definition of what a learning resource is, for purposes of this study, a learning resource is basically any tool or material added in the context of a course of curriculum that adds significant value to the teaching and learning experience in order to achieve a particular goal [19,20]. Digital learning resources could include text, audio, graphical images, photos, videos, simulations, animations, learning objects, programmed learning modules, etc.

3.2 Learning Objects

Learning objects have been a recurrent theme in e-learning for a long time. It was originated from the idea to solve the challenge of non-reusable open and distance-learning (ODL) content from an object-oriented programming approach [2,21]. What constitutes a learning object is largely debatable by the scientific community. However, a learning object can be seen as:

- "any digital resource that can be reused to support learning" [22]
- "any entity, digital or non-digital, that may be used for learning, education, or training" [23]
- "any entity, digital or non-digital, which can be used, re-used, or referenced during technology-supported learning" [24]
- "a small piece of learning material (e.g. visualisation, video clip, animation, interactive simulation, interactive exercises) that is a reusable, compact, as well as a unitary entity" [25]

Although there are disparities in how learning objects are defined, there seems to be some form of consensus in defining the properties in the design of learning objects. Hence, a learning object is not just a piece of text, a graphic, audio or video file; these are used in the creation of learning objects. It is neither a course curriculum on a subject; rather, LOs are aggregated to courses. The important properties of ideal LOs from these definitions are: reusability, modularity, interoperability, portability, and an educational goal. In [26], the authors differentiated between a reusable learning object (RLO) from a shareable learning object (SLO). They defined an RLO as having the basic properties of having educationally sound content, with a clear goal, and being able to be used on a learning platform. Furthermore, an SLO is an RLO, with metadata sufficient enough to interface with other learning platforms. We can summarise the main differences between digital learning resources and learning objects in Table 1.

Table 1. Digital Learning resources and learning objects

Digital learning resources	Learning objects
Learning objectives could be indefinite and general	Learning objectives are usually clear and concise
Potential for reusability or non-reusability is based on elemental aggregation	More potential for reusability in a particular context
Structure could be whole, inflexible, and have no restricting standards	Structure is mostly modular and standardised
More flexibility to be composed into complex units or decomposed to smaller units	Flexibility for composition or decomposition is dependent on structure and size
Complexity is well-defined by standards	Complexity is determined by content creator

3.3   Standards for Learning Objects

To create learning objects, information objects (concepts, procedures, facts, principles) contained in pieces of digital learning resources (text, audio, graphics, video, resources, etc.) are aggregated into units. A learning object can, thus, be a composition of different media resources. As digital learning resources move from their raw forms to a more standard form with specific and central learning objectives, context increases. As learning objects are aggregated into composite units such as courses and lessons, context and complexity further increase, thereby reducing potential for reuse [13]. Content creators, however, do not always meet the specifications of ideal LOs in the design of learning objects.

To ensure uniformity in the design of learning objects, various standards have been proposed for the description, structure, packaging, interactivity of learning objects, and learning information by international organisations. The most prominent ones, according to [2,5,13,21], are from Instructional Management System (IMS) Global Consortium [27], Advanced Distributed Learning (ADL) Initiative [28], IEEE Learning Technology Standards Committee (LTSC) [24], Aviation Industry CBT (Computer-Based Training) Committee (AICC) [28], and ARIADNE Foundation [29].

One of the most important aspects of a learning object is its description (general, technical, educational, proprietary, etc.), which is contained in its metadata. A widely-accepted standard for describing LOs is the Learning Object Metadata (LOM) [27], which was jointly developed by IMS and IEEE and has many similarities with the Dublin Core Standard [30]. A summary of the LOM standard is given in Table 2. ADL Initiative describes the structure of learning objects with the Shareable Content Object Reference Model (SCORM) differentiating SCOs (Shareable Content Objects) from assets (which are referred to as digital representation of learning content in text, image, sound, etc. delivered over the web) [28]. Assets are aggregated to form SCOs.

Table 2. Components of the LOM standard and their descriptions

No.	Category	Components	Description
1	General	1.1 Identifier, 1.2 Title, 1.3 Language, 1.4 Description, 1.5 Keyword, 1.6 Coverage, 1.7 Structure, 1.8 Aggregation Level	This specifies the information that describes the LO from a general perspective
2	Life cycle	2. 1 Version, 2.2 Status, 2.3 Contribute	This describes the background and the present state of the LO. It also specifies what contributors were involved in the process of transformation
3	Meta-metadata	3.1 Identifier, 3.2 Contribute, 3.3 Metadata Schema, 3.4 Language	This is used to describe the components of the metadata records
4	Technical	4.1 Format, 4.2 Size, 4.3 Location, 4.4 Requirement, 4.5 Installation Remarks, 4.6 Other Platform Requirements, 4.7 Duration	This describes the LO from a technical and computational perspective
5	Educational	5.1 Interactivity Type, 5.2 Learning Resource Type, 5.3 Interactivity Level, 5.4 Semantic Density, 5.5 Intended End User Role, 5.6 Context, 5.7 Typical Age Range, 5.8 Difficulty, 5.9 Typical Learning Time, 5.10 Description, 5.11 Language	This specifies the pedagogical components of the learning object
6	Rights	6.1 Cost, 6.2 Copyright and Other Restrictions, 6.3 Description	This describes the constraints and patent rights of the LO
7	Relation	7.1 Kind, 7.2 Resource	This describes the relationships between a LO and other LOs
8	Annotation	8.1 Entity, 8.2 Date, 8.3 Description	This specifies remarks made by users when using the LO
9	Classification	9.1 Purpose, 9.2 Taxon Path, 9.3 Description, 9.4 Keyword	This describes how the LO is categorised in a curriculum

To ensure interoperability and flexibility in the transfer of a collection of learning objects (individually or collectively) from one Learning Management System to another, IMS Content Packaging (IMS CP) describes a model called content packs [31,32]. IMS CP also provides the possibility of a hierarchical organisation of learning content which users can access through an LMS. SCORM Content Aggregation Model (CAM) (which is an extension of IMS CP) provides the structure of how learning content should be packaged to enable integration into a learning platform [28]. SCORM Run Time Environment (SCORM RTE) describes the possible operations of learning objects when they have been integrated into an LMS, while SCORM Sequence and Navigation (SCORM SN) provides rules for the sequencing and navigation of learning content for users in an LMS [2,31,32].

From a pedagogical point of view, information about individual or group learners are assembled in an IMS Learner Information Package (IMS LIP) [31]. Also, a model for specifying how assessments should be represented and reported are described by the IMS Question and Test Interoperability (IMS QTI) [31].

4 Adaptive Learning Objects

4.1 From Learning Objects to Adaptive Learning Objects

Learning objects have been previously considered to be static content [2]; however, one of the relatively recent property of LOs are its potentials for personalisation [6] which has generated a lot of research interest in the last two decades. This is also because of the possibility of extending the standards for designing LOs. An adaptive learning object (ALO) is a specialisation of a LO which is derived by adapting the learning content to specific features and different contexts to achieve a personalised and more effective teaching-learning experience.

4.2 Approaches to Adaptive Learning Objects

To delve further into the concept of adaptive learning objects, we'll look at the following aspects: what is adapted in learning objects, how it is adapted, and the components needed to achieve adaptation.

What Is Adapted? Adapting learning content to suit a particular purpose typically requires changing a learning object's semantic content, structure, or format. To further describe what is adapted in learning objects, we introduce the following categories: semantic content, presentation/navigation, organisation, and granularity described in Table 3.

How Is It Adapted? Adapting learning content to learner preferences is largely dependent on the definition and structure of the domain knowledge, information from the learner profile, and the instructional/teaching strategies that are employed [36]. The learner profile generally describes the cognitive, behavioural, and contextual information of the learner at any given time. In Sect. 2, we described the sources of adaptation usually employed in AEHS which are either from the user or user interactions with the system. Parameters from these sources can either be static (stable) or dynamic. Stable parameters do not change over long periods (or even at all) while dynamic parameters change

Table 3. Variables used for adaptation in learning objects

What is adapted	Examples
Semantic content	**Semantic density:** adding/removing concepts/ideas
	Redefining prerequisites, learning objectives, assessments
	Changing language and units of measurement and semantic interpretations suiting cultural peculiarities
Presentation	**Outlook:** preview, overview, review, summary, full view
	Format: text, audio, video
Navigation	**Different paths of navigation:** depth-first (exploring domain elements such as concepts/topics at different levels before proceeding to next element) vs breadth-first (exploring domain elements at the same level before proceeding to the next level)
Organisation	Reordering LO segments
Granularity	Smaller LOs combined to form LO with decreased granularity
	Larger LOs combined to form LOs with increased granularity

with respect to time, learning activities, medium of learning, and psychological/emotional states of the learner.

In [8, 37, 38], the authors describe personalisation criteria which are commonly used in adaptation in AEHS which include:

- **Learner preferences:** These are choices a learner makes according to available options. These could be language, content preferences (concepts, ideas in the knowledge domain), media preferences (text, audio, video, graphic options), learning styles (dependent on the learning style theory employed such as Felder and Silverman [39], Honey and Mumford [40], etc.), presentation preferences (options such as font colour, size, etc.), learning goals (intended purpose of learning acquisition), and navigational preferences (how the learner chooses to navigate through learning content—breadth-first or depth-first).

- **Learner status & history:** These are states of the learner before, during, and after different learning scenarios. They include previous level of knowledge, present level of knowledge, balance in participation and tasks (collaborative activities during group learning and tasks), cognitive traits (learner traits such as memory capacity, ability for inductive reasoning, speed of processing information, and skills of associative learning [41]), user status (features that relate to learner's emotional or physical state, time, or location. A learner, for instance, might prefer learning content for a particular length of time, one that might not require her full attention, or one specific in a current location or items in that location), and user history (log activities of a learner individually or in a group).

- **Learning medium parameters:** These relate to the features of the device used for learning at the particular time. They include device requirements (software and hardware requirements) and internet bandwidth of device.
- **Pedagogical/Domain parameters:** They include knowledge domain structure (the relationships and hierarchy between ideas and concepts in an ontology), motivation (parameters that drive the student—attention, relevance, confidence, satisfaction—during the learning process as represented in the ARCS Model [42]), and instructional approach (pedagogical theories and teaching strategies. For instance, employing a competence-based, collaborative, or an objectivist approach [36]).

A model of an adaptive learning object is shown below. In the next section, we'll describe some components in the architecture of an AEHS and also shown in the model (Fig. 1).

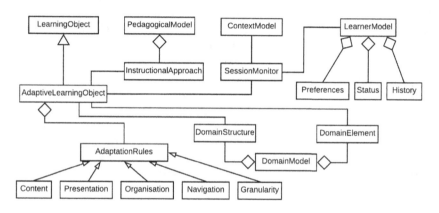

Fig. 1. A model of an adaptive learning object

Components for Adaptation: In addition to the learner, domain, and pedagogical models required for adaptation in AEHS, other components can be incorporated in the architectural design.

A *learner profile manager* component is necessary to manage the static and dynamic information from the user by updating the learner model after each learning process, assessment, and interaction that triggers adaptation rules [43]. A *context model* acquires and constantly updates user context values such as relation to time, location, or other external environmental factors [44]. A *session monitor* component keeps an account of the learner's activities during each learning session [45]. Such information is necessary to update the learner model or trigger the system to take necessary actions. Software agents have been gaining recent interest in AEHS designs for a while. Pedagogical agents (software agents specially designed for learning environments), which are adaptable and versatile, have been claimed to generate realistic simulations (as tutors, assistants, co-learners), encourage student engagement, motivation, and responsibility, and generally improve learning experience and performance by addressing learners' personal and sociocultural needs [46].

5   State-of-the-Art Models for ALOs

As the concept of ALO is gaining popularity in the design of AEHS, many studies have been developed towards designing models for ALO. Some of the recent works are being described below.

An ALO model is proposed in [2] which is specialised model of a learning object with metadata attributes from Dublin Core Standard and LOM standard. The model comprises a knowledge domain model, user model, context model, and session component. They also present two adaptation rules—navigation rules (which determine navigation options for certain users according to personalisation parameters) and content presentation rules (which present optimum learning content for learning scenarios), and evaluation rules (which, if triggered, can alter a learner's profile after an assessment).

The property of granularity is considered vital in the model proposed in [47], which consists of a domain model, learner model, and an adaptation model. They introduced four levels of aggregation: courses, documents, fragments, and multimedia pieces, in decreasing order of granularity, which can be composed or decomposed. A fragment comprises of pieces of multimedia such as text, image, audio, video, simulation, etc. and must not exceed 15 min. Adaptation is carried out by the navigation, presentation, and content models, which are sub-components of the adaptation model in relation to the static and dynamic preferences of the learner.

An ALOA (Adaptive Learning Objects Assembly) model is proposed in [48] which adapts learning content to user's learning styles and competency. The learning objects are organised hierarchically in an ontology with descriptions such as knowledge point, type, sequence relation, difficulty level, etc. A suggested difficulty level (E) and recommendation level (G) is given to each learning object by domain experts. Learning objects are then ordered using a sequence relation (S) which represents the order in which learning objects are to be studied. A PBIL (Population Based Incremental Learning) algorithm is used to get the most suitable learning path for users based on competences and learning styles.

A multi-agent system (MAS) model is proposed in [49] capable of adapting content to learner's preferences and needs whilst monitoring and giving feedback to students in real-time. The architecture comprises of three levels-the first level represents an interaction multi-agent system, the second level is the interface multi-agent system, and the final level is the human agent system (representing the learner and tutor). Within the Interaction MAS are agents such as the Profile Blackboard Agent which keeps a model of the learner's history and tracks the learner's performance and competences in the learning environment. The Learning Blackboard Agent tracks information used in adaptation during the learning process. A Course Generator Agent subsequently uses the information from the

Profile Blackboard Agent and the Learning Blackboard Agent to present learning content suited to a learner's preferences. The system utilises object Petri nets and an AI approach of a Blackboard System [50].

MALO (Model of Adaptation of Learning objects) [33], which is based on the micro-adaptive approach uses updated level of knowledge for each learner in addition to competencies/skills in achieving ALOs. The model is built by extending the LOM standard with an additional 'competence' specification. MALO basically consists of a learning object, units (small blocks of concepts which compose an LO), rules, and adaptation metadata. Two rules are defined, which are adaptation (semantics, presentation, organisation, and transformation) and conversion (composition and decomposition), for the creation of an ALO. Adaptation begins by ascertaining the competence of a learner and providing learning content to achieve a learning objective, which is the desired competence.

The authors in [51] propose an automatic generation of ALO for users by utilising the strengths of XML and Relational Databases (RDB). This is achieved by mapping the XML document of the course (with a Data Mapper) into an RDB, running SQL queries (with a Query Mapper) to find relationships between learner preferences and learning objects and reconstructing the SQL result (with a Relational to XMap Mapper) which contains the ALO. They define four levels of aggregation which include courses, units, learning objects, and concepts. Concepts are information objects which are composed of raw media elements (text, audio, video, etc.). Learning objects, which are aggregated from information objects, are assembled to form units, and which subsequently, collected, form courses.

6   Conclusion and Future Work

This paper describes learning content as it is used in adaptive hypermedia educational systems for personalised e-learning. Specifically, we have looked at the transition from digital learning resources (text, graphic, audio, video, presentation, simulation, etc.) in their raw form to adaptive learning objects that conform to characteristics of a learner. We considered important properties of learning objects and international standards that ensure interoperability between different platforms, whilst allowing proprietors of learning content to protect their work. Finally, we looked at different approaches towards adaptive learning objects, and briefly discussed theoretical and empirical implementations of models of adaptive learning objects.

Future work will involve developing a model of adaptive learning objects in an adaptive learning system, which combines multiple features of a learner and performs a weighing algorithm to determine which features are most important for adapting learning content for each learning scenario. We also intend to incorporate pedagogical agents which will serve as tutor assistants to foster a satisfying and effective teaching/learning experience.

References

1. UNESCO Global Education Monitoring Report: Education for people and planet: Creating Sustainable Futures for All, Paris, France, p. 73 (2016)
2. García-Valdez, J.M., Rodríguez-Díaz, A., Castañón-Puga, M., Cristóbal-Salas, A.: Adaptive learning objects. In: Proceedings of the International Conference on Artificial Intelligence ICAI04, pp. 105–109 (2004)
3. Wright, J.: Getting Personal: the role of personalization in online learning. http://www.insticc.org/portal/NewsDetails/TabId/246/ArtMID/1130/ArticleID/794/Getting-Personal-The-role-of-personalization-in-online-learning.aspx. Accessed 03 Apr 2019
4. Tseng, S.-S., Su, J., Hwang, G.-J., Hwang, G.-H., Tsai, C.-C., Tsai, C.-J.: An object-oriented course framework for developing adaptive learning systems. Educ. Technol. Soc. **11**, 171–191 (2008)
5. Andaloussi, K.S., Capus, L., Berrada, I.: Adaptive educational hypermedia systems: current developments and challenges. In: Proceedings of the 2nd International Conference on Big Data, Cloud and Applications - BDCA 2017, pp. 1–8. ACM Press, New York (2017). https://doi.org/10.1145/3090354.3090448
6. Shute, V.J., Zapata-Rivera, D.: Adaptive educational systems. In: Durlach, P.J., Lesgold, A.M. (eds.) Adaptive Technologies for Training and Education, pp. 7–27. Cambridge University Press, Cambridge (2012). https://doi.org/10.1017/CBO9781139049580.004
7. Medina-Medina, N., Garcia-Cabrera, L., Torres-Carbonell, J.J., Parets-Llorca, J.: Evolution in adaptive hypermedia systems. In: Proceedings of the International Workshop on Principles of Software Evolution - IWPSE 2002, p. 34. ACM Press, New York (2002). https://doi.org/10.1145/512035.512044
8. Vandewaetere, M., Desmet, P., Clarebout, G.: The contribution of learner characteristics in the development of computer-based adaptive learning environments. Comput. Hum. Behav. **27**, 118–130 (2011). https://doi.org/10.1016/j.chb.2010.07.038
9. Brusilovsky, P.: Adaptive hypermedia. User Model. User Adapt. Interact. **11**, 87–110 (2001). https://doi.org/10.1023/A:1011143116306
10. Brusilovsky, P.: Methods and techniques of adaptive hypermedia. User Model. User Adapt. Interact. **6**, 87–129 (1996). https://doi.org/10.1007/BF00143964
11. Henze, N., Nejdl, W.: Logically characterizing adaptive educational hypermedia systems. In: International Workshop on Adaptive Hypermedia and Adaptive Web-based Systems (AH 2003), pp. 20–24 (2003)
12. Sampson, D., Karagiannidis, C., Kinshuk, C.: Personalised learning: educational, technological and standardisation perspective. Interact. Educ. Multimed. **4**, 24–39 (2002)
13. Klašnja-Milićević, A., Vesin, B., Ivanović, M., Budimac, Z., Jain, L.C.: E-Learning Systems: Intelligent Techniques for Personalization. Springer, Switzerland (2017). https://doi.org/10.1007/978-3-319-41163-7
14. Ennouamani, S., Mahani, Z.: An overview of adaptive e-learning systems. In: 2017 Eighth International Conference on Intelligent Computing and Information Systems (ICICIS), pp. 342–347. IEEE (2017). https://doi.org/10.1109/INTELCIS.2017.8260060
15. Reategui, E., Boff, E., Campbell, J.A.: Personalization in an interactive learning environment through a virtual character. Comput. Educ. **51**, 530–544 (2008). https://doi.org/10.1016/j.compedu.2007.05.018

16. Beldagli, B., Adiguzel, T.: Illustrating an ideal adaptive e-learning: a conceptual framework. Procedia Soc. Behav. Sci. **2**, 5755–5761 (2010). https://doi.org/10.1016/j.sbspro.2010.03.939

17. Terzieva, T., Rahnev, A.: Basic stages in developing an adaptive e-learning scenario. Int. J. Innov. Sci. Eng. Technol. **5**, 50–54 (2018)

18. Vesin, B., Ivanović, M.: Modern educational tools. In: Proceedings of PRIM2004, 16th Conference on Applied Mathematics, Budva, Montenegro, pp. 293–302 (2004)

19. What do we mean by "digital learning resources"? https://flexiblelearning.auckland.ac.nz/learning_technologies_online/6/1/html/course_files/1_1.html

20. Association of American Publishers: What Are Learning Resources?—AAP. https://publishers.org/our-markets/prek-12-learning/what-are-learning-resources

21. Norman, S., Porter, D.: Designing Learning Objects for Online Learning: A Topical, Start-Up Guide to Distance Education Practice and Delivery. Commonwealth of Learning, Vancouver, BC, Canada (2007)

22. Wiley, D.A. (ed.): The Instructional Use of Learning Objects. Agency for Instructional Technology, Association for Educational Communications & Technology, Bloomington, Indiana (2002)

23. Barker, P.: What is IEEE Learning Object Metadata/IMS Learning Resource Metadata? Cetis Standards Briefings Series 1 (2005)

24. Learning Technology Standards Committee (IEEE): The Learning Object Metadata standard—IEEE Learning Technology Standards Committee. https://www.ieeeltsc.org/working-groups/wg12LOM/lomDescription

25. Pitkanen, S.H., Silander, P.: Criteria for pedagogical reusability of learning objects enabling adaptation and individualised learning processes, pp. 246–250 (2004). https://doi.org/10.1109/icalt.2004.1357412

26. Singh, R.G., Bernard, M., Gardler, R.: Creating sharable learning objects from existing digital course content. In: Proceedings of the 2004 Workshop on Computer Architecture Education Held in Conjunction with the 31st International Symposium on Computer Architecture - WCAE 2004, p. 8. ACM Press, New York (2004). https://doi.org/10.1145/1275571.1275582

27. IMS Global Learning Consortium. http://www.imsglobal.org/

28. ADL Initiative. https://www.adlnet.gov/

29. Ariadne Project EU—Foundation. https://www.ariadne-eu.org/

30. Miller, S.J.: Metadata for Digital Collections: A How-To-Do-It Manual, p. 56. ALA Neal-Schuman, Chicago (2011)

31. Learning object standard - EduTech Wiki. http://edutechwiki.unige.ch/en/Learning_object_standard

32. IMS Content Packaging - EduTech Wiki. http://edutechwiki.unige.ch/en/IMS_Content_Packaging

33. Guevara, C., Aguilar, J., González-Eras, A.: The model of adaptive learning objects for virtual environments instanced by the competencies. Adv. Sci. Technol. Eng. Syst. J. **2**, 345–355 (2017). https://doi.org/10.25046/aj020344

34. Ciolacu, M., Beer, R.: Adaptive user interface for higher education based on web technology. In: 2016 IEEE 22nd International Symposium for Design and Technology in Electronic Packaging, SIITME 2016, pp. 300–303 (2016). https://doi.org/10.1109/SIITME.2016.7777299

35. Marković, S., Jovanović, Z., Jovanović, N., Jevremović, A., Popović, R.: Adaptive distance learning and testing system. Comput. Appl. Eng. Educ. **21**, E2–E13 (2010). https://doi.org/10.1002/cae.20510

36. Essalmi, F., Ayed, L.J.B., Jemni, M.: A multi-parameters personalization approach of learning scenarios. In: Seventh IEEE International Conference on Advanced Learning Technologies (ICALT 2007), pp. 90–91. IEEE (2007). https://doi.org/10.1109/ICALT.2007.22

37. Essalmi, F., Ayed, L.J.B., Jemni, M., Kinshuk, Graf, S.: A fully personalization strategy of E-learning scenarios. Comput. Hum. Behav. **26**, 581–591 (2010). https://doi.org/10.1016/j.chb.2009.12.010

38. Thalmann, S.: Adaptation criteria for the personalised delivery of learning materials: a multi-stage empirical investigation. Australas. J. Educ. Technol. **30**, 45–60 (2014). https://doi.org/10.14742/ajet.235

39. Felder, R.M., Silverman, L.K.: Learning and teaching styles in engineering education. Eng. Educ. **78**(7), 674–681 (1988)

40. Honey, P., Mumford, A.: A manual of learning styles. In: Learning styles. Engineering Subject Centre. Peter Honey, Maidenhead (1986)

41. Rufer, R., Adams, R.H.: Adapting three-dimensional-virtual world to reach diverse learners in an MBA program. In: Handbook of Research on Practices and Outcomes in Virtual Worlds and Environments, pp. 606–619 (2011). https://doi.org/10.4018/978-1-60960-762-3.ch033

42. Keller, J.M.: Development and use of the ARCS model of motivational design. J. Instr. Dev. **10**, 2–10 (1987)

43. Ennouamani, S., Mahani, Z.: Designing a practical learner model for adaptive and context- aware mobile learning systems. IJCSNS Int. J. Comput. Sci. Netw. Secur. **18**, 84–93 (2018)

44. Ennouamani, S., Akharraz, L., Mahani, Z.: Integrating ICT in education: an adaptive learning system based on users' context in mobile environments. In: Farhaoui, Y., Moussaid, L. (eds.) ICBDSDE 2018. SBD, vol. 53, pp. 15–19. Springer, Cham (2019). https://doi.org/10.1007/978-3-030-12048-1_3

45. Klašnja-Milićević, A., Vesin, B., Ivanović, M., Budimac, Z.: E-Learning personalization based on hybrid recommendation strategy and learning style identification. Comput. Educ. **56**, 885–899 (2011). https://doi.org/10.1016/j.compedu.2010.11.001

46. Veletsianos, G., Russell, G.S.: Pedagogical agents. In: Spector, J.M., Merrill, M.D., Elen, J., Bishop, M.J. (eds.) Handbook of Research on Educational Communications and Technology, pp. 759–769. Springer, New York (2014). https://doi.org/10.1007/978-1-4614-3185-5_61

47. Battou, A., El Mezouary, A., Cherkaoui, C., Mammass, D.: Towards an adaptive learning system based on a new learning object granularity approach. Int. J. Adv. Comput. Sci. Appl. **2**, 8–14 (2011). https://doi.org/10.14569/IJACSA.2011.020902

48. Wan, S., Niu, Z.: Adaptive learning objects assembly with compound constraints. In: 2014 IEEE Computers, Communications and IT Applications Conference, pp. 34–39. IEEE (2014). https://doi.org/10.1109/ComComAp.2014.7017166

49. Hammami, S., Mathkour, H.: Adaptive e-learning system based on agents and object Petri nets (AELS-A/OPN). Comput. Appl. Eng. Educ. **23**, 170–190 (2015). https://doi.org/10.1002/cae.21587

50. Hayes-Roth, B.: A blackboard architecture for control. Artif. Intell. **26**, 251–321 (1985). https://doi.org/10.1016/0004-3702(85)90063-3

51. Bousalem, Z., El Guabassi, I., Cherti, I.: Toward adaptive and reusable learning content using XML dynamic labeling schemes and relational databases. In: Ezziyyani, M. (ed.) AI2SD 2018. AISC, vol. 915, pp. 787–799. Springer, Cham (2019). https://doi.org/10.1007/978-3-030-11928-7_71

Agile-Based Product Line Tool Development

Detlef Streitferdt[1]([✉]) [iD], Livia Sangeorzan[2], and Johannes Nau[1]

[1] Department of Computer Science and Automation,
Technische Universität Ilmenau, 98693 Ilmenau, Germany
{detlef.streitferdt,johannes.nau}@tu-ilmenau.de
[2] Department of Mathematics and Computer Science,
Transilvania University of Brasov, 500036 Brasov, Romania
sangeorzan@unitbv.ro

Abstract. The product line domain and agile software development created a well-received product line concept with complex toolchains and the agile development idea that fosters a rather pragmatic development style with less documentation. Both parts have been included in two student projects targeting the development of a configurator product line. This paper presents requirements for configurator product lines and evaluates the two projects towards these requirements. The positive results of the projects lead to the proposal to broaden the support and acceptance of special project types in the product line domain where the source code and structure is enough to understand and maintain the project. We even propose this to be the better solution.

Keywords: Product line tools · Agile development · C++

1 Introduction

Product lines date back to Kang's [7] early technical report about Feature-Oriented Domain Analysis. The basic idea to structure the design of a system along its features introduced a new view to software development and a new way of designing and developing such software systems. One of the key ideas is the interaction of software developers with users using the term "features". Features were introduced as elements that should be understood by both parties, the users and software developers, and they describe elements customers are willing to pay for. Additionally, a product line is modeled by its mandatory and optional features. Of course, another economic reason for product lines is the cost savings if the product line architecture can be reused and variants of it can be derived by only configuring a needed product instead of developing it from scratch. The product line design idea was of advantage for software systems [1], and it was also adopted in several industrial projects [9]. Despite these positive results, the complexity of setting up and maintaining product line development environments is still high enough for the corresponding tools or toolchains to

© Springer Nature Switzerland AG 2020
D. Simian and L. F. Stoica (Eds.): MDIS 2019, CCIS 1126, pp. 33–47, 2020.
https://doi.org/10.1007/978-3-030-39237-6_3

be a point for optimization. In [5] the complexity of product line development projects in the automotive domain is described, and the tool setup is explicitly mentioned to be a "substantial effort" and still a challenge.

Based on our own experiences in the automation industry, the tool-setup for product line development projects was orchestrated centrally for all development teams in the company but still with team specific tools. The complexity of the tool chain resulted in about 15% of the overall development effort which was spent for its setup and maintenance. Developers questioned the toolchain handling, demanding a decentralized tool approach.

Requirements for this type of development are elaborated in Sect. 2. A decentralized tool approach automatically leads towards more tool responsibility for development teams. This is in line with the currently well-known agile software development approach, which has been adopted for product lines as well, as described in [12] with an enhanced Scrum process for product lines.

The integration of decentralized tool management into the agile development approach is a high-level goal. This paper starts with a smaller sub-goal, the domain of configurators using the product line approach. They require less overhead than a complete product line and could be seen as a *lightweight product line*.

Configurators keep the information of many components with their constraints to validate whether a set of components could work correctly together. Configurators can be used in current web-systems or desktop machines. For example, car-configurators, PC-configurators, or the configuration of the Linux Kernel can be modeled with the product line approach. The realization of one product based on the product line requires the validation of the selected components and will create different outputs. A car-configurator could generate the order of documents for the customer, plans for the assembly of the selected car, or even test cases for single components or their integrated sub-systems. The Linux kernel configuration would create build scripts and parameterized code. In any case, the feature model needs to be validated, whereas the realization of a member of the product line, e.g., the car or a Linux kernel, is an individual programming task.

This paper is based on the experiences out of the collaboration with over ten companies within research projects as well as two student projects done in the research group of the author. As the bottom line, more than half of the companies are using *configuration approaches* with a product line background, in contrast to the complete product line approach, industrial examples can be found in [9]. The idea is to use a lightweight approach for product lines, with the lowest possible effort for its integration. Thus, the agile approach with a developer-friendly, coding-oriented approach seemed very promising and was evaluated by the two student projects. The resulting research question reads as follows:

Research Question. *What are the benefits of using an agile approach for the development of configurators in the product line domain?*

The novel idea of the response to this research question is to strengthen the agile principle of less documentation and focus more on programming. The examples given in this paper are of a special type, which allows the source code to be a document itself indeed. The examples are explained and evaluated against requirements to show that they fulfill their intended task while they are developed according to the agile approach in a sense explained above.

In Sect. 2, the configuration aspect is described by requirements for the development and implementation of this specific product line approach. In Sect. 3, an overview of the product line development is given together with agile product line approaches. As a result, the agile approach is considered a valid solution for the product line development according to the requirements elaborated in Sect. 2. Two implementations based on student projects are presented in Sect. 4. These projects have been developed as part of the research work in the research group of the first author of this paper. The students developed a lightweight product line tool within the short timeframe of a Master's thesis (six months). Their research question was how would software experts support themselves with the task of developing a product line configurator-tool if they have the freedom to decide upon the architecture and implementation of the tool.

Finally, in Sect. 5, conclusions are drawn about the two projects in relation to the requirements given in Sect. 2. The paper finishes with the future work section.

2   Requirements

In this section, requirements for a product line configurator, as discussed in the last section, are given. The requirements have been elicited within the two student projects based on our industry cooperation.

The configuration aspect of product line engineering targets feature models to derive variants, comparable to the Linux kernel configuration or the car configurators on the Internet. The idea is to support a complex composition, like the composite design pattern, but with the most possible degrees of freedom for the features themselves, as well as the constraints for the feature model.

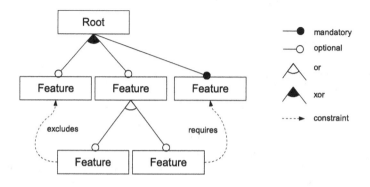

Fig. 1. Feature model notation as presented in [11]

A feature model, as shown in Fig. 1, is a hierarchical structure of features referring to selectable components of the desired product, e.g., a car. The edges connect features, either mandatory or optional. All the mandatory features are always present in each variant derived from the feature model. All optional features may be selected by the customer. Taking a car as example, it could be the chassis that needs to be present in all configuration, whereas several types of tires can be optional and thus, selectable by the customer. The constraints in the given notation might *require* or *exclude* one or more features for a given feature. Such constraints need to be checked when a variant is derived. Thus, a variant can only be derived if all constraints are met.

All parts of the feature model in Fig. 1 need to be supported. The following requirements have been elicited.

R1 The learning/ramp up effort for the approach should be minimal.
R2 Using the new approach should require the least possible management effort for the tool.
R3 A feature should be able to carry additional, arbitrary information (e.g., a description).
R4 A feature should be able to hold (numeric) parameters to specify e.g. the size.
R5 Constraints should enable an n-to-m relationship between a set of features.
R6 Constraints should behave like arbitrary functions evaluating to *true* or *false*.
R7 The feature model should be editable (add/delete/change).
R8 A given selection of features should be analyzable whether it is a valid variant.
R9 A subset of features (currently or, xor) should have arbitrary selection criteria.

This list contains the requirements relevant for our *configurator*. Additional requirements for feature modeling in general can be found in [13]. There, modeling (mandatory features, optional features, feature cardinality, attributes, feature versions, layers, external features, binding times, resource mapping, alternative-groups, or-groups, group cardinality, multiple groups) and constraint language (expressiveness, representation) requirements are discussed.

3   State of the Art

Software product lines are a broad concept for re-use, and the literature review in [10] on software product line evolution reveals a domain with increased maturity, but a still reduced tool support with a low level of automation and rather heavy-weight development processes. Large and worldwide operating companies using the software product lines approach have been analyzed in [2]. As one result, a demand for integrative solutions for the distributed working style has been identified, again emphasizing the tools for the product line. At the same time and due to nowadays disruptive changes regarding flexibility and short project time requirements, there are small and worldwide operating teams, which require flexible processes, as delivered by the agile approach [4]. Thus, the situation changed from companies formerly working with large headquarters and most engineers being on-site, towards smaller teams, distributed worldwide. These small teams are organizationally composed to form engineering departments in their companies.

The combination of both, software product lines and the agile development approach was analyzed in [5] and further enhanced in [8]. The resulting transformation model, to transform standard projects to the agile software product line approach, is divided into four layers, an organizational, a team, a management and team, as well as a pure management layer. One of the proposed software product line extensions given for the last two layers emphasizes the agile idea of teams to organize and decide by themselves, especially about their infrastructure. Such infrastructure includes tools which will be organized by the team itself. Based on our own project management experiences and many student projects, the relation of responsibility given to the members of a development team, and their satisfaction with their tasks is very tight. Thus, the agile development approach will support requirements R1 and R2. In this paper, the proposal for requirements R1 and R2 is to choose the language of the developers and let them describe and solve the task in their language. Of course, the language of developers is their programming language. This eliminates the learning effort for the language. The tool management effort depends on the quality of the code, but here we expect the self-regulation of the developers to reduce this effort since the developer's responsibility for his own tool directly corresponds with the effort he needs to spend for any maintenance.

Small teams will form larger organizational engineering structures with the responsibility but also the wish of companies to take care and maintain their own tool set. Depending on the task given to a team, tools might not even have to interact beyond the team scope. Such tools will be unique for this team. This is true in many product line examples in the industry [9]. These success stories often include home-made tools with high efficiency for the hosting team. Thus, current development teams are given more responsibility for their own toolchain, which now becomes a success factor for the development of product lines. Again this is related to requirements R1 and R2 with the same argumentation as in the previous paragraph.

The implementation of feature-oriented product lines is presented in [1] and includes modeling but also many programming parts. It is apparent that the coding domain has a better motivating potential for the developers than other tasks, for example, documentation, which is in line with the agile approach.

As an example chosen for this paper, online computer configurators offer the service of putting together a complete computer system for customers without detailed knowledge about the compatibility of components. Here, the features of the product line are the PC components the end-user wants and is willing to pay for. The selection process is guided by a web tool, and any constraints are maintained and hidden by the same tool. Finally, the customer is only able to select his desired components. The web system validates the configuration.

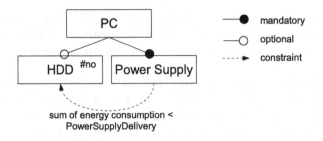

Fig. 2. Example: configuration of a PC

The example in Fig. 2 shows two PC components and a constraint. A PC will have a power supply, which needs to have a parameter to identify the maximum energy output. The HDD-feature also needs a parameter, the number of harddisks built into the PC. This number has an upper limit given by the PC case chosen. The constraint between the power supply and the installed harddisks is now more complex than the initially available *excludes* and *requires* constraints. The sum of the energy consumption of all the harddisks needs to be smaller than the energy the power supply can deliver. The parameters refer to requirement R4 and the constraint to requirement R6.

Two commercial tools, *pure::variants*[1] and *Gears*[2], as well as an open-source tool, *FeatureIDE*[3], are described in [1]. Another 26 tools are just listed. The tools are able to handle the described scenario of the PC configurator but at the expense of an initial learning curve and continuous maintenance effort, which contradicts requirements R1 and R2. The tools partly even support the OCL (Object Constraint Language), which was specifically developed to enable constraints for arbitrary models. But this approach requires the knowledge of the domain-specific OCL, which would again require additional efforts.

It is easy to see that more complex constraints very soon demand programming languages to cover all problem domains. The approach presented in [11] is based on the validation of feature models by transforming these models into a Constraint Satisfaction Problem (CSP) and solving them with a Constraint Programming Solver (CP). This approach is very advanced to address feature model analysis requirements. For now, these analyses are beyond the scope of this paper, but they might be in future enhancements and research.

To sum up, the current product line domain offers tools to develop and maintain product lines. However, for the special case of configurators, the tools are too heavyweight, causing additional and unneeded efforts to use them. Based on the agile concept of a simplified development and the presented agile adaptations to product lines, the approach can be taken to the next level, to support the complete set of requirements given in Sect. 2. After analyzing the state-of-the-art developing agile configurators with the product line approach is very well

---

[1] www.pure-systems.com.

[2] biglever.com.

[3] www.featureide.com.

possible when we use only the programming approach instead of complex product line toolchains.

In the following sections, two student projects will be presented. With the basic knowledge of the product line approach and the programming tools available, the agile and in this case, pragmatic approach was used for the development of a configuration product line tool, relevant and usable for developers within their team.

4   Solutions

The programming solution is a pragmatic view onto software product lines, made for software development experts and made for the domain of configurators. Two software architectures to model and use feature models, will be presented in this paper, along with the analysis results of their usage.

The task given to the two master students was the development of a product line configurator. The students were free to choose whichever example they wanted and implement it with their approach. They were told to use the agile development process and any communication was meant to be amongst developers, thus, extensive written documents were not needed.

Two lightweight product line tools will be presented, compared, and assessed. They are both developed in C++ and require the skills of a software developer for their usage. In exchange, these lightweight solutions will work on the source code level and can be integrated into toolchains with, based on our experience, an effort of less than three days.

4.1   1st Project: Feature Toolset

The first project was developed in C++ as part of a master's thesis by Johannes Hein [3] and was released on *github*[4]. This solution is straight forward and uses classes to build and analyze feature models.

The feature model is based on two classes, see the left side in Fig. 3. The class *Feature* for the basic elements of the model and the class *Dependency* to model relations between features. This class-structure represents the underlying meta-model. By inheritance, a feature model can be developed and stored as C++ code. The instantiation of a concrete model is the equivalent to deriving a variant, and again a variant will be stored in a C++ code file.

Feature Class. This class is the template for all features in feature models. Concrete features are simply subclasses of *Feature*. The boolean attribute _selected reflects whether a feature was chosen as part of a variant of the product line. It has the std::list attribute _dependencies for each feature to store zero to many *Dependency*-objects, with the helper methods *getDependencies* and *addDependecy*.

---

[4] https://github.com/johanneshein/feature-toolset.

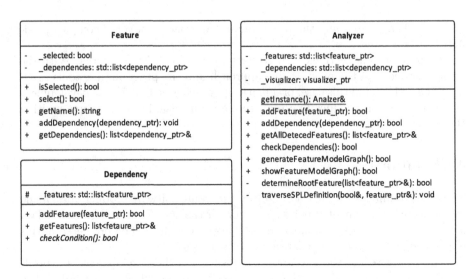

Fig. 3. Feature model with the corresponding design

The class layout allows us to build simple feature models as is but also to extend the meta-model to enable more complex feature models with different feature-types by inheriting from *Feature*.

Dependency Class. The relationships amongst features are realized by the *Dependency*-class. The hierarchy of feature models, as shown in Fig. 1, is not implemented by the very common aggregation association from and to the *Feature*-class, since this would have required one aggregation per dependency type. Instead, the current version was realized by the dependencies MANDATORY, OPTIONAL, OR and XOR, all of which are subclasses of *Dependency*.

Using Feature and Dependency. The variables ending on "_ptr" make use of C++ shared pointers to ease memory handling. The usage of the two classes *Feature* and *Dependency* is divided into the following steps.

1. Develop the feature model by creating any desired feature classes and dependencies.
2. Instantiate the feature model.
3. Derive a variant by selecting the desired features.
4. Check the variant for its validity.

The first step results in the source code of the corresponding feature model project. After this, the first part of the second step starts with the instantiation of the features, as shown for the first three features in Listing 1.1.

Listing 1.1. Feature Model Instantiation

```
1  feature_ptr pc (new PC);
2  feature_ptr drive (new Drive);
3  feature_ptr mainboard (new Mainboard);
```

Listing 1.2 finalizes the second step, the setup of the structure of the feature model. By convention, the dependency has to be created first (see source line 1). All features belonging to the dependency will be added to the dependency (see source line 2), and then the dependency will be added to its feature (see source line 3).

Listing 1.2. Design of the Feature Meta-Model

```
1  dependency_ptr m1(new Mandatory);
2  m1->addFeature(drive);
3  pc->addDependency(m1);
4
5  dependency_ptr m2(new Mandatory);
6  m2->addFeature(mainboard);
7  m2->addFeature(processor);
8  pc->addDependency(m2);
9
10 dependency_ptr m3(new Optional);
11 m3->addFeature(hid);
12 pc->addDependency(m3);
13
14 dependency_ptr or1(new OR);
15 or1->addFeature(Keyboard);
16 or1->addFeature(mouse);
17 hid->addDependency(or1);
18
19 dependency_ptr xor2(new XOR);
20 xor2->addFeature(i7);
21 xor2->addFeature(athlon);
22 processor->addDependency(xor2);
```

Finally, the feature model can be traversed to let the user select the desired features by the *select*-method of the *Feature*-class what is implemented in the service methods of the *Analyzer*-class in the next subsection.

Analyzer Class. The key component of the approach is the *Analyzer* class, implemented as *singleton*. All the features and dependencies are kept in an object of this class (see the *_feature* and *_dependency* attributes). The selection of a product line variant is analyzed in the *traverseSPLDefinition* method. Starting with the root-feature (see *determineRootFeatures*), all the features will be traversed in a top-down manner, and for each dependency, the *checkCondition* method will be called. Thus, the validity of a product variant according to the product line model will be evaluated. The two remaining methods for the generation and visualization of a feature model graph use the *Graphviz dot*[5] tool.

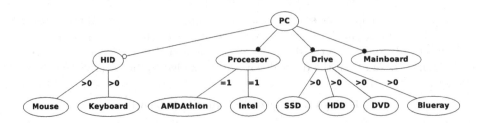

Fig. 4. Generated feature model graph

With the implemented visualization capabilities the generated feature model graph in Fig. 4 was automatically constructed.

All the features were instantiated according to Listing 1.2. The structure of the feature model was implemented as in Listing 1.2. Lines 1 to 12 of the code Listing 1.1 create the first level of the feature model, the three mandatory features, and the single optional *HID* feature. There are two OR-connected features sets below the *HID* and *drive* feature, as well as the XOR-connected features set below the *processor* feature.

The only step left is the selection process with the dependency checking, which is done by calling the corresponding method in the *Analyzer* object.

```
1 || Analyzer :: getInstance () . checkDependencies () ;
```

A successful call to *checkDependencies* indicates a valid product line variant. Any features of the own product line can be extended with any data possible, and this data can be checked with all the language constructs of our, in this case C++ , programming language. Thus, the flexibility of this approach is maximized.

4.2 2nd Project: Product Line Generator

The second approach to product line engineering is a master's thesis developed in C++ and documented with doxygen[6] by Tobias Hüttl [6]. The structure for the feature model is comparable, but the approach for the constraints of a model is different and XML-based.

In Fig. 5 the development of a product line starts with an XML-file (*Feature Model(XML)*), shown in Listing 1.3. This file will be used by the central component of the solution, the *Feature Model Selector*. The tool reads the model and offers a guided selection of features to the user. The selection and also any

---

[5] www.graphviz.org.
[6] www.doxygen.nl.

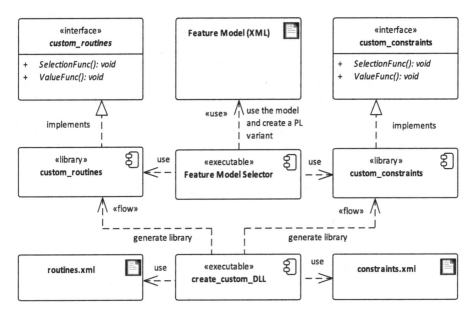

Fig. 5. Generative product line tool

selected or set values are stored in an extended version of the Feature Model XML-file using new XML-elements and additional attributes. As in the previous solution, constraints are implemented directly in C++ . The difference is the fully externalized data model, present as XML-file.

The library *custom_constraints* contains the code that will be executed while the user is selecting features for the desired variant. For each selection, the constraints attached to features will be executed to check whether they hold or break the feature model, programmed as conditions in C++ evaluating to true/false.

The library *custom_routines* contains the code that will be executed when a variant is selected. The execution is an additional step that was implemented in this solution, which is not yet part of the solution presented in Subsect. 4.1. The selection of a variant might only lead to an order process for different hardware components or it might lead to a code generation process. Since these are different tasks, *routines* can be attached to features to take care of anything which needs to be done for the execution of a feature. Again the *routines* are programmed in C++ for full flexibility.

Listing 1.3. Feature Model (XML)

```
1  <objekt name="PC" mandatory="true" rule="or">
2  <dll-run>custom_routines.dll</dll-run>
3  <dll-constraint>custom_constraints.dll</dll-constraint>
4  <element name="drive" mandatory="true" rule="xor">
5          <data> descriptive text for drive </data>
6          <element name="SSD">
7                  <data> descriptive text for SSD</data>
8          </element>
9          <element name="HDD">
10                 <data> descriptive text for HDD</data>
11         </element>
12         <element name="DVD">
13                 <data> descriptive text for DVD</data>
14         </element>
15         <element name="Blueray">
16                 <data> descriptive text for Blueray</
                        data>
17         </element>
18 </element>
19 </objekt>
```

Both libraries, *custom_routines* and *custom_constraints*, implement an interface which enables to check for the value of a feature, the *ValueFunc* method and the *SelectionFunc* method enable to check the selection status of a feature and further evaluate its constraints.

Listing 1.4. Constraints.xml

```
1  <constraints>
2          <constraint name="Elektro">
3                  return selection("Verbrenner");
4          </constraint>
5  </constraints>
```

Listing 1.5. Routines.xml

```
1  <routines>
2          <routine name="Elektro">
3                  print("Elektro test");
4          </routine>
5  </routines>
```

The code for the *custom_constraints* as well as the *custom_routines* library is organized in the *constraints.xml* and the *routines.xml* files, shown in Listings 1.4 and 1.5. Both files are processed by the *create_custom_DLL* tool which automatically generates the code for both libraries, *custom_constraints* and *custom_routines*, and finally compiles the libraries.

Table 1. Comparison and Evaluation of the two Projects

ReqID	Evaluation	Conclusion
1, 2	The creation time for both projects has been six months, the programming time $\sim$ two months	For the students, the initial programming time was rather high due to the final thesis type of work. In an industrial setting, our estimation is a two week initial setup time, given the coding character of the project
3, 4	Both projects offer a fully flexible, object-oriented data model	Requirements are met completely
5, 6	The constraint modeling is fully flexible in both projects. The 2nd project has programmable constraints as part of an XML-file but from there on an automated code generation	The 1st project has less overhead towards the implementation of a constraint. Both projects implemented n-to-m relations and fully programmable constraints
7	Editing the feature model as well as feature variants has to be done in the chosen programming editor or IDE	Both projects met the requirement. The editing experience is dependent on the chosen programming environment. Thus, no additional efforts are introduced by this approach
8	Both projects implemented the validation of a selected variant according to the feature model - checking the constraints	Additional analyses are possible but need to be implemented as required. This is future work. The requirements were partly met
9	The tree structure is fully flexible for the 1st project and bound to XML in the 2nd project	The requirement is met, but the relation of efforts is yet unknown and needs to be investigated in future research projects

5   Comparison of Approaches and Conclusion

Both projects successfully developed a functional product line tool. The solutions show a clean and understandable design, although the second project is slightly more complex. The initially stated requirements are evaluated in Table 1.

The agile idea of keeping things simple and working with code towards goals has been perfectly implemented in both projects. With the few clean code rules, reading and understanding the projects is very efficient. Compared to the tools discussed in the state-of-the-art, the vital concept of flexible constraints could be successfully addressed and realized within the short timeframe of a thesis. The results of the student projects show that the best way to address constraints is by using a programming language with all its capabilities. The integration of such constraints into a product line tool needs a data model hosting features and constraints which has been developed in both projects.

Finally, C++ with its new language features, like smart pointers and the extensive standard libraries, offers an excellent platform to develop product line tools for small (in our case even one-man) projects from scratch and gain the internal knowledge about the own tools used. This is a soft factor in the software development domain, which leaves a favorable ground for good team communication, and based on the communication, the team cohesion. Product line configuration tools are located inside a development team - only developers are building and using this tool. The simplicity of the design and the clarity of the code allow such projects only to exist as code. With the complexity of the product line tool domain discussed in the state-of-the-art section, the expectation of an increased number of project types, as presented in this paper, is easily visible. To react as flexibly as needed, we propose to actively support such project types, starting with the education of developers and computer scientists up to industrial teams.

6   Future Work

As stated in the Table 1, effort/timing measurements in upcoming projects need to be added. As of today, the limitations of the programming approach are given only by the implemented feature model, which had up to 200 features. We will further investigate agile software development by lightweight tool projects, especially in the teaching domain, for adaptable componentized lectures. Lectures developed as a product line can be configured to the needs of students and the resulting teaching and learning material can be generated. Such tools are best developed in-house and they will also support software engineering courses as they will be taken as examples.

References

1. Apel, S., Batory, D., Kästner, C., Saake, G.: Feature-Oriented SoftwareProduct Lines. Springer (2013)
2. Galindo, J.A., Benavides, D., Trinidad, P., Gutiérrez-Fernández, A.M.,Ruiz-Cortés, A.: Automated analysis of feature models: Quo vadis? Computing**101**(5), 387–433 (2019).https://doi.org/10.1007/s00607-018-0646-1
3. Hein, J.: Feature Toolset in C++. Master's thesis, Technische Universit ät Ilmenau (2019)
4. Hohl, P., Munch, J., Schneider, K., Stupperich, M.: Real-Life Challenges on Agile Software Product Lines in Automotive, Lecture Notes in Computer Science, vol. 10611, pp. 28–36. Springer International Publishing Ag, Cham (2017). https://doi.org/10.1007/978-3-319-69926-4_3

5. Hohl, P., Stupperich, M., Münch, J., Schneider, K.: Combining agile development and software product lines in automotive: Challenges and recommendations. In: 2018 IEEE International Conference on Engineering, Technology and Innovation (ICE/ITMC). pp. 1–10 (June 2018). https://doi.org/10.1109/ICE.2018.8436277

6. Hüttl, T.: Feature Model Analysis. Master's thesis, Technische Universität Ilmenau (2019)

7. Kang, K.C., Cohen, S.G., Hess, J.A., Novak, W.E., Peterson, A.S.: Feature-oriented domain analysis (foda) feasibility study. Carnegie-Mellon Univ Pittsburgh Pa Software Engineering Inst, Tech. rep. (1990)

8. Klunder, J., Hohl, P., Schneider, K.: Becoming Agile While Preserving Software Product Lines An Agile Transformation Model For Large Companies. Proceedings of the 2018 International Conference on Software and System Process, Assoc. Computing Machinery, New York (2018). https://doi.org/10.1145/3202710.3203146

9. van der Linden, F.J., Schmid, K., Rommes, E.: Software Product Lines in Action:The Best Industrial Practice in Product Line Engineering. Springer (2007)

10. Marques, M., Simmonds, J., Rossel, P.O., Bastarrica, M.C.: Software product line evolution: A systematic literature review. Information and Software Technology **105**, 190–208 (2019). https://doi.org/10.1016/j.infsof.2018.08.014

11. Navarro, J.C., Chavarriaga, J.: Using Microsoft Solver Foundation to Analyse Feature Models and Configurations. 8th Euro American Conference on Telematics and Information Systems, Ieee, New York (2016)

12. Santos Jr., A., Lucena Jr., V.: Scrumpl - software product line engineering with scrum. In: Proceedings of the Fifth International Conference on Evaluation of Novel Approaches to Software Engineering - Volume 1: ENASE, pp. 239–244. INSTICC, SciTePress (2010). https://doi.org/10.5220/0003038302390244

13. Seidl, C., Winkelmann, T., Schaefer, I.: A software product line of featuremodeling notations and cross-tree constraint languages. Modellierung 2016(2016)

Conceptual Modelling

Conceptual Model Engineering for Industrial Safety Inspection Based on Spreadsheet Data Analysis

Nikita O. Dorodnykh⬤, Aleksandr Yu. Yurin$^{(\boxtimes)}$⬤, and Alexey O. Shigarov⬤

Matrosov Institute for System Dynamics and Control Theory, Siberian Branch
of the Russian Academy of Sciences, 134, Lermontov st., Irkutsk 664033, Russia
`iskander@icc.ru`

Abstract. Conceptual models are the foundation for many modern intelligent systems, as well as a theoretical basis for conducting more in-depth scientific research. Various information sources (e.g., databases, spreadsheets data, and text documents, etc.) and the reverse engineering procedure can be used for creation of such models. In this paper, we propose an approach to support the conceptual model engineering based on the analysis and transformation of tabular data from CSV files. Industrial safety inspection (ISI) reports are used as examples for spreadsheets data analysis and transformation. The automated conceptual model engineering involves five steps and employs the following software: TabbyXL for extraction of canonical (relational) tables from arbitrary spreadsheet data in the CSV format; Personal Knowledge Base Designer (PKBD) for generation of conceptual model fragments based on analysis and transformation of canonical tables, and aggregating these fragments into domain model. Verification of the approach was carried out on the corpus containing 216 spreadsheets extracted from six ISI reports. The obtained conceptual models can be used in the design of knowledge bases.

Keywords: Spreadsheet data · Conceptual models · Class diagram · UML · Model transformation · Industrial safety inspection

1 Introduction

Conceptual models are the foundation for many modern knowledge-based systems, as well as a theoretical basis for conducting more in-depth scientific research on the nature of domain concepts and relationships between them. These models in the form of concept and mind maps, UML class and entity relation diagrams and others are actively used for the knowledge base engineering at the acquisition and structuring stages. The conceptual modeling results, on the one hand, contain special knowledge that can be used for automated source codes generation, on the other hand, they are a convenient and understandable way for representation of the domain-specific knowledge.

© Springer Nature Switzerland AG 2020
D. Simian and L. F. Stoica (Eds.): MDIS 2019, CCIS 1126, pp. 51–65, 2020.
https://doi.org/10.1007/978-3-030-39237-6_4

One of the domains requiring designing conceptual models is the reliability and safety provision of industrial facilities. The safety provision problem of industrial facilities remains relevant in many industries, in regard to the degradation and aging of technical equipment, which rate is ahead of the pace of modernization and re-placement. This is especially true for long-running technical equipment at oil refiner-ies, petrochemical and chemical plants. This technical equipment is dangerous for people and environment and requires periodic assessment of technical condition, its monitoring, diagnosing, and forecasting. These tasks are parts of the industrial safety inspection (ISI) procedure, and the complete and adequate subject domain models are required for their proper solving.

Conceptual models remain a main technique for visualization and formalization of the basic concepts and relationships of any subject area, performing a communicative function between domain experts and software developers. An in the case of ISI they can be used for decision support systems engineering, including design of databases, ontologies (local taxonomies) and knowledge bases [1–3].

The ISI results are presented in the form of conclusions (reports) containing heter-ogeneous information in the form of texts, tables, charts, and graphs and can be used for designing conceptual models. Herewith, tables form ISI reports provide the most structured and formalized representation of domain entities and can be used for con-ceptual model engineering.

Methods and tools for extracting and transforming data from spreadsheets have been actively developed in the last decade. However, there are still limitations, both in the spreadsheet layouts and in the domains covered. At the same time, solving the problem of extracting spreadsheet information from ISI reports makes it possible to consider new spreadsheet layouts and a new subject domain, providing support for conceptual modeling.

In this paper, we present an approach for conceptual models engineering based on automated analysis and transformation of spreadsheet data. Main results of transformation are conceptual model fragments, which can be aggregated into a complete domain model. The automated conceptual model formation involves five steps and employs the following software: TabbyXL [3, 4] for extraction of canonical (relational) tables from arbitrary spreadsheet data in the CSV format; Personal Knowledge Base Designer (PKBD) [2] for generation of conceptual model fragments and their aggregation.

The paper is organized as follows: Sect. 2 presents related works, while Sect. 3 illustrates the approach proposed. Section 4 presents discussion and concluding remarks.

2   Related Works

Spreadsheets are a common way for representing information, and they are widely used in documents and web in HTML, PDF, EXCEL, CSV formats. A big volume and structure properties of such spreadsheets make them a valuable source in data science and business intelligence applications. However, they are not accompanied by explicit semantics necessary for the machine interpretation of their content. The analysis of these data requires their preliminary extraction and transformation to a structured representation with a certain formal model.

Due to the widespread use of spreadsheets in various subject domains, there is a strong interest in the analysis and transformation of tabular data. Recently, several studies have been conducted that deal with spreadsheet data transformation for designing conceptual models. In particular, methods for the role and structural spreadsheets analysis (restoration of relations between cells) are proposed in [5–13]. The research in this area is also focused on specialized tools for extraction and transformation of arbitrary spreadsheet data into a structured form, including spreadsheet data transformation systems [14–22].

In particular, Chen and Cafarella [7] describe relational data extraction system from spreadsheets with header hierarchies. Systems for transformation of arbitrary spreadsheets to a relational form based on the search for critical cells are presented in [8,11]. Hung et al. [15] propose TranSheet approach for data model generation from spreadsheets with the use of a spreadsheet-like formula language. Cunha et al. [19] present an approach for spreadsheet data transformation based on the search the functional dependences between data cells, the results of transformation are relational models.

Also we can note the paper [21], the authors present a technique to automatically extract information from spreadsheet data and transform it into UML class diagrams. This technique is based on two-dimensional patterns, which regard layout, data and formulas included in the spreadsheets. The resulting class diagram can be used by software engineers to understand, to refine, or to re-implement the spreadsheet's functionality. Amalfitano et al. [22] describe a heuristic- based reverse engineering process for inferring a data model from spreadsheet data in the Excel format. This process was used to obtain the UML class diagrams representing the conceptual data models of three different spreadsheet-based information systems.

All these approaches and tools have similar goals (to transform spreadsheet data from an arbitrary form to a relational one). However, they use specified models of source spreadsheets with mixed physical and logical layouts. This fact limits the use of these tools for processing arbitrary spreadsheets presented in statistical reports.

Our review showed that the solutions considered above (each separately) fail to process the layouts from ISI reports. The use of the authors' software, namely, TabbyXL [4] is promising in this aspect. TabbyXL is a command-line tool for spreadsheet data canonicalization. This tool is used to produce flat relational (normalized) spreadsheet tables from semi structured tabular data. The tool operates with CSV format documents. TabbyXL provides a domain-specific rule language (Cells Rule Language, CRL) for analysis and interpretation of arbitrary tables by using user-defined properties of their layout, style, and text content.

3 The Methodology

We propose to use the TANGO approach [23] as a methodological basis and qualitatively redefine the main stages to support conceptual model engineering based on the analysis and transformation of spreadsheet data from the ISI reports. Despite some ideological similarity between our approach and [23], it is necessary to highlight its novelty, such as: the CSV files processing; an ability to handle any spreadsheet layouts (due to the use of CRL); focus on the designing conceptual models describing the ISI tasks; integration with knowledge base design systems (PKBD).

3.1 Main Steps

Designing conceptual models on the basis of analysis and transformation of spreadsheet data can be presented as a workflow diagram (Fig. 1) and contains five main steps.

Step 1: Extracting tables. At this step a set of tables is formed for further analysis and transformation. The method for formation is not strictly defined: user can use text recognition systems or manual copying and retyping.

Step 2: Recognizing of arbitrary tables presented in the CSV format and their transforming to canonicalized (normalized) form. In this connection, the following structure of canonical table is used (this structure is formed on the basis [23]):

$$CT^{CSV} = \{DATA, RowHeading, ColumnHeading\}, \qquad (1)$$

where $DATA$ is a data block that describes literal data values (named "entries") belonging to the same data type (e.g., numerical, textual, etc.), $RowHeading$ is a set of row labels of the category, $ColumnHeading$ is a set of column labels of the category. The values in cells for heading blocks can be separated by the "|" symbol to divide categories into subcategories. Thus, the canonical table denotes hierarchical relationships between categories (headings). This step results in tables in the unified (canonicalized) form prepared for their further automated processing. In the general case, this transformation includes all the enumerated stages [4]:

1. Detection. A spreadsheet document may contain several arbitrary tables surrounded by text and graphics.
2. Recognition. A human-readable structure of an arbitrary table can differ from its machine-readable structure presented in a spreadsheet, e.g. one logical cell can be visually composed of several physical cells through drawing their borders.
3. Role (functional) analysis. A spreadsheet cell stores a text, where a human can distinguish one or more data items that play some functional roles in a table (e. g. values or attributes). However, there are no spreadsheet metadata that separate data items from a cell value and determine their functional roles.

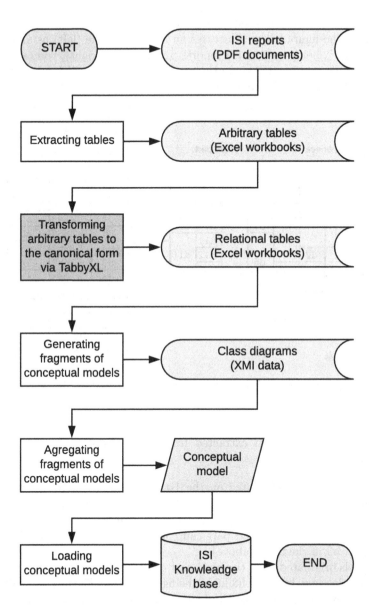

Fig. 1. Diagram of the workflow for analysis and transformation of spreadsheet data from ISI reports

4. Structural analysis. A spreadsheet also contains no metadata for representing relationships between data items of a table.

In our case, all tables can be separated into two types by their layout forms.

Form 1. The figure below illustrates an arbitrary table (left) as an example of the "Form 1" being used in ISI reports. In the figure (right), you can also see a corresponding relational table in the canonicalized form which is generated as a result of the table transformation.

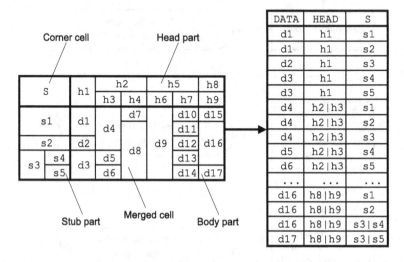

Fig. 2. Scheme of the "Form 1" table recognition and transforming them to the canonicalized form

The tables of this form extracted from ISI reports satisfy the following assumptions:

1. There is a corner cell located on the 1st column and 1st row. The bottom border of this corner cell is also the bottom border of *the head part* of a table. Its right border is also the right border of *the stub part* of the table.
2. Any cell located in the head part can contain only one "column" label (e.g. h1, h2,..., h9 in the figure above).
3. The labels originated from the head part can be read as paths of parent-child relationships (e.g. h2|h3 or h8|h9 in the figure above). The cell of a child label is nested by columns in the cell of the corresponding parent label (e.g. h4 is the child of h2).
4. Any path of column labels belongs to the undefined category HEAD.
5. Any cell located in the stub part of a table can contain only one "row" label (e.g. s1, s2, ..., s5 in the figure above).
6. The labels originated from the stub part can be read as paths of parent-child relationships (e.g. s3|s4 or s3|s5 in the figure above). The cell of a child label

is nested by rows in the cell of the corresponding parent label (e.g. h4 is the child of h2). Moreover, only two consecutive columns constitute the stub part.

7. Any path of raw labels belongs to the named category defined by a value of the corner cell (e.g. S in the figure above).
8. Any cell located in *the body part* of a table (i.e. under the head and right the stub) can contain only one entry (e.g. d1, d2,..., d17 in the figure above). A merged cell can be considered as a set of tiles split by rows (e.g. d16 in the figure above). Each tile can be considered as a separate cell with a duplicate of entry presented in the corresponding merged cell.
9. Each entry is addressed by one path of column labels and one path of row labels (e.g. d17 is addressed by two paths of labels: h8|h9 and s3|s5).

The assumptions listed above allowed us to develop two rulesets for transforming tables for both arbitrary forms to the canonicalized form.

CRL transformation rules were developed for dedicated layouts (see Fig. 2). For example, for "Form 1" :

1. Generate and categorize "column" labels from cells located in the head part of a table.
2. Associate child "column" labels with parent ones.
3. Generate "row" labels from cells located in the stub part of a table.
4. Associate child "row" labels with parent ones.
5. Split merged cells located in the body part into tiles.
6. Generate entries from cells located in the body part.
7. Associate entries with "column" and "row" labels.

Form 2. The figure below illustrates an arbitrary table (left) as an example of the "Form 2" being used in ISI reports. In the figure (right), you can also see a corresponding relational table in the canonicalized form that is generated as a result of the table transformation (Fig. 3).

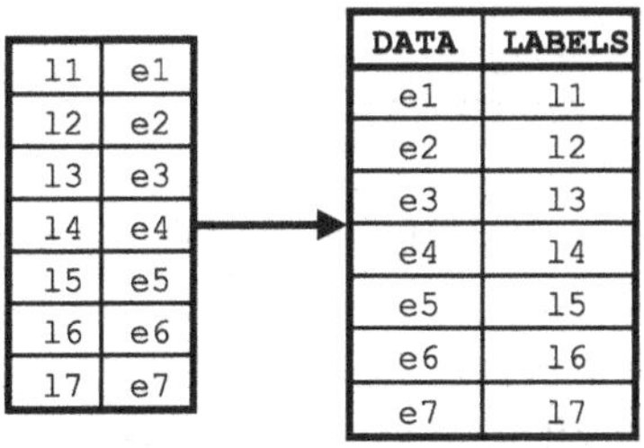

Fig. 3. Scheme of the "Form 2" table recognition and transforming them to the canonicalized form

This form is a simple list of pairs, where keys (labels) are placed in the left column (e.g. l1,..., l7 in the figure above) and their values (entries) are placed in the right column (e.g. e1,..., e7 in the figure above).

A detailed description of transformation rules for form layouts on CRL is provided in [3].

Step 3: Generating conceptual model fragments. The analysis of canonical tables is carried out line by line. At the same time, cells can contain a several values (concepts) with the separator ("|"). A cell value with the separator ("|") is interpreted as a hierarchy of either classes (concepts) or attributes (properties). The examples of a string analysis procedure are presented in Figs. 4, 5, 6 and 7.

The following typical structures for "Form 1" are identified and relevant transformation algorithms are proposed:

1. Simple structure, when the cell located in the head and stub parts can contain only one "column" label (Fig. 4).
2. Simple structure, when labels originated from the head part can be read as paths of parent-child relationships, and the cell located in the stub part can contain only one "column" label (Fig. 4).
3. Structure, when labels originated from the head and stub parts can be read as paths of parent-child relationships (Fig. 5).
4. Structure, when labels originated from the stub parts can be read as paths of multiple parent-child relationships (Fig. 6).

Only one structure for "Form 2" is identified (Fig. 7).

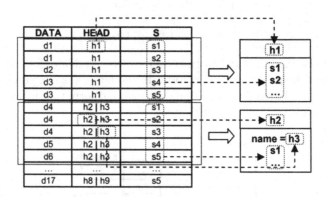

Fig. 4. Generating conceptual model fragments for the "Form 1" table (structures 1 and 2)

In UML class diagrams, all obtained parent-child relationships are interpreted as the association and the cardinality of "1..*" is determined by default.

By default attribute values are set based on the DATA column.

Step 4: Aggregating conceptual model fragments. This step includes operations for clarifying the names of concepts, their properties and relationships, and also their possible merging and separation.

The following rules used for automatic aggregation of conceptual models fragments:

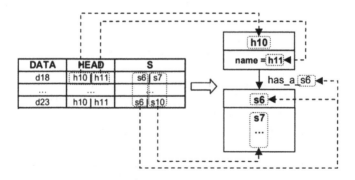

Fig. 5. Generating conceptual model fragments for the "Form 1" table (structure 3)

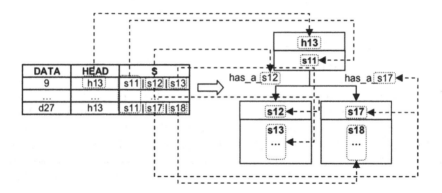

Fig. 6. Generating conceptual model fragments for the "Form 1" table (structure 4)

DATA	LABELS
e1	l1
e2	l2
e3	l3
e4	l4
e5	l5
e6	l6
e7	l7

Fig. 7. Generating conceptual model fragments for the "Form 2" table

1. Classes with equal names are merged (a common list of attributes is formed).
2. When the names of a class and attribute are equal, the attribute of the same name is removed; the corresponding relationship between classes is created.

Manual merging and separation operations are performed by the user using PKBD.

Step 5. Loading conceptual model. The obtained complete conceptual model can be used for the knowledge base source codes generation in the CLIPS (C Language Integrated Production System) format. This step is an important task, but it is not a purpose of this paper. More information about this problem can be found in [2].

Steps 3–5 are implemented as an extension module for the software of prototyping rule-based expert systems – Personal Knowledge Base Designer (PKBD) [2]. PKBD provides serializing conceptual model fragments in different formats, in particular, in the form of UML class diagrams. The obtained class diagram fragments are presented and stored in XMI (XML Metadata Interchange) format.

3.2   Example

Next, consider an example of the proposed methodology.

To illustrate conceptual model engineering on the basis of spreadsheet analysis and transformation we use ISI reports in the form of PDF documents. These documents were processed with the use of standard recognition tools and manual post-processing. We processed six ISI reports of Irkutsk Research and Design Institute of Chemical and Petrochemical Engineering (IrkutskNIIHimMash) [1] and obtained the dataset with 216 tables. The extracted arbitrary tables are presented in the CSV format. Figure 8 presents tables from our dataset containing information about elements of the inspected object and results of hardness measurement.

The following canonical tables are obtained (Fig. 9) with the use of TabbyXL.

Domain concepts are defined by the analysis of canonical tables (Fig. 9). These concepts can be presented as a UML class diagram (see Fig. 10).

Further modification of the conceptual models fragments allows us to obtain a complete domain model, for example, Fig. 11.

4   Discussion and Conclusions

Verification of the approach proposed was carried out on the data set formed by the analysis of the ISI petrochemical facilities reports. The data set includes 216 spreadsheets extracted from six reports. TabbyXL successfully processed all tables from this data set. TabbyXL experiment results on precision and recall for other data sets, in particular, TANGO [23] are presented in [4].

PKBD was used to transform canonical tables. 92 classes and 20 relationships were allocated. Resulted fragments (classes and relationships) were validated

Structural element	Amount	Pressure, MPa	Material	
			Marka	Standard
Pipe 159x4,5-180 for the output of the rest of the product	1	25	Steel 20	1050-88
Pipe 273x8-200 for the output of the vapour product				
Pipe 159x4,5-190 for the input of the coolant	3			
Pipe 57x4-110 for the drainage	1			
Main hatch 480x10-200			09G2C	5520-79
Place for the level control	2	-	Steel20	1050-88
Place for magnometer	1	25		
Mounting hatch 219x6-258	3			
Place for level indicator	2	-		
Pipe bundle inlet fitting (1,2,3)700x36-335	3	25	09G2C	5520-79

Measurment location	Material	Hardness, HB Min-Max
Base material of the corpus	BSt3	138-146
Ring welds	-	153-159
Longitudinal welds		151-161
Base material of the bottom of the corpus		151-155
Base material of the distribution chamber shell		145-153
Base material of the bottom of the distribution chamber shell	09G2C	149-157
Ring welds of the distribution chamber shell		150-158
Longitudinal welds of the distribution chamber shell	-	152-162

Fig. 8. Examples of arbitrary source tables

by experts and compared with models obtained earlier [24] when performing research projects with the Irkutsk research and design institute of chemical and petrochemical engineering (IrkutskNIIHimmash). 15 classes from the extracted set were used for further processing.

A qualitative comparison of approaches was also carried out (Table 1).

The results obtained show the prospects of using our approach to support the conceptual modeling for prototyping knowledge bases, developing software and ontologies [1–3].

The scientific novelty of the approach proposed is its universality: TabbyXL provides analysis and interpretation of arbitrary tables by using user-defined properties of their layout, style, and text content; PKBD provides transformation of obtained canonical tables into conceptual model fragments in the form of UML class diagrams and its aggregation into a complete domain model. The resulting domain model can be then transformed into the CLIPS format. These features provide an opportunity to transfer the approach proposed to another subject domain.

DATA	Row Heading	Column Heading
1	structural element | pipe 159x4,5-180 for the output of the rest of the product	amount
25	structural element | pipe 159x4,5-180 for the output of the rest of the product	pressure, mpa
steel 20	structural element | pipe 159x4,5-180 for the output of the rest of the product	material | marka
1050-88	structural element | pipe 159x4,5-180 for the output of the rest of the product	material | standard
1	structural element | pipe 273x8-200 for the output of the vapour product	amount
25	structural element | pipe 273x8-200 for the output of the vapour product	pressure, mpa
steel 20	structural element | pipe 273x8-200 for the output of the vapour product	material | marka
1050-88	structural element | pipe 273x8-200 for the output of the vapour product	material | standard
3	structural element | pipe 159x4,5-190 for the input of the coolant	amount
25	structural element | pipe 159x4,5-190 for the input of the coolant	pressure, mpa
steel 20	structural element | pipe 159x4,5-190 for the input of the coolant	material | marka
1050-88	structural element | pipe 159x4,5-190 for the input of the coolant	material | standard
1	structural element | pipe 57x4-110 for the drainage	amount
25	structural element | pipe 57x4-110 for the drainage	pressure, mpa
steel 20	structural element | pipe 57x4-110 for the drainage	material | marka

DATA	Row Heading	Column Heading
вst3	measurment location | base material of the corpus	material
138-146	measurment location | base material of the corpus	hardness, hb | min-max
-	measurment location | ring welds	material
153-159	measurment location | ring welds	hardness, hb | min-max
-	measurment location | longitudinal welds	material
151-161	measurment location | longitudinal welds	hardness, hb | min-max
09g2c	measurment location | base material of the bottom of the corpus	material
151-155	measurment location | base material of the bottom of the corpus	hardness, hb | min-max
09g2c	measurment location | base material of the distribution chamber shell	material
145-153	measurment location | base material of the distribution chamber shell	hardness, hb | min-max
09g2c	measurment location | base material of the bottom of the distribution chamber shell	material
149-157	measurment location | base material of the bottom of the distribution chamber shell	hardness, hb | min-max
-	measurment location | ring welds of the distribution chamber shell	material
150-158	measurment location | ring welds of the distribution chamber shell	hardness, hb | min-max
-	measurment location | longitudinal welds of the distribution chamber shell	material
152-162	measurment location | longitudinal welds of the distribution chamber shell	hardness, hb | min-max

Fig. 9. Fragments of canonical tables resulted from tables on Fig. 8

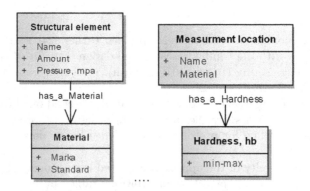

Fig. 10. Fragments of conceptual models

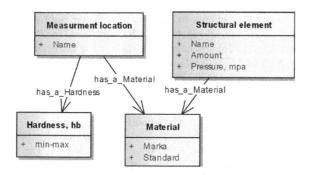

Fig. 11. A fragment of an aggregated conceptual model

Table 1. A qualitative comparison of approaches (*depends on PKBD modules, **CRL provides to handle any spreadsheet layouts)

Comparison criteria	TANGO [23]	Amalfitano et al. [22]	Our
Data source	Web	Microsoft Excel	PDF documents
Source table format	HTML	Microsoft Excel	CSV
Target format	OWL ontology	UML class diagram	UML class diagram,concept map, CLIPS*
Constraints for spreadsheet layouts	Yes	Not defined	No**

Acknowledgments. This work was supported by the Russian Science Foundation, grant number 18-71-10001.

References

1. Berman, A.F., Nikolaichuk, O.A., Yurin, A.Y., Kuznetsov, K.A.: Support of decision-making based on a production approach in the performance of an industrial safety review. Chem. Petrol. Eng. **50**(11–12), 730–738 (2015). https://doi.org/10.1007/s10556-015-9970-x
2. Yurin, A.Y., Dorodnykh, N.O., Nikolaychuk, O.A., Grishenko, M.A.: Prototyping rule-based expert systems with the aid of model transformations. J. Comput. Sci. **14**(5), 680–698 (2018). https://doi.org/10.3844/jcssp.2018.680.698
3. TabbyXL wiki. https://github.com/tabbydoc/tabbyxl/wiki/Industrial-Safety-Inspection. Accessed 13 Sept 2019
4. Shigarov, A.O., Mikhailov, A.A.: Rule-based spreadsheet data transformation from arbitrary to relational tables. Inf. Syst. **71**, 123–136 (2017). https://doi.org/10.1016/j.is.2017.08.004
5. Mauro, N., Esposito, F., Ferilli, S.: Finding critical cells in web tables with SRL: trying to uncover the devil's tease. In: 12th International Conference on Document Analysis and Recognition, pp. 882–886 (2013). https://doi.org/10.1109/ICDAR.2013.180

6. Adelfio, M., Samet, H.: Schema extraction for tabular data on the web. VLDB Endowment **6**(6), 421–432 (2013). https://doi.org/10.14778/2536336.2536343

7. Chen, Z., Cafarella, M.: Integrating spreadsheet data via accurate and low-effort extraction. In: 20th ACM SIGKDD International Conference Knowledge Discovery and Data Mining, pp. 1126–1135 (2014). https://doi.org/10.1145/2623330.2623617

8. Embley, D.W., Krishnamoorthy, M.S., Nagy, G., Seth, S.: Converting heterogeneous statistical tables on the web to searchable databases. IJDAR **19**(2), 119–138 (2016). https://doi.org/10.1007/s10032-016-0259-1

9. Rastan, R., Paik, H., Shepherd, J., Haller, A.: Automated table understanding using stub patterns. In: Navathe, S.B., Wu, W., Shekhar, S., Du, X., Wang, X.S., Xiong, H. (eds.) DASFAA 2016. LNCS, vol. 9642, pp. 533–548. Springer, Cham (2016). https://doi.org/10.1007/978-3-319-32025-0_33

10. Goto, K., Ohta, Yu., Inakoshi, H., Yugami, N.: Extraction algorithms for hierarchical header structures from spreadsheets. In: Workshops of the EDBT/ICDT 2016 Joint Conference, vol. 1558, pp. 1–6 (2016)

11. Nagy, G., Seth, S.: Table headers: An entrance to the data mine. In: 23rd International Conference Pattern Recognition, pp. 4065–4070 (2016). https://doi.org/10.1109/ICPR.2016.7900270

12. Koci, E., Thiele, M., Romero, O., Lehner, W.: A machine learning approach for layout inference in spreadsheets. In: Proceedings of 8th International Joint Conference Knowledge Discovery, Knowledge Engineering and Knowledge Management, pp. 77–88 (2016). https://doi.org/10.5220/0006052200770088

13. de Vos, M., Wielemaker, J., Rijgersberg, H., Schreiber, G., Wielinga, B., Top, J.: Combining information on structure and content to automatically annotate natural science spreadsheets. Int. J. Hum.-Comput. Stud. **130**, 63–76 (2017). https://doi.org/10.1016/j.ijhcs.2017.02.006

14. Kandel, S., Paepcke, A., Hellerstein, J., Heer, J.: Wrangler: interactive visual specification of data transformation scripts. In: SIGCHI Conference on Human Factors in Computing Systems, 3363–3372 (2011). https://doi.org/10.1145/1978942.1979444

15. Hung, V., Benatallah, B., Saint-Paul, R.: Spreadsheet-based complex data transformation. In: 20th ACM International Conference on Information and Knowledge Management, pp. 1749–1754 (2011). https://doi.org/10.1145/2063576.2063829

16. Harris, W., Gulwani, S.: Spreadsheet table transformations from examples. ACM SIGPLAN Notices **46**(6), 317–328 (2011). https://doi.org/10.1145/1993316.1993536

17. Astrakhantsev, N., Turdakov, D., Vassilieva, N.: Semi-automatic data extraction from tables. In: Proceedings 15th All-Russian Conference Digital Libraries, pp. 14–20 (2013)

18. Barowy, D.W., Gulwani, S., Hart, T., Zorn, B.: FlashRelate: extracting relational data from semi-structured spreadsheets using examples. ACM SIGPLAN Notices **50**(6), 218–228 (2015). https://doi.org/10.1145/2813885.2737952

19. Cunha, J., Erwig, M., Mendes, M., Saraiva, J.: Model inference for spreadsheets. Autom. Softw. Eng. **23**, 361–392 (2016). https://doi.org/10.1007/s10515-014-0167-x

20. Jin, Z., Anderson, M.R., Cafarella, M., Jagadish, H.V.: Foofah: Transforming data by example. In: ACM International Conference Management of Data, pp. 683–698 (2017). https://doi.org/10.1145/3035918.3064034

21. Hermans, F., Pinzger, M., van Deursen, A.: Automatically extracting class diagrams from spreadsheets. In: D'Hondt, T. (ed.) ECOOP 2010. LNCS, vol. 6183, pp. 52–75. Springer, Heidelberg (2010). https://doi.org/10.1007/978-3-642-14107-2_4

22. Amalfitano, D., Fasolino, A.R., Tramontana, P., De Simone, V., Di Mare, G., Scala, S.: A reverse engineering process for inferring data models from spreadsheet-based information systems: an automotive industrial experience. In: Helfert, M., Holzinger, A., Belo, O., Francalanci, C. (eds.) DATA 2014. CCIS, vol. 178, pp. 136–153. Springer, Cham (2015). https://doi.org/10.1007/978-3-319-25936-9_9

23. Tijerino, Y.A., Embley, D.W., Lonsdale, D.W., Ding, Y., Nagy, G.: Towards ontology generation from tables. World Wide Web Internet Web Inf. Syst. 8(8), 261–285 (2005). https://doi.org/10.1007/s11280-005-0360-8

24. Yurin A.Y., Dorodnykh N.O., Nikolaychuk O.A., Berman A.F., Pavlov A.I.: ISI models, mendeley data, v1 (2019). https://doi.org/10.17632/f9h2t766tk.1

Data Mining

Nonlinearity Estimation of Digital Signals

Kiril Alexiev$^{(\boxtimes)}$ (iD)

Institute of Communication and Information Technologies, Bulgarian Academy of Sciences, 25A Acad. G. Bonchev Str., 1113 Sofia, Bulgaria
alexiev@bas.bg
http://iict.bas.bg

Abstract. Assessing the nonlinearity of one signal, system, or dependence of one signal on another is of great importance in the design process. The article proposes an algorithm for simplified nonlinearity estimation of digital signals. The solution provides detailed information to constructors about existing nonlinearities, which in many cases is sufficient to make the correct choice of processing algorithms. The programming code of the algorithm is presented and its implementation is demonstrated on a set of basic functions. Several steps to further development of the proposed approach are outlined.

Keywords: Nonlinearity estimation · Nonlinear dependencies · Nonlinear models

1 Introduction

In a seminal article in 2004 Simon Haykin defined the main problems in signal processing for the 21-st century. He stated that the main difference in signal processing will be in the processing of non-linear, non-Gaussian and non-stationary signals [1]. Other scientists also spoke for the curse of the three "non". However, it is clear that the modern signal processing is concerned about these three "non". Why do these problems attract the attention of the specialists in the signal processing? This is primarily due to the fact that in real life, the systems we observe, evaluate, or control are most likely nonlinear, non-Gaussian, and non-stationary. Therefore, solving these types of problems is possible through the use of new methods and algorithms whose implementation is feasible, thanks to the constantly increasing power of the modern computers. To solve the problems, mentioned above, it is required to be designed:

- Correct mathematical model of the observed dynamic process or dynamic system;
- Correct statistical description of the received signals and the noise;
- Reflect the changes in statistics over time.

This article is limited only to considering primarily nonlinearities in the behavior of the observed system or process. The task of estimating nonlinearities can be interpreted in various ways.

D. Simian and L. F. Stoica (Eds.): MDIS 2019, CCIS 1126, pp. 69–80, 2020.
https://doi.org/10.1007/978-3-030-39237-6_5

The simplest definition of a nonlinearity is the geometric representation. For this representation we are looking for an estimate how close the function is to linear one.

In the design and the analysis of systems, the deviation of the output of the system is often considered, depending on the input signal. In such systems, a test is performed for SISO (single input single output) or BIBO (bounded input bounded output) systems in order to describe the (non)linear dependence of the system output from input.

The mathematical description of the problem definitely looks for an estimate how one variable depends on another one.

Nevertheless the origin of the description is coming from, the task is to find affordable method for nonlinearity estimation. The nonlinear functions are well-known from many years and there are several methods to describe them. Brook Taylor, a British mathematician, proposed a description of nonlinear function near a point more than 3 centuries ago ($\sim$1715 year)[2]. Two centuries later, Vito Volterra devised a mathematical tool for modeling of non-parametric and non-linear systems [3]. Named in honor of the Italian mathematician, the Volterra's series makes it possible to express the dependence of a given data point in a time series not only on the closest preceding one but also on all the preceding ones (the so-called memory effect). The output signal representation is expressed as a sum of integral operators from the input signal. However, the both methods are applicable only for "weak enough" nonlinear signals and they are unfeasible for strongly nonlinear ones. Later, an extended Kalman filter (EKF) appeared, followed by EKF with Expectation Maximization (EM) supplementation [4].

The development of new algorithms does not stop and many other versions of the KF were created like Generalized Pseudo-Bayesian (GPB) estimators of different orders, Fixed Structure Interactive Multiple Models (IMM), Variable Structure IMM, Probabilistic Data Association IMM, and so on [5–9]. All of them are estimating the nonlinear system parameters. Although there is rich variety of methods and algorithms, they are mainly based on linear approximation. This makes the algorithms particularly sensitive to large nonlinearities in system behavior. In some conditions the convergence of the estimated uncertainty is slow, sometimes could not be reached at all. Most often this happens because linear or near linear dependencies between some of the main variables are assumed in the considered interval. Linearity helps us to construct easily the simpler mathematical model of the observed phenomena, but sometimes the system behavior is very different from the behavior of the linear model and the mathematical model leads to erroneous conclusions. It would still be good to distinguish these two cases and to know when we can use linear approximation and to what extent and when cannot use it.

The article addresses this issue by evaluating the degree of nonlinearity of a function. With this estimate, the algorithms with appropriately selected parameters can be applied, without the risk of divergence of the realized nonlinear filter.

2   The State of the Problem

In [10], the first found paper on this topic, a numerical measure of the non-linearity of a model was introduced. The general problem description, given by the author, is:

$$y_u = \eta(\xi_u, \theta) + \epsilon_u, u = 1, \ldots, n, \tag{1}$$

where y_u is a set of observations, $\eta(\xi_u, \theta)$ is the set of corresponding theoretical mean values, ϵ_u is random error vector. We are looking for θ parameters which simultaneously satisfy two conditions:

1) The model is approximately linear;
2) The choice minimizes the sum of squares of residuals:

$$S(\theta) = \sum_{u=1}^{n} \{y_u - \eta(\xi_u, \theta)\}^2 \tag{2}$$

The proposed confidence regions are defined for a set of values of θ, holding the difference $S(\theta) - S(\tilde{\theta})$ less than a value. Desoer and Wang proposed the concept of nonlinearity measure in 1980 [11]. According this article, the nonlinearity measure of a nonlinear function N over $u \in V$ with respect to a bounded time interval $[0, T]$ is the non-negative real number defined by:

$$\delta_T(N, V) = \inf \sup_{u \in V} |N_u - L_u|_T, \tag{3}$$

where L is the best linear approximation of N over V. The best linear approximation L of a nonlinear function N minimizes the mean square error:

$$\lim_{\tau \to \infty} \frac{1}{\tau} \int_0^\tau [N_u(t) - L_u(t)]^2 dt. \tag{4}$$

Further, the authors defined a second nonlinearity measure as:

$$\delta_T(N, V) = \inf \sup_{u \in V} \frac{|N_u - L_u|_T}{|u|_T} \tag{5}$$

In 1980 Bates and Watts developed new measures of nonlinearity based on the geometric concept of curvature - the maximum curvature measure [12]. A quantitative measure of nonlinearity was proposed in 1993 in the next form [13]:

$$L = \frac{\sqrt{\int_{x_1}^{x_n} [f(x) - ax - b]^2 dx}}{x_n - x_1} \tag{6}$$

Here the parameters a and b must be chosen in order to minimize L. The values x_1 and x_n determine the interval of the argument change. Tugnait proposed a novel approach for linearity testing of stationary time series. It was based on data power spectrum estimate [14]. Similar approach is proposed in [17]. Frank

Allgower propose a new normalized measure of nonlinearity in [15,16]. If we use already used notation this measure can be expressed by:

$$\delta_T(N,V) = \inf_{} \sup_{u \in V} \frac{|N_u - L_u|_T}{|L_u|_T} \tag{7}$$

In [18] a wonderful overview of the methods from correlation analysis, harmonic analysis and higher order spectrum analysis for nonlinearity estimation was written. Each described method has been analyzed for its advantages and disadvantages. The authors proposed also modifications of the known metrics and some new indices were introduced. Their analysis begins with cross correlation function in frequency with Haber metrics [19]:

$$NLI1 = 1 - \max_{\omega} \frac{|\phi_{yu}(j\omega)|^2}{\phi_{uu}(j\omega)\phi_{yy}(j\omega)}. \tag{8}$$

Here $\phi_{..}(j\omega)$ are the auto- and cross-spectral densities associated with the system input/output data. The measure has to be zero for linear system. The corresponding measure in time domain is [19]:

$$NLI4 = 1 - \frac{[\sum_{r=0}^{N-1} \phi_{yu}(r)]^2}{\sum_{r=0}^{N-1} \phi_{uu}(r) \sum_{r=0}^{N-1} \phi_{yy}(r)}. \tag{9}$$

Particularly valuable in their analysis is that they explore different approaches to noise vulnerability.

Smith used the mutual information in measuring of the total dependence [20]. In a recent paper Liu and Li considered especially measuring the degree of nonlinearity for estimation [21]. They proposed a more general definition of the measure of the signal nonlinearity, based on the distance between the nonlinear function and linearity. They formulated the minimization task as follows:

$$\min_{A,b} \left(E[\|g(x,v) - (Ax+b)\|_2^2]\right) + \min_{\psi(w,v)} \left(E[\|w\|_2^2] - 2E[g(x,v)'w]\right). \tag{10}$$

They confessed that the numerical minimization of Eq. (10) is difficult.

In [23] time series from economics are considered. The author proposed a measure which exploits the decomposition of a conditional expectation into its linear and nonlinear components.

The measuring of nonlinearity is especially important in the nonlinear estimation. Summarizing the literature review on the subject, we can conclude that a robust indicator of the degree of nonlinearity has not be designed. The proposed till now estimates of the nonlinearity are not sufficiently convenient or well-functioning. Usually, the divergence of the estimating filter is considered as a rough indicator of the nonlinearity of the observed process. Unfortunately, when such a divergence is detected, the estimation procedure has to be stopped and the filter must be restarted, losing the benefits of applying the filter.

3   Nonlinearity Estimation of Digital Signals

The linear interpolation has long been known in the mathematics and in the signal processing. It is the most natural instrument for reconstructing a function/signal with known points/measurements. It follows from the Taylor series that any smooth (differentiable) function can be represented with a given accuracy by a finite set of linear functions. Increasing the accuracy of the approximation will lead to an increase in number of approximating linear functions. It is also true that increasing the nonlinearity of a function leads to an increase in the residual error in the Taylor series, used for linear approximation, and therefore will require a corresponding increase in the number of approximating linear functions. Therefore, if we fix the accuracy of approximation of a nonlinear function, then the degree of nonlinearity can be estimated by the number of approximating linear functions required.

Let denote the approximation accuracy of a nonlinear function by ε. In the case of linear approximation, the function is split in several parts. The signal is approximated by a straight line for each part and the approximation error does not exceed ε. Let's now look at two adjacent approximated signal parts. For each of them the approximation error does not exceed ε.

Consequently the sum of both errors should not exceed $2 * \varepsilon$, when the function under consideration is smooth. And vice versa if the sum of errors exceeds $2 * \varepsilon$ the function is continuous at the middle point but it is not differentiable at that point.

The nonlinearity estimation algorithm is built on the base of two measures of nonlinearity, described in Eqs. (3) and (7). The structure of nonlinear estimator, however, is quite different. In order to find an estimate of local nonlinearity, the input signal is segmented on a special way. The segments are chosen in the way to preserve signal monotonicity (every signal segment is a monotone function). It is simple to find the segment border point - they are signal extrema. They can be found by an extrema detection algorithm, which identifies all local peaks and troughs of the observed input signal. Every segment is enclosed between one maximum and one minimum or vice versa - between one minimum and one maximum. The segments have two properties:

1) They have not overlapping parts;
2) The gradient sign remain the same for all segment points.

The signal has also two additional segments - the first part of signal before the first found peak and the last one - after the last peak which are also monotone functions. The nonlinearity will be estimated on every segment.

These basics are embedded in the newly proposed nonlinearity estimation algorithm.

The basic processing steps of the proposed algorithm are shown on Fig. 1.

The **first step** of the algorithm consists of preliminary denoising and resampling. The importance of this step arises when the noise in the system is stronger. If the noise level is high enough the extrema detection algorithm may detect

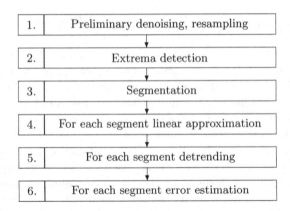

Fig. 1. Basic processing steps of the proposed algorithm

much more signal extrema. Something more, the algorithm could not localize accurately the signal extrema. In order to assure correct detection of the fast system changes, the electronic designers select suitable signal sampling rate, guaranteeing a full representation of the observed system (Nyquist - Kotelnikov theorem states that for a particular signal, the sampling rate must be no less than twice the frequency of the composite in the highest frequency band). If the fast processes predominate, it is possible that some segments may contain not big enough number of measurements. In these cases, a resampling is required. It is realized with two different interpolating functions depending on the type of signal being processed. For a typical analogous signal the spline approximation is used. For a pulse train signal the linear interpolation is more suitable to be applied.

On the **second step** an extrema detection algorithm finds the signal extrema. All maxima and minima are selected and ordered. The first and the last signal measurements are added to them. All these points are marked on the signal. Based on extrema points the segments are determined on the **third step**.

The next three steps are repeated for every detected segment.

On the **fourth step** a linear interpolation is realized. We have already postulated that the function corresponding to the measurements in each segment is monotonic. To maintain smooth transitions from one segment to another and in order to preserve function continuity, the linear interpolation is not based on linear regression analysis. A simplified method is used to draw a straight line through the end points of the segment. As a result of this interpolation, the transition points between the segments are saved and the computational cost is significantly reduced. Naturally, this is at the expense of deterioration the interpolation quality (the interpolation error increases).

On the **fifth step** the signal in each segment is detrended by subtracting the corresponding interpolated values from the signal measurements. As a result, the detrended segment signal has null values in its first and last points.

The **last step** is devoted on error estimation. Two different measures are used for error estimation. The first one is based on Eq. (3). We are looking for maximum deviation of the detrended signal on the segment. This metric is an absolute one and it does not depend on the length of the segment. The second measure is based on Eq. (7). It is normalized to the length of the segment and shows the deviation of the error per unit length of the segment.

The received error measure compares with a threshold. If it surpasses the threshold, the error signal goes to the step two for extrema detection. If the error is small enough, the algorithm finishes its work for this segment.

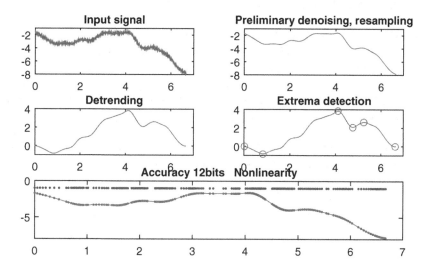

Fig. 2. Demonstration of algorithm (Color figure online)

These steps are shown on Fig. 2. On the last graph on this figure the non-linearity estimate is visualized with blue ink (points) above the signal (with red ink). The results are received using 12 bits ADC (analog-to-digital converter), limiting the maximal interpolation accuracy. The qualitative description of the nonlinearity measure is given by the density of points above the signal. On these parts of signal, where the points are rare, the nonlinearity is low. The parts of signal with dense set of points have bigger nonlinearity. The quantitative nonlinearity measures can be expressed by the distances between neighboring points, their density for a chosen part of the signal, etc.

The idea of the proposed algorithm is similar in some sense to the so called polylines simplification algorithms. These algorithms approximate a curve by line segments. They use different approaches and heuristics in order to minimize the number of linear segments while maintaining a given level of approximation accuracy. The most popular between them are the algorithm like Ramer-Douglas-Peucker, Visvalingam-Whyatt, Reumann-Witkam, Zhao-Saalfeld, Opheim simplification algorithm, Lang simplification algorithm, etc. [22]. The newly proposed algorithm is similar to the listed polyline approximation algorithms. However it uses different linearization criterion and it has different implementation. A distinctive feature of the proposed algorithm is the preliminary special segmentation of the curves, securing the monotonicity of the signal in the individual segments. This segmentation preserves also the extrema of the curve in the reduced set of points. The second characteristic feature of this algorithm is its final goal - to create/calculate trustworthy estimate of the degree of nonlinearity of the signal.

4 MATLAB Realization

An recursive algorithm is realized according the description, given in previous section. The demonstration code is written on MATLAB and displayed on Fig. 3, where a fragment from the main program is given. The heart of the algorithm is the recursive procedure, shown on Fig. 4. The main program inserts the input signal, detrend it and prepare work arrays. The signal is detrended by a simplified procedure, described in the previous section. The main program calls the recursive procedure, sending the detrended signal, the sampling points, the approximation accuracy of a nonlinear function ε. The approximation accuracy is given in an engineering manner - the number of bits, used by ADC for signal representation.

```
%============ normalization =============
s_lin = interp1([t_in(1) t_in(end)], [s_in2(1) s_in2(end)], t_in, Int_method);
Err_val = s_in2 - s_lin;
subplot(3,2,3), plot(t_in, Err_val);
title('Detrending');
NonLinearEstimator(Err_val, t_in, epsilon);
[Log_t,Loc_t] = ismember(t_out,t_in);
subplot(3,1,3);
plot(t_in,s_in2,t_out,s_in2(Loc_t),'-r.',t_out, Log_t*(max(s_in)+delta/10),'b.');
title(['Accuracy ' num2str(k) 'bits   Nonlinearity']);
```

Fig. 3. Fragment of main programm

The recursive procedure detects the signal extrema. In the set of signal extrema the first and the last signal measurements are also included. Then the signal is segmented. In a cycle for each segment a linear interpolation is fulfilled. The signal points are compared with the interpolated ones and an estimate of interpolation error is received. If the interpolation error is smaller than a threshold, the segment is regarded linear and its processing finishes. If the error is greater than the threshold, the procedure calls itself in order to treat this segment further. When the procedure finishes its work it collects the border points. Their density on the signal serves as indicator for nonlinearity of the observed signal.

```
function NonLinearEstimator(s_in, t_in, epsilon)

    global t_out
    Int_method = 'linear';
    %=============== Find extr =====================
    [extr_loc, extr_ind] = find_extr1(s_in, t_in, epsilon);

    %============ for every segment =======================
    N_extr = length(extr_loc);
    for i = 1:N_extr-1
        %========= fetch segment =======================
        s = s_in(extr_ind(i):extr_ind(i+1));
        t = t_in(extr_ind(i):extr_ind(i+1));
        %========= interpolation =====================
        s_lin = interp1([t(1) t(end)], [s(1) s(end)], t, Int_method);
        %============ Is it good interpolation? ================
        Err_val = s - s_lin;
        max_err = max(abs(Err_val));
        if max_err > epsilon
            NonLinearEstimator(Err_val, t, epsilon);
        else
            if isempty(t_out)
                t_out = [t_out; t(1); t(end)];
            else
                t_out = [t_out; t(end)];
            end
        end
    end
end
```

Fig. 4. Recursive program for nonlinearity estimation

5   Experimental Results

The new algorithm is applied to several demonstrative signals of diverse types
(Fig. 5). The first signal is a sine function. The segments' boundary points, used
for linear approximation are placed on signal curve and additionally are depicted
on the top of drawing because they play role of nonlinearity indicator. The
density points out the local function nonlinearity. The density grows up near to
the extrema and diminishes on the signal slopes. It is important to note, that
the density depends on the approximation accuracy. On the cited drawing the
chosen accuracy (very low) enhances the visualization of different densities.

On the next demonstrative example a pulse train is analyzed. This function
is continuous, but not differentiable. Due to its linearity the segments' boundary
points are placed only on the transition points from one state of the signal to
another. Something more, due to the bigger approximation error difference (sum)
in neighboring segments, it is very easy to detect the non differentiable points.
In this way the system model and the filtering algorithms could be prevented
from divergence.

The last example concerns processing of real ECG signal. The ECG signal
characterizes with both type of features - smooth parts and sharp peaks. This
sophisticated example demonstrates the capabilities of the proposed nonlinearity
estimator. The nonlinearity indicator successfully outlines the largest nonlinearities, as well as the segments with smooth behavior.

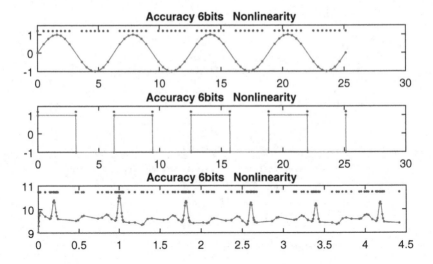

Fig. 5. Demonstration examples - sine, pulse train, ECG signal

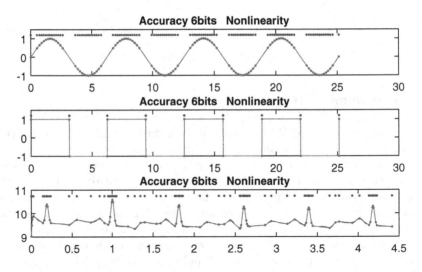

Fig. 6. Demonstration examples - sine, pulse train, ECG signal, second threshold

Summarizing the results of the demonstration examples, we can say that the proposed algorithm successfully handles different types of signals when evaluating their nonlinearity. It gives a local estimate of the nonlinearity at a given point of the signal or an interval estimate of nonlinearity.

The next Fig. 6 displays the results from the same examples, when the second threshold is applied. A careful comparison of the results of the last two figures shows that the application of the second threshold leads to more precisely reproduction of the nonlinearities.

6   Conclusions

In this article a new algorithm for nonlinearity estimation is proposed. Four basic assumptions are used in developing:

- The linear approximation of a signal gives information about the changes in the signal. The error of approximation signalizes how big the nonlinearity is;
- The linear approximation of a signal is realized through the signal splitting into non-overlapping segments. The signal extrema are used as boundary points of segment. These points carry the biggest nonlinearities of the signal. They are special feature points, which fragment a signal into monotonicity parts.
- The linear approximation is realized by splitting the signal until given accuracy is achieved. The signal splitting depends entirely on signal nonlinearity. The density of boundary segment points is a perfect indicator of signal nonlinearity.
- If two neighboring signal segments have sum/difference of errors exceeding twice the error threshold, it can be considered, that the function is not differentiable in the border point splitting these segments.

The algorithm is realized as a recursive procedure. Two types of approximation errors are considered. The first one considers absolute error deviation for a segment. The second approximation error is normalized and it expresses signal nonlinearity more correctly. The proposed algorithms has simple implementation and it does not have high requirements to the computer resources.

References

1. Haykin, S.: Signal processing in a nonlinear, nongaussian, and nonstationary world. In: Chollet, G., Esposito, A., Faundez-Zanuy, M., Marinaro, M. (eds.) NN 2004. LNCS (LNAI), vol. 3445, pp. 43–53. Springer, Heidelberg (2005). https://doi.org/10.1007/11520153_3
2. http://www.17centurymaths.com/contents/taylorscontents.html
3. Xiong, X.Y.Z., Jiang, L.J., Schutt-Aine, J.E., Chew, W.C.: Volterra series-based time-domain macromodeling of nonlinear circuits. IEEE Trans. Compon. Packag. Manuf. Technol. **7**(1), 39–49 (2017). https://doi.org/10.1109/TCPMT.2016.2627601
4. Roweis, S.T., Ghahramani, Z.: Learning nonlinear dynamical system using the expectation-maximization algorithm. In Haykin, S. (ed.) Kalman Filtering and Neural Networks, First published: 01 October 2001. Wiley, Hoboken (2001). https://doi.org/10.1002/0471221546.ch6, https://cs.nyu.edu/~roweis/papers/nlds.pdf
5. Bar-Shalom, Y., Forthmann, T.: Tracking and Data Association. Academic Press, San Diego (1988)
6. Bar-Shalom, Y. (ed.): Multitarget-Multisensor Tracking: Advanced Applications. Norwood, Chicago (1990)
7. Bar-Shalom, Y., Li, X.R.: Multitarget-Multisensor Tracking: Principles and Techniques. Artech House, Boston (1993)

8. Li, X.R.: Engineers' Guide to Variable-Structure Multiple-Model Estimation and Tracking (2000). http://citeseerx.ist.psu.edu/viewdoc/download?doi=10.1.1.61.8701&rep=rep1&type=pdf

9. Blom, H.A.P., Bloem, E.A.: Joint IMM and coupled PDA to track closely spaced targets and to avoid track coalescence. In: Proceedings of the Seventh International Conference on Information Fusion, pp. 130–137 (2005)

10. Beale, E.M.L.: Confidence regions in non-linear estimation. J. Roy. Stat. Soc. Ser. B (Methodol.) **22**(1), 41–88 (1960)

11. Desoer, C.A., Wang, Y.T.: Foundations of feedback theory for nonlinear dynamical systems. IEEE Trans. Circ. Syst. **27**(2), 104–123 (1980)

12. Bates, D.M., Watts, D.G.: Relative curvature measures of nonlinearity. J. Roy. Stat. Soc.: Ser. B (Methodol.) **42**(1), 1–25 (1980). Wiley for the Royal Statistical Society. https://www.jstor.org/stable/2984733

13. Emancipator, K., Kroll, M.H.: A quantitative measure of nonlinearity. Clin. Chem. **39**(5), 766–772 (1993)

14. Tugnait, J.K.: Testing for linearity of noisy stationary signals. IEEE Trans. Signal Process. **42**(10), 2742–2748 (1994)

15. Allgower, F.: Definition and Computation of a Nonlinearity Measure. IFAC Nonlinear Control Systems Design, Tahoe City, California, USA (1995)

16. Helbig, A., Marquardt, W., Allgower, F.: Nonlinearity measures: definition, computation and applications. J. Process Control **10**, 113–123 (2000)

17. Barnett, A.G., Wolff, R.C.: A time-domain test for some types of nonlinearity. IEEE Trans. Signal Process. **53**(1), 26–33 (2005)

18. Hosseini, S.M., Johansen, T.A., Fatehi, A.: Comparison of nonlinearity measures based on time series analysis for nonlinearity detection. Model. Identif. Control **32**(4), 123–140 (2011). ISSN 1890-1328

19. Haber, R.: Nonlinearity test for dynamic process. In: IFAC Identification and system Parameter Estimation (1985)

20. Smith, R.: A mutual information approach to calculating nonlinearity. The ISI's Journal for the Rapid Dissemination of Statistics Research. https://doi.org/10.100X/sta.0000, (http://wileyonlinelibrary.com)

21. Liu, Y., Li, X.R.: Measure of nonlinearity for estimation. IEEE Trans. Signal Process. **63**(9), 2377–2388 (2015)

22. Shi, W., Cheung, C.: Performance evaluation of line simplification algorithms for vector generalization. Cartographic J. **43**(1), 27–44 (2006)

23. Kotchoni, R.: Detecting and measuring nonlinearity. MDPI, Econometrics **6**, 37 (2018). https://doi.org/10.3390/econometrics6030037

Aggregation on Learning to Rank for Consumer Health Information Retrieval

Hua Yang[1,2(✉)] and Teresa Gonçalves[1]

[1] Computer Science Department, University of Évora, Évora, Portugal
huayangchn@gmail.com, tcg@uevora.pt
[2] School of Computer Science, Zhongyuan University of Technology,
Zhengzhou, China

Abstract. Common people are increasingly acquiring health information depending on general search engines which are still far from being effective in dealing with complex consumer health queries. One prime and effective method in addressing this problem is using Learning to Rank (L2R) techniques. In this paper, an investigation on aggregation over field-based L2R models is made. Rather than combining all potential features into one list to train a L2R model, we propose to train a set of L2R models each using features extracted from only one field and then apply aggregation methods to combine the results obtained from each model. Extensive experimental comparisons with the state-of-the-art baselines on the considered data collections confirmed the effectiveness of our proposed approach.

Keywords: Learning to Rank · Rank aggregation · Consumer health · Information Retrieval

1 Introduction

A 2013 report from the Pew Research Center shows that 73% of US people use the Internet, and 71% of them use the Internet to search health information [9]. It is a common activity for consumers to use the World Wide Web as a source for health information and general search engines are popularly used with this goal.

However, despite the popularity of consumer health search in daily activity and its topic interest in the Information Retrieval (IR) research community, the development of search technologies remain challenging in the area of Consumer Health Information Retrieval (CHIR) [10]. The methodologies and techniques applied are still far from being effective in addressing complex consumer health queries [10,35]. Access mechanisms for factual health information search have developed greatly and it is easy to get an answer to 'what is gout?' or 'what are the symptoms of gout?'; nevertheless, for complex health searches (like 'does daily aspirin therapy prevent heart attack?'), which do not have a single definitive answer, it is still indefinable.

© Springer Nature Switzerland AG 2020
D. Simian and L. F. Stoica (Eds.): MDIS 2019, CCIS 1126, pp. 81–93, 2020.
https://doi.org/10.1007/978-3-030-39237-6_6

During the past years, Learning to Rank (L2R) techniques, which apply machine learning methods on ranking problems, have been successfully used to improve retrieval of Web pages [5,15,27]. Likewise, L2R has also been studied in the context of consumer health search. This approach has been recently used to promote understandability in medical health queries [19] and to train models using syntactic and semantic features [25].

Creating a feature list is an important task in applying the L2R approach. Traditionally, explored potential features are defined and combined to create a feature list which is used to train a L2R model afterwards. A vast amount of research has been done into crafting new features, but this is a costly job in Learning to Rank. Compared with this research line that aims to find new good features, little work has been done on studying how to make good use of the explored features (like, for instance, the classification of features based on field information).

Since a document field (e.g.: title, H1 or body) contributes differently to the document, we assume that:

- Raw combination of features extracted from different fields into one single feature list will make the features blur;
- An aggregated model over a set of pre-trained field-based models (a field-base model is a model trained using single field features) is more effective than a model trained with all features from different fields.

In this work, we study this practical challenge by applying rank aggregation methods on field-based L2R models with a focus on Consumer Health Search. Based on the above ideas, we propose a two-stage L2R framework: we first train a set of field-based L2R models and then apply aggregation functions on these models. Our extensive experimental comparisons with the state-of-the-art baselines on the considered data collections show that the aggregated models achieve much better results than the models that blindly join all features. The main contribution of this work is a proposal of a two-stage L2R framework where aggregation methods are applied to field-based L2R models. This approach significantly outperforms the strongest baseline and prior works.

The rest of the paper is organized as follows. In Sect. 2, previous work on Learning to Rank in health search and the rank aggregation techniques are reviewed. The proposal is introduced in Sect. 3. The experiments and the results are described in Sects. 4 and 5. Finally, the conclusion is made and the future work is discussed in Sect. 6.

2   Related Work

In this section, previous work on Learning to Rank in health search domain are first reviewed; then, the rank aggregation techniques are discussed.

2.1 Learning to Rank in Health Search

During the past decade, Learning to Rank has shown its effectiveness in solving the ranking problems in the IR area. Recently, this technique has also gained the great interest of researchers in health search area [12,21,22,36].

In this paper, we mainly review the work applying L2R techniques in CLEF eHealth IR lab[1] from teams that participated in the lab from 2015 to 2018. This evaluation lab aims at gathering researchers working on consumer health search topics and providing datasets available for research in this area.

In 2015 two teams explored L2R techniques in their work. One team explored combining scores and ranks from BM25, PL2 and BB2 into a six-dimensional vector [26]; the results show that this method achieved under-performed performance compared with query expansion techniques explored by the same team. The second team investigated L2R along with a Markov Random Field approach [28]; no clear results were reported.

In 2016, one group proposed a L2R algorithm to re-rank the results; no clear evaluation over the results was reported [32]. Moreover, Zuccon *et al.* demonstrated in his work [36] that L2R did not work as well as query expansion techniques.

Soldaini *et al.* [25] proposed a combination of statistical and semantic features to train a L2R model; their methods were tested on CLEF eHealth 2016 dataset. The results showed that their approach outperforms the best baseline approach by 26.6%.

Palotti *et al.* [19] researched the effectiveness of the L2R method which exploited retrieval features as well as readability features. They used standard weighting models features for learning topical relevance and additional features based on readability measures and medical lexical aspects to learn understandability. They concluded that the combination of retrieval features and readability features improve search engine results.

In 2017, Scells *et al.* [23] proved that the use of the PICO-based features within L2R provides improvements over the use of baseline features alone.

For the 2018 task, Pallotti *et al.* [20] performed a personalized retrieval in a L2R setting and concluded that using this technique did not always improved the baseline.

Other related work by Abacha [1] concluded that the L2R approach could slightly improve the baseline. Jo and Lee [24] developed certain strategies for using L2R methods, but no clear performance improvement was reported; moreover, their performance compared with other techniques were not clarified.

Traditional L2R techniques usually depend on manual judgments when training a model. In the last several years, another trend, namely online L2R has also attracted attention in the IR research community. Online L2R gathers information from the implicit user feedback like clicks and can directly make use of the returned search results [2,31,33].

From the above discussion, we can see that although L2R methods have shown its success in Information Retrieval, their performance in health search is

---

[1] https://sites.google.com/site/clefehealth/.

not quite clear and more research work is needed to prove its usefulness in this specific IR area.

Our research is based on traditional L2R and the judgments are still heavily depending on explicit medical experts.

2.2 Rank Aggregation Techniques

Rank aggregation means combining the results information available from multiple retrieval models and producing a single ranking list. In the area of IR, there is a long history of using aggregation techniques over different weighting models. Moreover, rank aggregation techniques have been applied in different applications nowadays such as meta-search [18].

The output information from a ranking model can be a valued score or a sorting regarding to a document. Based on the output, the techniques applied can be classified as score-based combination [8,13,14,17,18,30,34] or the sort-based combination[2] [4,6,7]. Our work is mainly based on sort-based combination and the readers are asked to distinguish them.

In the early years, rank aggregation techniques were mainly used to combine ranking results obtained from different retrieval weighting models inside a search engine [8,14,30]. Later, rank aggregation techniques were extended and used for meta-search where ranking results from different search engines or meta-search engines [17,18] are combined. Recently, some research work also showed its effectiveness in other applications [13,34].

Early in 1993, Fox and Shaw [8] presented their method for combining the similarity values from multiple retrieval runs. They proposed six combining strategies in their work: CombMAX, CombMIN, CombSUM, CombANZ, CombMNZ and CombMED. Although simple, these combination strategies showed their efficiency and are still popularly used by other researchers in this area. These strategies are still the classic methods for score-based combination. Table 1 describes these strategies.

Table 1. Rank aggregation functions by Fox and Shaw'94

Agg. function	Description
CombMAX	Maximum of documents scores in learners
CombMIN	Minimum of documents scores in learners
CombSUM	Sum of documents scores in learners
CombANZ	CombSUM ÷ number of learners
CombMNZ	CombSUM × number of learners
CombMED	Median of documents scores in learners

---

[2] Sort-based combination is also known as rank-based combination in the literature.

Following this work, Lee [14] further observed that CombMNZ worked best among all these combination techniques, then CombSUM; CombMIN and Comb-MAX perform the worst. Vogt and Cottrell [30] thoroughly analyzed these methods by Fox and Shaw [8] using a linear combination model for information retrieval systems; in their work, the linear combination model combined results from multiple IR systems and a weighted sum of scores was used.

Later these strategies were extended and applied in meta-search aiming to combine the ranking lists from multiple search engines. Montague and Aslam [18] empirically stated that they improved the performance of meta-search algorithms using CombMNZ and CombSUM. They improved these strategies by using more statistics than max and min in the normalization scheme. Manmatha and Feng [17] used a model of score distributions for combining results from various search engines to produce a meta-search engine.

Work by Xia et al. [34] adopted CombSUM CombMNZ and CombANZ in their work for cross-language bug localization, where their methods combined the top-100 files from each ranked lists into one list. Kuzi et al. [13] proposed to use combination strategies on fusion-based term scoring. Resulting term lists were fused and CombSUM, CombMNZ and CombMAX were mainly used in their work. These techniques were used for words selecting and applied on word embedding based query expansion application. The experiments tested on the TREC dataset proved the effectiveness of using these techniques in word scoring and selecting.

Vogt and Cottrell [29,30] pointed out that aggregation allowed a significant reduction in the number of features and enumerated three beneficial effects of combining multiple models:

- **The Skimming Effect.** Skim means only top-ranked items are selected. Documents are represented by different retrieval methods and thus retrieve different relevant items. A combination model taking the top-ranked items from each of the retrieval approaches can increase recall as well as precision.
- **The Chorus Effect.** A number of retrieval approaches suggest that an item is relevant to a query provides stronger evidence for relevance than that of a single approach. A combination model can explore this effect when ranking documents in the intersection of the retrieved lists higher.
- **The Dark Horse Effect.** Compared to other retrieval approaches, a retrieval approach may produce effective estimates of relevance for some documents.

3   Proposal

To prove the assumptions put forward in Sect. 1, we propose a two-stage L2R framework where aggregation is applied on a set of L2R models:

- During the first stage, the defined features are grouped and a set of field-based L2R models is generated; each model is trained using single field features. Meanwhile, following the traditional way, one L2R model is trained using all features together;

– During the second stage, the scores obtained from the pre-trained field-based
  models are aggregated employing various aggregation strategies.

3.1 Features Extracted

Following a similar feature exploring way as in L2R Benchmark dataset [15],
here we extract features from each of the four fields: Title, H1, Else[3] and full
text of a document[4]. We also take into account the features that perform well in
consumer health search applications as mentioned in [19,25]. We have 9 features
per field, which totals 36. These extracted features are mostly based on classic IR
weighting models including TF-IDF, BM25, the language models HiemstraLM
and DirichletLM, BB2 and PL2 [3]. All features, except 4, 13, 22 and 31, are
query independent and are extracted from text length information.

   An overview is presented in Table 2, where they are clustered into four groups
based on the fields they are extracted from.

Table 2. Ids of the features extracted and grouped for L2R processing.

Feature	Field group			
	Title	H1	Else	full doc
TF	1	10	19	28
BM25	2	11	20	29
TF-IDF	3	12	21	30
Dl	4	13	22	31
HiemstraLM	5	14	23	32
DirichletLM	6	15	24	33
IDF	7	16	25	34
PL2	8	17	26	35
BB2	9	18	27	36

3.2 Aggregation Strategies

As aggregation strategies we chose the score-based combination strategies first
proposed by Fox and Shaw [8]; these are shown in Table 1. Although simple, these
combination strategies show their efficiency and are still used for score-based
combination. We employ them to aggregate the scores obtained from different
field-based L2R models.

---

[3] These are the texts that do not belong to Title or H1.
[4] We regard the full text as one field information as well.

4   Experiments

This section presents the experiments done. It introduces the used data collections and the chosen experimental setup and describes the baselines and the developed rankers.

4.1   Data Collections

The proposal is evaluated using the CLEF 2016−2018 eHealth Evaluation Lab IR collections [12,21,36]. CLEF eHealth organizes evaluation tasks in consumer health search since 2013; these IR tasks follow the TREC-style evaluation process with a shared IR data collection containing a dataset, a query set and assessment files available to participants. The statistics of these three data collections are presented in Table 3.

Table 3. Statistics of data collections for experiments.

	CLEF'2016−2017 collection	CLEF'2018 collection
Dataset	ClueWeb12-B13	5,535,120 Web pages
Query set	300	50
Qrels files	269,232	18,763

CLEF'2016−2017 Collection. LEF'2016 and CLEF'2017 collections include the same dataset and query set, but CLEF'2017 one has an increased assessment pool with more topic-documents pairs. We combined the two assessment files into one for this work and named it CLEF'2016−2017 Collection. The query set was issued by general public[5] and expressed their real health information needs. Preferable posts serving as base queries were selected and a total of 300 medical queries were created to resemble laypeople health queries. CLEF'2016 & CLEF'2017 collections used ClueWeb12-B13[6] as the dataset which contained about 52 million web pages. The topic-document pairs were assessed by senior medical majors. Relevance between a topic and a document was graded as *highly relevant, somewhat relevant* and *not relevant*.

CLEF'2018 Collection. his collection was generated following the same procedure as CLEF'2016−2017 collection. It contains 5,535,120 web pages obtained from the CommonCrawl[7] as the dataset, 50 medical queries issued by the general public and gathered from Health on the Net (HON) search engine[8] and 18,763 topic-documents pairs for the assessment.

---

[5] https://www.reddit.com/r/AskDocs/.
[6] http://lemurproject.org/clueweb12/.
[7] http://commoncrawl.org.
[8] https://www.hon.ch/.

4.2   Experimental Setup

We used the learning to rank framework provided in Terrier 4.2[9] with Jforest and LambdaMART [16]. All rankers were trained and tuned with a separate validation set from CLEF'2016−2017 collection and tested on CLEF'2018 collection. The Okapi BM25 weighting model was used with all the parameters set to default values. All queries were pre-processed by lower-casing characters, removing stop words and applying stemming with the Porter Stemmer. The default stop word list available in the Terrier platform was used.

The performance measures adopted in this work include three important and classically used ones in IR: mean average precision (MAP), the normalized discounted cumulative gain at the top 10 retrieved documents (NDCG@10) [11] and precision at the top 10 retrieved documents (P@10).

4.3   Baselines

Six baselines were built using three state-of-the-art information retrieval models in the Terrier platform: DirichletLM, TF-IDF and BM25. We built the baselines with and without using query expansion techniques. Pseudo relevance feedback was used for the query expansion and the top 10 terms from the top 3 documents in the retrieved ranked list were selected to expand the original query. The seventh baseline BaseBing was provided by organizers of the CLEF eHealth 2016 IR task.

4.4   Developed Rankers

Table 4 describes the rankers built for our experiments. First, we trained 4 field-based L2R rankers using CLEF'2016−2017 collection: R_T, R_H, R_E and R_F, each trained using features from a specific field as presented in Subsect. 3.1. R_A was built following the traditional way and using all 36 features. Next, these field-based L2R rankers were used to perform retrieval on CLEF'2018 collection and the scores returned from these rankers were aggregated following the strategies presented in Subsect. 3.2. Three groups of aggregated rankers were generated: R_{TH}, R_{THE} and R_{THEF}. Each aggregated ranker group contained 6 rankers each using a different aggregation strategy, totalling 18 aggregated rankers.

5   Results

In this section, we first compare the performance among all built rankers and with the baselines. Then, we analyze the effect of how different aggregation methods vary aggregation performance.

---

[9] http://terrier.org/.

Table 4. Description of developed rankers.

Ranker	Description
R_T	L2R model trained with Title features
R_H	L2R model trained with H1 features
R_E	L2R model trained with Else features
R_F	L2R model trained with full doc features
R_A	L2R model trained with all 36 features
R_{TH}	Aggregation on R_T and R_H
R_{THE}	Aggregation on R_T, R_H and R_E
R_{THEF}	Aggregation on R_T, R_H, R_E and R_F

5.1 Aggregated Rankers Evaluation

As already mentioned, the baselines and the built rankers were assessed using three adopted evaluation measures; the results are presented in Table 5. Due to space restrictions, not all aggregated rankers but only the most effective solutions in our experiments, are presented here; they are the aggregated rankers using CombSUM/CombMED strategy (both CombSUM and CombMED present the same performance in our experiments).

We start by considering aggregated rankers. As it can be observed, R_{THEF} outperformed the strongest baseline TF-IDF$_{noqe}$ in all three evaluation measures. Then, ranker R_{THE} outperformed the baseline BM25$_{qe}$ in all cases using the same retrieval model and query expansion techniques as R_{THE}. Also, R_{TH} outperformed baseline BM25$_{qe}$ for the MAP measure.

Turning our attention to R_A, which was trained with all 36 features, it failed to exceed all baseline except BaseBing for P@10; for NDCG@10 and MAP measures, this ranker was only able to exceed the lowest baselines, DirichletLM$_{qe}$ and BaseBing, underperforming all the other baselines.

Looking at the L2R models trained with single field features, we observe that R_T trained with the `Title` field outperformed the BM25$_{qe}$ baseline for NDCG@10 measure. Rankers R_H, R_E and R_F performed almost similarly, failing to exceed most baselines. Nevertheless, when comparing these field-based rankers to R_A, some of them, namely R_T and R_F, still outperformed R_A.

In sum, for all three evaluation measures, the results clearly show that the aggregated rankers produce very competitive results as the best solutions. These aggregated rankers exceed the ranker trained using all features R_A with a large amount and shows to be superior in all cases.

5.2 Aggregation Methods Analysis

To better understand the effectiveness of how different aggregation methods performed, we conducted an empirical evaluation by trying all six strategies. Figure 1 presents their performance for each of the three evaluation measures on

Table 5. P@10, NDCG@10 and MAP results for built rankers.

Algorithm	Ranker	P@10	NDCG@10	MAP
Baselines	DirichletLM$_{noqe}$	0.7120	0.6054	0.2507
	DirichletLM$_{qe}$	0.6520	0.5521	0.1455
	TF-IDF$_{noqe}$	<u>0.7360</u>	<u>0.6292</u>	<u>0.2586</u>
	TF-IDF$_{qe}$	0.7200	0.6080	0.2526
	BM25$_{noqe}$	0.7100	0.5919	0.2575
	BM25$_{qe}$	0.6900	0.5698	0.2471
	BaseBing	0.4940	0.4856	0.0185
L2R (field-based features)	R$_T$	0.6820	0.6131+	0.2428
	R$_H$	0.6340	0.5683	0.2279
	R$_E$	0.5700	0.4753	0.2115
	R$_F$	0.6620	0.5395	0.2404
L2R (all features)	R$_A$	0.6420	0.5687	0.2177
Aggregation	R$_{TH}$	0.6740	0.6101	0.2492+
(CombMED/CombSUM)	R$_{THE}$	0.7040+	0.6246+	0.2500+
	R$_{THEF}$	0.7440+	0.6630+	0.2660+

=: the strongest baseline of all
+: better than the strongest baseline
_: baseline using the same experimental settings as our built rankers
+: better than the baseline using the same experimental settings

rankers R$_{TH}$, R$_{THE}$ and R$_{THEF}$. The results were compared with the strongest baseline TF-IDF$_{noqe}$ and the baseline using same experimental setting as the rankers (BM25$_{qe}$).

As it can be observed, and for all three evaluation measures, CombMED and CombSUM performed the same and achieved the best scores. Considering P@10 only, we can observe that the CombMIN strategy performed the worst, underperforming the baseline BM25$_{qe}$ in all three rankers; for NDCG@10 we can see that all rankers using these aggregation methods were able to outperform the baseline BM25$_{qe}$. Finally, for MAP measure, CombANZ and CombMNZ performed almost the same and far worse than the baseline; CombMAX achieved almost similar results as CombMED and CombSUM strategies.

6   Conclusion and Future Work

In this paper, we propose the application of aggregation methods on field-based L2R models. Experimental results carried out on the health collections show that aggregated models are able to outperform state-of-the-art baselines and exceed the L2R model trained using all features. Some field-based L2R models (such as the ones built using Title and full doc information) achieve better performance

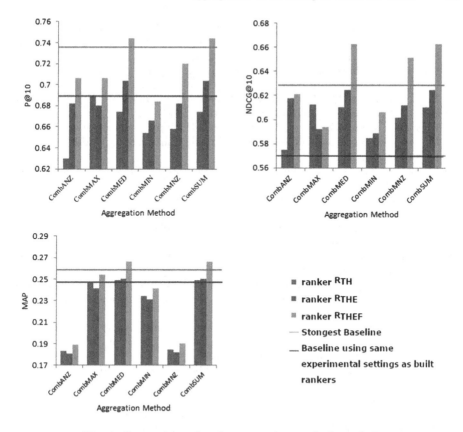

Fig. 1. Comparison of rank aggregation methods on L2R.

than the L2R model using all features; this shows that feature grouping can be
an effective technique for L2R.

As a future work, it would be interesting to investigate the approach with
other data collections to test how its scalability. It would also be interesting to
include other features and test the proposed approaches with those features in
the future. For example, Header and Meta field information could be explored.
Moreover, it would also be interesting to group features using other categories
besides the fields of the document.

References

1. Abacha, A.B.: NLM NIH at TREC 2016 clinical decision support track. In: TREC
   (2016)
2. Ai, Q., Bi, K., Luo, C., Guo, J., Croft, W.B.: Unbiased learning to rank with
   unbiased propensity estimation. arXiv preprint arXiv:1804.05938 (2018)
3. Amati, G.: Probabilistic models for information retrieval based on divergence from
   randomness. Ph.D. thesis, University of Glasgow, UK (2003)

4. Aslam, J.A., Montague, M.: Models for metasearch. In: Proceedings of the 24th Annual International ACM SIGIR Conference on Research and Development in Information Retrieval, pp. 276–284. ACM (2001)
5. Chapelle, O., Chang, Y.: Yahoo! learning to rank challenge overview. In: Proceedings of the Learning to Rank Challenge, pp. 1–24 (2011)
6. Deng, K., Han, S., Li, K.J., Liu, J.S.: Bayesian aggregation of order-based rank data. J. Am. Stat. Assoc. 109(507), 1023–1039 (2014)
7. Dwork, C., Kumar, R., Naor, M., Sivakumar, D.: Rank aggregation methods for the web. In: Proceedings of the 10th International Conference on World Wide Web, pp. 613–622. ACM (2001)
8. Fox, E.A., Shaw, J.A.: Combination of multiple searches. NIST special publication SP 243 (1994)
9. Fox, S., Duggan, M.: Health online 2013. Pew Internet & American Life Project, Washington, DC (2013)
10. Goeuriot, L., Jones, G.J., Kelly, L., Müller, H., Zobel, J.: Medical information retrieval: introduction to the special issue. Inf. Retr. J. 1(19), 1–5 (2016)
11. Järvelin, K., Kekäläinen, J.: Cumulated gain-based evaluation of IR techniques. ACM Trans. Inf. Syst. 20(4), 422–446 (2002)
12. Jimmy, Zuccon, G., Palotti, J.: Overview of the CLEF 2018 consumer health search task. In: Working Notes of Conference and Labs of the Evaluation (CLEF) Forum. CEUR Workshop Proceedings (2018)
13. Kuzi, S., Shtok, A., Kurland, O.: Query expansion using word embeddings. In: Proceedings of the 25th ACM International on Conference on Information and Knowledge Management, pp. 1929–1932. ACM (2016)
14. Lee, J.H.: Analyses of multiple evidence combination. In: ACM SIGIR Forum, vol. 31-SI, pp. 267–276. ACM (1997)
15. Liu, T.Y., Xu, J., Qin, T., Xiong, W., Li, H.: LETOR: benchmark dataset for research on learning to rank for information retrieval. In: Proceedings of SIGIR 2007 Workshop on Learning to Rank for Information Retrieval, vol. 310. ACM, Amsterdam (2007)
16. Macdonald, C., Santos, R.L., Ounis, I., He, B.: About learning models with multiple query-dependent features. ACM Trans. Inf. Syst. (TOIS) 31(3), 11 (2013)
17. Manmatha, R., Rath, T., Feng, F.: Modeling score distributions for combining the outputs of search engines. In: Proceedings of the 24th Annual International ACM SIGIR Conference on Research and Development in Information Retrieval, pp. 267–275. ACM (2001)
18. Montague, M., Aslam, J.A.: Relevance score normalization for metasearch. In: Proceedings of the Tenth International Conference on Information and Knowledge Management, pp. 427–433. ACM (2001)
19. Palotti, J., Goeuriot, L., Zuccon, G., Hanbury, A.: Ranking health web pages with relevance and understandability. In: Proceedings of the 39th International ACM SIGIR Conference on Research and Development in Information Retrieval, pp. 965–968. ACM (2016)
20. Palotti, J., Rekabsaz, N.: Exploring understandability features to personalize consumer health search. In: CEUR-WS, Working Notes of CLEF 2017 - Conference and Labs of the Evaluation Forum (2018)
21. Palotti, J., et al.: CLEF 2017 task overview: the IR task at the ehealth evaluation lab. In: Working Notes of Conference and Labs of the Evaluation (CLEF) Forum. CEUR Workshop Proceedings (2017)
22. Roberts, K., Simpson, M.S., Voorhees, E.M., Hersh, W.R.: Overview of the TREC 2015 clinical decision support track. In: TREC (2015)

23. Scells, H., Zuccon, G., Deacon, A., Koopman, B.: QUT ielab at CLEF ehealth 2017 technology assisted reviews track: Initial experiments with learning to rank. In: CEUR Workshop Proceedings: Working Notes of CLEF 2017: Conference and Labs of the Evaluation Forum. vol. 1866, Paper-98. CEUR Workshop Proceedings (2017)

24. Jo, S.-H., Lee, K.S.: CBNU at TREC 2016 clinical decision support track. In: Text Retrieval Conference (TREC 2016) (2016)

25. Soldaini, L., Goharian, N.: Learning to rank for consumer health search: a semantic approach. In: Jose, J.M., et al. (eds.) ECIR 2017. LNCS, vol. 10193, pp. 640–646. Springer, Cham (2017). https://doi.org/10.1007/978-3-319-56608-5_60

26. Song, Y., He, Y., Hu, Q., He, L., Haacke, E.M.: ECNU at 2015 ehealth task 2: user-centred health information retrieval. In: CLEF (Working Notes) (2015)

27. Tax, N., Bockting, S., Hiemstra, D.: A cross-benchmark comparison of 87 learning to rank methods. Inf. Process. Manage. **51**(6), 757–772 (2015)

28. Thuma, E., Anderson, G., Mosweunyane, G.: UBML participation to CLEF ehealth IR challenge 2015: Task 2. In: CLEF (Working Notes) (2015)

29. Vogt, C.C., Cottrell, G.W.: Predicting the performance of linearly combined IR systems. In: Proceedings of the 21st Annual International ACM SIGIR Conference on Research and Development in Information Retrieval, pp. 190–196. ACM (1998)

30. Vogt, C.C., Cottrell, G.W.: Fusion via a linear combination of scores. Inf. Retrieval **1**(3), 151–173 (1999)

31. Wang, H., Langley, R., Kim, S., McCord-Snook, E., Wang, H.: Efficient exploration of gradient space for online learning to rank. arXiv preprint arXiv:1805.07317 (2018)

32. Wang, R., Lu, W., Ren, K.: WHUIRgroup at the CLEF 2016 ehealth lab task 3. In: CLEF (Working Notes), pp. 193–197 (2016)

33. Wang, X., Bendersky, M., Metzler, D., Najork, M.: Learning to rank with selection bias in personal search. In: Proceedings of the 39th International ACM SIGIR Conference on Research and Development in Information Retrieval, pp. 115–124. ACM (2016)

34. Xia, X., Lo, D., Wang, X., Zhang, C., Wang, X.: Cross-language bug localization. In: Proceedings of the 22nd International Conference on Program Comprehension, pp. 275–278. ACM (2014)

35. Yang, H., Goncalves, T.: Promoting understandability in consumer health information search. In: Jose, J.M., et al. (eds.) ECIR 2017. LNCS, vol. 10193, pp. 727–734. Springer, Cham (2017). https://doi.org/10.1007/978-3-319-56608-5_72

36. Zuccon, G., et al.: The IR task at the CLEF ehealth evaluation lab 2016: user-centred health information retrieval. In: CLEF 2016-Conference and Labs of the Evaluation Forum, vol. 1609, pp. 15–27 (2016)

Intelligent Systems for Decision Support

Intelligent System for Generation and Evaluation of e-Learning Tests Using Integer Programming

Daniela Borissova[1,2]($\boxtimes$) [iD] and Delyan Keremedchiev[1,3] [iD]

[1] Institute of Information and Communication Technologies at Bulgarian Academy of Sciences,
1113 Sofia, Bulgaria
dborissova@iit.bas.bg, delyan.keremedchiev@gmail.com
[2] University of Library Studies and Information Technologies, 1784 Sofia, Bulgaria
[3] New Bulgarian University, 1618 Sofia, Bulgaria

Abstract. The major challenge in e-learning is the assessment as a tool to measure students' knowledge. In this regard an intelligent system for generation and evaluation of e-learning tests using integer programming is proposed. The described system aims to determine a number of questions with different degree of difficulty from a predefined set of questions that will compose the test. It allows also generating tests with different level of complexity. To realize the selection of the questions for different levels of tests two optimization models are proposed. Both of these models are of linear integer programming. The first of them determines the minimum number of questions by selecting among more difficult questions, while the second one aims to maximize the number of questions by selecting among less difficult questions. The proposed intelligent system for generating and evaluating e-learning tests with different levels of complexity is implemented as web-based application. The numerical testing of the developed prototype of the intelligent system for generation of tests for e-learning purposes is demonstrated in a web programming course.

Keywords: Intelligent system · E-tests · Algorithm · Integer programming · Mathematical models

1 Introduction

The assessment as a tool for feedback about the acquired students' knowledge related to learning objectives plays the central role in the teaching and learning process. The students' knowledge can be evaluated considering theoretical knowledge and practical skills [1]. The most common way to assess theoretically the learners' progress is via tests. Tests as a tool of verifying knowledge and subsequent evaluation are often used not only in traditional training but also in various forms of e-learning. The new e-learning challenges require the incorporation of modern technologies into business intelligence tools to improve product quality and user satisfaction. Therefore, the current trends in e-learning are focused not only on the e-learning content but they also

© Springer Nature Switzerland AG 2020
D. Simian and L. F. Stoica (Eds.): MDIS 2019, CCIS 1126, pp. 97–110, 2020.
https://doi.org/10.1007/978-3-030-39237-6_7

integrate some modules for code training [2] and different tools for testing the acquired knowledge [3, 4].

It is shown that the students who use the tests have better performance compared with those who do not use them and the result is 85.7% vs. 77.8% for the students who used the tests [5]. The advance of ICT makes possible to use different types of questions that could be easily checked and then evaluated, e.g. questions of multiple-choice type, true-false questions, short-answer, essay, and questions provided by test banks [6]. Since true-false questions provide 50% chance of guessing the right answer, multiple choice ones are often preferred. The usage of alternatives through multiple choice questions has some benefits for the learner. These tests give the opportunity to learn new information from the test: for example, if the learner does not know the answer to the question and cannot generate the exact answer but is able to justify the path to the knowledge-based answer for other alternatives [7].

Apart from the traditional form of questions, the game-based quizzes have recently become more interesting and popular. Gamification in e-learning provides better learning experience and better learning environment, instant feedback and can be applied for most learning needs. These advantages are proved by the results from peer and self-assessment in the Moodle e-learning environment [8, 9]. It is shown that usage of JavaScript and AJAX could successful implements distributed computing due to modern web browsers' advantages [10]. To get feedback about the e-learning outcome a web-based examination system is proposed [11]. In addition, another system for e-learning and online exam management and evaluation is proposed [12]. It allows to automatically assessing essays semantically, using pair-wise approach.

In contrast to the other approaches that are focused on the generation of the questions [13], the proposed intelligent system emphasizes on the optimal selection of questions for generation of tests with different level of complexity. A predefined number of questions to choose from are needed to compose the tests. There are different models to implement such question selection. For example, the problem of test construction is formally represented as an optimization problem with an objective function that could maximize the amount of information in the test or minimize the amount of items in a test [14]. Due to the nature of the selection problems, the integer programming approach seems to be the most suitable. The selection of questions for assembling the tests could be viewed also as a multi-objective problem [15]. Independently from the type of questions that will compose the test, each question should have predetermined level of difficulty. The determination of the intervals for assessment the tests levels of difficulty is set by the instructor who prepares the test taking into account the purpose of the test [16]. Considering this the current paper aims to propose an intelligent system for generation and evaluation of e-learning tests using integer programming. The core of this system is the formulation of mathematical models for generation of tests with more questions but with lower degree of difficulty and for generation of tests with fewer questions but with higher degree of difficulty.

The rest of this paper is structured as follows. In the next section, an algorithm of an intelligent system for generation and evaluation of e-learning tests is presented. The formulation of mathematical models based on integer programming for generating and evaluating e-learning tests is described in Sect. 3. The case studies of the proposed models are then presented in Sect. 4. Section 5 provides a comparative analysis for the described models. Finally, the paper ends with concluding remarks in Sect. 6.

2 Algorithm of Intelligent System for Generating and Evaluating e-Learning Tests

The proposed algorithm of intelligent system for generating and evaluating e-learning tests with different levels of complexity is illustrated in Fig. 1.

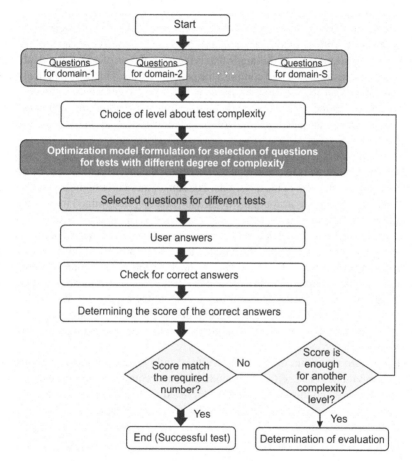

Fig. 1. Algorithm of intelligent system for generating and evaluating e-learning tests.

In order to generate e-learning tests, the requirement is the existence of already formulated questions. The type of questions – multiple-choice questions, true-false questions, short-answer questions, etc. does not matter. There is a requirement for a questions set and each of the questions should be evaluated toward its level of difficulty. When these two requirements are satisfied, the proposed intelligent system could be applied to generate and put in sequent order questions for an e-learning test used for evaluation. The set of questions and their difficulty could be prepared in advance in a separate module. The determination of the questions levels of difficulty is set by the instructor who prepares the test [15].

Depending on the particular area of interest, each user should choose from the set of different question databases within the interested domain/s. If the question data-bases domains are already known, the intelligent system could start. The second stage of this system allows generating the tests with different level of complexity. This can be done by selection of the level of test complexity. Several levels of complexity could be formed that correspond to different degrees of test difficulty. The six-point marking system seems to be suitable for the purposes of knowledge assessment as a result of e-learning. There are no obstacles to differentiating as many levels of the generated tests as needed.

The next important stage of this algorithm is the formulation of a mathematical model for selection of questions that will compose the particular tests. This mathematical model should guarantee that the selected questions will not be repeated within the generated test. This means that the special case of 0–1 integer linear programming technique could be best fitted. Once the questions that compose the test level are known, the user can give his answers.

After the answers are given the system checks how many questions are answered correctly. The next stage is to determine the scores for the test depending on the number of obtained correct answers of the questions. The sum of the scores of the correct answers is calculated by taking into account the questions difficulty determined in the first stage of the proposed algorithm and correct answers. Then verification is needed to check whether the correct answers calculated score sum matches the required score number for the selected test level. If this is the case the algorithm ends, but if this is not the case verification should be done. This verification checks whether the obtained scores from the test are within acceptable range for another level of test complexity. If this is the case the algorithm ends with a proposal for corresponding evaluation. When this is not the case, the algorithm of the proposed intelligent system allows the user to select a new test with less complexity and to make another test. This scenario is possible only when the given time for testing is not over.

The proposed algorithm of intelligent system could be used in self-testing, training and final exam modes. The self-testing mode does not require sending the evaluation to the tutor or lecturer and the user can test his knowledge as many times as he needs. The final exam mode sets predetermined time limits for making the test and the evaluation is saved and sent by e-mail.

3   Mathematical Model Based on Integer Programming for Generating and Evaluating e-Learning Tests

The input data for the mathematical model formulation for generating and evaluating e-learning tests are shown in Table 1.

The predefined question set concerning the particular domain is denoted by $Q \in \{q_1, q_2;..., q_M\}$. This set consists of M number of different questions. Each question has its

Table 1. Questions, difficulty and levels of test complexity.

Set of questions	Questions difficulty	Binary decision variables	Levels of tests complexity
q_1	d_1	x_1	
...	...	...	
q_i	d_i	x_i	$L^1, L^2, ..., L^K$
...	...	...	
q_M	d_M	x_M	

own degree of difficulty, which takes values in the range $1 \leq d_i \leq N$ where the lowest degree of difficulty of the questions is 1 and the value corresponding to the highest degree of difficulty is expressed by N. It should be noted that there is no relation between the total number of questions (Q) and degrees of difficulty.

3.1 Mathematical Model for Selection of Fewer Questions with Higher Degree of Difficulty

Taking into account the described above input data the following generalized integer linear programming optimization model for selection of questions in generating e-learning tests is formulated:

$$\text{minimize} \sum_{i=1}^{m} x_i = K^k \tag{1}$$

subject to

$$\sum_{i=1}^{m} x_i d_i = L^k \tag{2}$$

$$L^k \leq L_{max}^k \tag{3}$$

$$L^k \geq L_{min}^k \tag{4}$$

$$x_i \in \{0, 1\} \tag{5}$$

The objective function (1) aims to identify as few questions as possible considering their difficulty, while satisfying the particular test level. The Eq. (2) determines the test level complexity as the sum of the selected questions by decision variables (x_i) and their corresponding difficulties (d_i). The restrictions (3) and (4) define the lower $\left(L_{min}^k\right)$ and upper $\left(L_{max}^k\right)$ limit for the score number needed to form the chosen degree of test complexity. The k-th index in these boundaries denotes the levels of tests complexity. The binary integer variables x_i expressed by the Eq. (5) is used to determine the questions that will compose the particular test. The usage of the binary variables guarantees that the questions within the generated test will not be repeated.

The formulated above optimization model expresses a special case of 0–1 integer linear programming where the variables (x_i) are restricted to integers and are unknown.

3.2 Mathematical Model for Selection of More Questions with Less Degree of Difficulty

If as many as possible questions are needed to compose the test, the proposed above mathematical model (1)–(5) should be modified. In this case the correct mathematical model will have the following maximizing objective function:

$$\text{maximize} \sum_{i=1}^{m} x_i = K^k \qquad (6)$$

subject to (2)–(5).

The mathematical formulation with objective function (6) subject to (2)–(5) will determine as many questions as possible taking into account the levels of test complexity. The main idea of this scenario is to select a greater number of questions, but with less degree of difficulty.

The usage of the model (1)–(5) will generate the tests with fewer questions with more difficulty, while the second model (6) subject to (2)–(5) will generate the tests with more questions with less difficulty. Both models can be applied to test the students' acquired knowledge in accordance to the required level of test complexity.

4 Numerical Application

To demonstrate the applicability of the proposed algorithm of an intelligent system for generating and evaluating e-learning tests, a case study is used. The numerical application of the proposed two optimization models is illustrated by the use of a limited number of questions equal to 40. The range for their degree of difficulty is between 1 and 10 (i.e. $1 \leq d_i \leq 10$), where the greater means higher level of difficulty. The used input data concerning the question difficulty and obtained results for binary integer variables (x_i) for three different levels for test complexity are shown in Table 2.

Table 2. Set of questions, their difficulties and determined values for decision variables.

Set of questions	Difficulty	Minimization			Maximization		
		Level 1	Level 2	Level 3	Level 1	Level 2	Level 3
1	5	0	1	1	1	1	0
2	7	1	1	1	1	1	1
3	10	1	1	1	0	0	1
4	9	1	1	1	0	1	1
5	7	1	0	0	1	1	1
6	6	0	0	0	1	1	0
7	3	0	0	0	0	0	0
8	5	0	1	1	1	1	1
9	8	1	1	1	1	1	0

(continued)

Table 2. (*continued*)

Set of questions	Difficulty	Minimization			Maximization		
		Level 1	Level 2	Level 3	Level 1	Level 2	Level 3
10	9	1	0	0	0	1	1
11	6	0	1	1	1	1	0
12	7	1	1	1	1	1	1
13	8	1	0	0	1	0	0
14	3	0	1	1	1	0	1
15	10	1	0	0	0	0	1
16	5	0	1	0	1	1	1
17	7	0	1	1	1	1	1
18	10	1	1	1	0	1	1
19	9	1	1	1	0	1	1
20	8	1	0	0	1	0	0
21	6	0	0	0	1	1	0
22	3	0	0	0	1	1	1
23	5	0	0	0	1	1	1
24	4	0	1	0	1	0	1
25	7	1	0	0	1	1	1
26	5	0	1	1	1	1	1
27	10	1	0	0	0	0	0
28	6	0	1	1	1	1	0
29	8	1	0	0	1	0	0
30	3	0	1	1	1	1	1
31	8	1	0	0	1	0	0
32	4	0	1	1	1	0	0
33	8	1	1	1	1	0	0
34	10	1	0	0	1	0	0
35	6	0	0	0	1	1	0
36	5	0	1	1	1	1	1
37	10	1	0	0	0	1	1
38	6	0	1	1	1	1	1
39	7	1	1	0	1	1	1
40	7	1	1	1	1	1	1

The overall score for all questions in this excerpt is equal to 270. The numerical testing is performed at three different levels of complexity of the tests with predefined upper and lower boundaries for each test level. The number of the selected questions and corresponding scores for each test level using both formulated optimization models with minimization and maximization functions are shown in Table 3.

Table 3. Test levels, acceptable boundaries and selected questions number.

Levels of tests complexity	Levels of tests complexity	Levels of tests complexity	Levels of tests complexity	Levels of tests complexity
Minimization				
L1	200	185	190	23
L2	184	170	170	20
L3	169	155	156	18
Maximization				
L1	200	185	192	32
L2	184	170	183	31
L3	169	155	167	29

5   Result Analysis

The proposed mathematical models based on integer programming allow generating and evaluating e-learning tests with different level of complexity. The first model with objective function (1) subject to (2)–(5) can be used when fewer questions have to be determined but with higher degree of difficulty, while the second one with objective function (6) subject to (2)–(5) is intended to determine as many questions as possible but with less degree of difficulty.

The comparisons between generated tests under three levels of complexity for both models are shown in Fig. 2.

5.1   Application of the Mathematical Model for Minimization/Maximization of the Questions' Number Within the Generated Test

For the highest level of test complexity (*L1*) the determined number of questions is equal to 23. The sum of difficulties of these questions is within determined boundaries (Table 3) and it is equal to 190 scores. The graphical visualization of the relation between the selected number of questions and the corresponding test scores is shown in Fig. 2a.

The generation of the test for the medium level (*L2*), requires reduction of the test score. The results from the optimization task solving are as expected. The selected number of questions is equal to 20 and the overall question scores are equal to 170. The results for the generation of a test with a lower level of difficulty (*L3*) show that the test is composed of 18 questions with difficulty scores 156. The questions selected by the developed system for level *L3* are visualized in Fig. 2b.

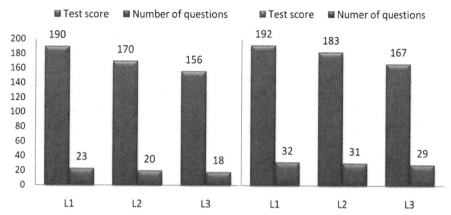

Fig. 2. Comparison between generated tests by minimization and maximization model (a) selected number of questions and corresponding score in case minimization; (b) selected number of questions and corresponding score in case of maximization

It could be noted that the obtained scores for the generated tests are close to the lower boundary for each test level. For example, in case of a test with $L1$ level, the scores are 190, while the lower boundary is set 185. For level $L2$ of the generated test, the scores are 170 and the lower boundary is also 170, and for a test with $L3$ level the scores are 156 with lower boundary of 155.

The usage of the second model with an objective function (6) is also tested for three different cases of test generation. The aim of this model is to determine as many questions as possible with lower degree of difficulty. The obtained results for this model for different cases of test complexity are illustrated in Fig. 2b.

For the highest level ($L1$) the determined number of questions is 32, while the sum of their difficulties is close to those in the first model and the score is equal to 192. When a test from the medium level (L2) is generated, the optimization task solution determines 31 questions and 183 scores for them. The results for the generation of a test with lower level of difficulty ($L3$) show that the test is composed of 21 questions with scores from their difficulties 167.

The numerical application of the second model with objective function (6) subject to (2)–(5) shows that the obtained scores for the generated tests are close to the upper boundary for each test level. For example, when generating a test with level $L2$ the scores are 183 with upper boundary 184, and for a test with $L3$ level the scores are 167 with upper boundary 169. The scores of 192 for the test with $L1$ level are in the middle of the lower and the upper boundaries.

5.2 Application of the Developed Prototype of the Intelligent System for Generation and Evaluation of e-Learning Tests Using 0–1 Integer Programming

In this section the applicability of the developed and tested prototype of the intelligent system for generation of tests with deferent degree of complexity is described. The main interface of this web-based system involves: (1) the possibility to select different domain area; (2) the level of test complexity; (3) selection of questions difficulties. The developed prototype was tested in self-testing regime and the second regime for official exam is under development.

The demo version of the system was tested in a web programming course. The system is realized to generate tests with four degrees of complexity that correspond to level *L1* for excellent and to level *L4* for satisfied evaluation. Nevertheless, the developed system integrates the proposed two integer programming models that allow generation

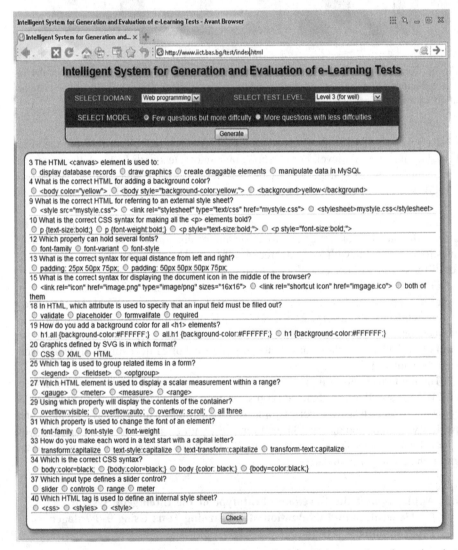

Fig. 3. Selected questions for test with level *L3* of complexity with less number of questions but more difficulty

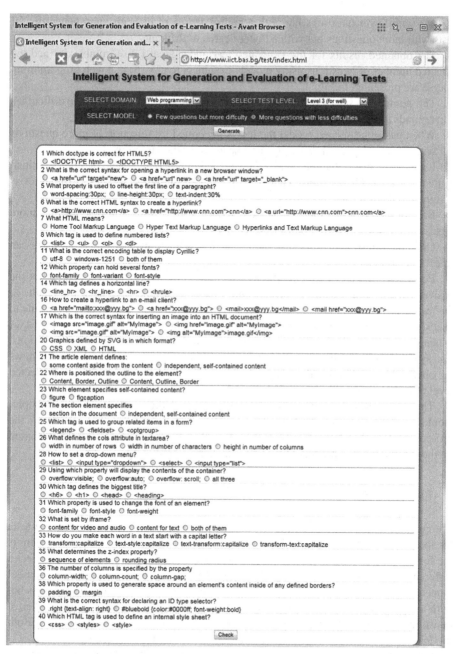

Fig. 4. Generated test of level L3 complexity with more questions number but less difficulty

of tests with fewer questions but with a higher degree of difficulty and generation of tests with more questions but with a lower degree of difficulty.

The obtained results for the generated test under level L3 of complexity and the selected number of questions using model (1) subject to (2)–(5) in a web programming course are presented in Fig. 3.

The number of selected questions is equal to 18 and the sum of their difficulties corresponds to the score 156 accordingly to the input data given in Table 2.

When using the second model the test is generated by selection of more questions but with a lower degree of difficulty. This scenario is shown in Fig. 4.

It should be noted that the obtained results are highly dependable on predetermined difficulties for each question. That is why the determination of these difficulties is assigned to the relevant specialists.

Both of the proposed models can be extended with additional restrictions for more precise application of different user preferences.

Once the questions composing the required test level are visualized the users can select the answers.

For all of the generated tests there is a limited time when the users can point the answers. If the user finishes the test within this time, he/she can check the result for the test level. Activating the button "check" sends the answers to the server machine to check the correctness of the for answers and the result is shown in a pop-up window. When the time is over, the system does not permit the user to answer more questions. The system automatically sends the given answers to the server, checks them and shows the obtained result. The results can be of type "successfully passed test" for the selected level of complexity or "score for lower level".

The business logic concerning the verification of the correct answers is implemented server-side using Node.js. This functionality proves the applicability of the pro-posed algorithm for generation of tests with different level of complexity based on the formulated two models of type 0–1 integer programming.

6 Conclusions

The current article describes an intelligent system for generation and evaluation of e-tests for the purposes of e-learning. The main purpose of the proposed intelligent system is the formulation of mathematical optimization models according to the need to select a different number of questions a big or a small one to compose the tests. The first model aims to minimize the number of questions by the determination of fewer questions but with a higher degree of difficulty. The second model aims to maximize the number of questions by the determination of more questions with a lower degree of difficulty. Both models could be used to implement the tests with different level of complexity.

The numerical application of the first model shows that the obtained scores for the generated tests are close to the lower boundary for each test level. The results from the second model demonstrate the opposite situation where the obtained scores for the generated tests are close to the upper boundary for each test level.

Regardless of the chosen model for selection of questions for the generated tests the time for answering is the same. Thus, the proposed intelligent system provides the flexibility in generation of tests with different level of complexity. It also gives the user the possibility to choose what type of questions to answer – a smaller number but with higher level of difficulty or a bigger number but with a lower level of difficulty. It could be implemented in a Learning Management System or used as a separate tool for the e-learning and e-testing purposes.

References

1. Borissova, D., Keremedchiev, D.: Group decision making in evaluation and ranking of students by extended simple multi-attribute rating technique. Cybern. Inf. Technol. **18**(3), 45–56 (2019)
2. Mustakerov, I., Borissova, D.: A framework for development of e-learning system for computer programming: application in the C programming language. J. e-Learn. Knowl. Soc. **13**(2), 89–101 (2017)
3. Mustakerov, I., Borissova, D.: A conceptual approach for development of educational web-based e-testing system. Expert Syst. Appl. **38**(11), 14060–14064 (2011)
4. Marinova, G., Guliashki, V., Chikov, O.: Concept of online assisted platform for technologies and management in communications OPTIMEK. Int. J. Bus. Technol. **3**(1) (2014). https://doi.org/10.33107/ijbte.2014.3.1.02
5. Hennig, S., Staatz, C., Bond, J.A., Leung, D., Singleton, J.: Quizzing for success: evaluation of the impact of feedback quizzes on the experiences and academic performance of undergraduate students in two clinical pharmacokinetics courses. Curr. Pharm. Teach. Learn. **11**, 742–749 (2019). https://doi.org/10.1016/j.cptl.2019.03.014
6. ClassMarker. https://www.classmarker.com/. Accessed 30 Aug 2019
7. Marsh, E.J., Cantor, A.D.: Learning from the test: dos and don'ts for using multiple-choice tests. In: McDaniel, M., Frey, R., Fitzpatrick, S., Roediger, H.L. (eds.) Integrating Cognitive Science with Innovative Teaching in STEM Disciplines (2014). https://doi.org/10.7936/k7z60kzk
8. Tuparov, G., Keremedchiev, D., Tuparova, D., Stoyanova, M.: Gamification and educational computer games in open source learning management systems as a part of assessment. In: 17th International Conference Information Technology Based Higher Education and Training (ITHET), pp. 1–5. IEEE (2018)
9. Paunova-Hubenova, E., Terzieva, V., Dimitrov, S., Boneva, Y.: Integration of game-based teaching in Bulgarian schools state of art. In: Ciussi, M. (ed.) 12th European Conference on Game-Based Learning, ECGBL 2018, pp. 516–525 (2018)
10. Balabanov, T., Keremedchiev, D., Goranov, I.: Web distributed computing for evolutionary training of artificial neural networks. In: International Conference InfoTech-2016, pp. 210–216 (2016)
11. Ma, J., Liu, Q.: The design and development of web-based examination system. In: Wang, Y. (ed.) Education Management, Education Theory and Education Application. Advances in Intelligent and Soft Computing, vol. 109, pp. 117–121. Springer, Heidelberg (2011). https://doi.org/10.1007/978-3-642-24772-9_17
12. Tashu, T.M., Esclamado, J.P., Horvath, T.: Intelligent on-line exam management and evaluation system. In: Coy, A., Hayashi, Y., Chang, M. (eds.) ITS 2019. LNCS, vol. 11528, pp. 105–111. Springer, Cham (2019). https://doi.org/10.1007/978-3-030-22244-4_14
13. Stancheva, N., Stoyanova-Doycheva, A., Stoyanov, S., Popchev, I., Ivanova, V.: A model for generation of test questions. Comptes rendus de l'Academie bulgare des Sciences **70**(5), 619–630 (2017)
14. Veldkamp, B.P.: Computerized test construction. In: Wright, J.D. (ed.) The International Encyclopedia of Social and Behavioral Sciences, 2nd edn, pp. 510–514. Elsevier, Amsterdam (2015)

15. Veldkamp, B.P.: Multiple objective test assembly problems. J. Educ. Meas. **36**(3), 253–266 (1999)
16. Kubiszyn, T., Borich, G.D.: Educational Testing and Measurement: Classroom Application and Practise. Harper Collins Publishers, New York (1990)

Developed Framework Based on Cognitive Computing to Support Personal Data Protection Under the GDPR

Soraya Sedkaoui[1]([⊠]) and Dana Simian[2]

[1] Department of Economics, University of Khemis Miliana, Khemis Miliana, Algeria
soraya.sedkaoui@gmail.com
[2] Department of Mathematics and Informatics, Lucian Blaga University, Sibiu, Romania
dana.simian@ulbsibiu.ro

Abstract. The General Data Protection Regulation (GDPR) has entered into force in the European Union (EU) since 25 May 2018 in order to satisfy present difficulties related to private information protection. This regulation involves significant structural for companies, but also stricter requirements for personal data collection, management, and protection. In this context, companies need to create smart solutions to allow them to comply with the GDPR and build a feeling of confidence in order to map all their personal data. In these conditions, cognitive computing could be able to assist companies extract, protect and anonymize sensitive structured and unstructured data. Therefore, this article proposes a framework that can serve as an approach or guidance for companies that use cognitive computing methods to meet GDPR requirements. The goal of this work is to examine the smart system as a data processing and data protection solution to contribute to GDPR compliance.

Keywords: GDRP · Data protection · Cognitive computing · Data processing · Framework

1 Introduction

More than ever before, the use of data is increasing rapidly in all areas of our daily lives. To harmonize data protection and preserve data privacy [1] across the EU, the new General Data Protection Regulation (GDPR) was introduced in May 2018. The GDPR, which replaced the Data Protection Directive 95/46/EC (see [2] and [3]), introduces a number of changes that require significant efforts from companies that explore personal data, to comply.

From an IT point of perspective, all specifications cover the entire solution, including apps, platforms, and infrastructure, particularly if some companies deal on a direct or indirect basis with personal data. Consequently, compliance with this regulation will certainly have a significant effect on the processes of information management [4], including identification and categorization of data, data encryption, data masking, information tracking, data security and protection, and compliance and reporting audits.

© Springer Nature Switzerland AG 2020
D. Simian and L. F. Stoica (Eds.): MDIS 2019, CCIS 1126, pp. 111–130, 2020.
https://doi.org/10.1007/978-3-030-39237-6_8

Companies cannot achieve compliance by using only specific products. They must stop the personal data of clients from being lost, altered or disseminated. A repository that defines the mapping between each sensitive data element and the respective anonymization rule will need to be maintained and updated (see Sect. 4 for the definition of anonymization). They also need to discover new ways of managing the data gathered by mailing lists, online forms, etc. That's why today's technologies need to be powerful and smart.

It is clear that many technological solutions that enable GDPR compliance can be adopted. With the increasing demand for a new technology generation to better IT security, cognitive technology might be a good solution for achieving comprehensive GDPR compliance.

Applied to massive volumes of data, cognitive computing can enable companies to process data faster and make better decisions. It is also increasingly used in risk management, to analyze often ambiguous and sensitive data, and to identify risk indicators. Cognitive computing technology provides a better mapping for data security and data protection.

As a result, this study attempts to investigate the dynamism of such technology by developing an approach through which smart systems can assist companies to guarantee compliance with the new requirements for their private data management and data protection procedures. The main research objective can be formulated as follows:

How can cognitive computing help companies to comply with the Data Protection Regulation (GDPR) and improve the collection, processing and use of personal data?

Through this research question and to create the foundations of a framework, we intended to identify where cognitive technology can contribute to the GDPR compliance process. More precisely, we set out to identify and define those personal data requirements in the GDPR, whose fulfillment could be simplified, using cognitive computing technology.

Therefore, the main contribution of this work is the creation of a framework that combines cognitive computing approaches and methods to enable companies to attain effectiveness and protect sensitive data in the GRDP context. The aim of the proposed framework is to demonstrate cognitive computing capacities and possibilities for companies to ensure personal data protection under GDPR.

This framework will be developed through the integration of autonomic and cognitive systems, based on a systematic review and assessment of the key elements implemented by the GDPR. The review and meta-analysis of the GDPR literature and the various concepts associated with this research enable us to define changes in personal data, data management, and their technological context. We embraced this meta-analysis approach in order to achieve a comprehensive description of the GDPR requirements that could be of concern to our research. Also, consideration should be given to a number of challenges including data complexity, management of the resulting heterogeneous data, as well as system scalability.

The remainder of this article is structured as follows. Section 2 covers the literature review related to this research by identifying the several changes implemented by the GDPR and outlining a short data protection history. Section 3 handles the associated works that played an important part in the development of the proposed framework.

Section 4 provides an overview and describes the framework design and the adopted methodology. Section 5 presents a brief discussion to provide the needed support and background to develop the proposed framework as well as the role of cognitive computing in maintaining compliance. Section 6 concludes with implications, practical impacts, and limitations of the current study for further research directions.

2 Literature Review

Before discussing how computing technology can be applied to support compliance with the GDPR, a brief overview of data protection and the GDPR requirements, is needed. This section outlines a historical background related to data protection in the developing IT context. It also discusses the main changes of the GDPR that companies must take into consideration when they develop their business strategies. This section is constructed with the intent to provide comprehension of the context of this research.

2.1 Personal Data Protection in the IT Context

Advanced technology and smart devices have become an important part of our daily activities. The number of internet users is similarly rising across the globe thanks to the ubiquitous smartphone and supporting networks [5]. In large part, the rapid evolution of the use of advanced technologies and smart devices is to be attributed to the exponential growth of datafication [6].

Increasingly large amounts of personal data are being stored and transmitted in and through smart devices. This would include the fact that breaches of personal data are common, often cross-border and rarely efficiently sanctioned in the IT context [7]. Consequently, personal data protection has become a field of interest to almost all sectors, services, and technologies. But, what personal data means?

It presents information that can be directly or indirectly related to an individual identified ([3] and [8]). It can be a name, a photo, blood type, IP address, a phone number, a mailing address, a voice recording, a social security number, email, religion, etc.

Table 1. Sensitive data by sector

Sector	Sensitive data
Business: Bank, Insurance, Telecom, Industry, e-Commerce	Names, emails, surveys, CV, phone number, etc
Academia	Names, photos, emails, CV, list of papers, affiliations, composition, and schedules of the study formations
Research	Names, emails, professional addresses, the field of interest, CV, etc
Legal	Court decisions, contracts, etc.
Health	Patient records, medical forums, data held by a hospital or doctor

Depending on the business sector, some contents represent real pools of sensitive data. Some examples of contents are shown in Table 1. Some of them are sensitive as they relate to information that may give rise, for example, to discrimination.

The use of personal data by companies creates various societal benefits, both for the businesses and for individuals. But, it is evident that this usage poses also some challenges related to personal data protection. This presents serious data protection ramifications as such data is regarded as particularly sensitive when stored in systems that keep electronic records. It is, therefore, clear that its storage, processing, and analysis can be at the heart of the business model [9].

All concerns and risks must be considered carefully taking into account the provisions of several regulations, such as the GDPR. Some of the main risks include [10]:

- Intrusive use of smart devices by controllers and processors;
- Unauthorized access to personal data;
- Unlawful surveillance and hacking;
- Data losses, etc.

In smart environments, it is the hyper-connected active user who creates and produces huge amounts of data [11]. Furthermore, the personal data on which GDPR can be applied are highly unstructured (text, documents, images, etc.), and companies are now struggling with managing and protecting it ([12] and [13]).

In this context, advanced technology raises a number of concerns from a data protection perspective. It introduces basic questions about its ethical, social and legal effects, thus posing new issues to data protection and privacy. Also, the form of automatic communication between smart devices makes it difficult to apply fundamental transparency and fairness principles.

Along with the increasing use of smart technology, data uses are typically associated with stringent security requirements and privacy sensitivities, especially in the case of the internet of things (IoT) applications that involve the collection and processing of personal data [13].

In addition, advanced technology and smart devices pose challenges to personal data protection in view of the different sources from which data is gathered. Another important point, related to the use of large scale cloud infrastructure with a diversity of software platforms, spread across large networks of computers, increases the entire system's attack surface as well. Also, manipulation and loss of equality have been identified as two major issues that new technologies cause personal data protection.

So, the story of using personal information is, therefore, is the technology story itself. Personal data protection is, therefore, emerging as an area of significant interest in recent years as many countries adopt data protection regulations in order to protect data because data is an organization's most valuable asset. In this context, companies must develop new approaches to upgrade their business strategies and make them compliant with these regulations.

2.2 What Changes with the GDPR?

The reform of the European legislation seemed necessary in view of its dilapidated state, revealed by the digital explosion, the emergence of new uses and the introduction of new economic models. The main idea comes from the European Commission's finding that the legislation, which entered into force in 1995, needed to be updated to deal with technological developments [14].

Then, the GDPR is the new European framework for the processing and circulation of personal data [15], elements on which companies rely to offer their services and products. It also concerns the harmonization of the European legal panorama on the privacy of personal data. The definitions of the key concepts of GDPR (data processing and personal data protection) are developed in a broadly flexible and adaptable manner so that they can be applied to the technological context ([16] and [8]).

GDPR gives more authority to people, clients, and staff over their data and less power to organizations collecting, using, and monetizing such data. The goal of GDPR is to better adapt users' rights to the growing digital context and, in particular, to the development of big data e-commerce and connected devices, and more mainly based on personal data collection and processing.

It should also be noted that sensitive data are described in the GDPR as personal information revealing political views, religious or philosophical beliefs, racial or ethnic origin, and trade union membership. The GDPR's general provisions include new definitions for pseudonymization, sensitive personal data types, data protection policies, and data breach [13].

It also includes a recognition of a right and the reassuring of personal data in case of invasion of privacy, the right to the data portability, to be able to pass from a network social to another, from one ISP to another or from one streaming site to another, etc., without losing information, as well as the right to be informed in case of data piracy. Globally, Table 2 summarizes and explains the main individuals' rights and the company's responsibilities under the GDPR.

Globally, the GDPR changes how personal data is defined. Therefore, it contains important rights for users regarding the processing of their personal data [11]. It presents some significant new concepts linked to personal data processing; pseudonymization, data minimization, transparency, and consent of minors.

In this case, any entity handling personal data concerning Europeans must comply with the regulations [17]. Giants like Google, Facebook, Amazon or Uber must, therefore, take into account the GDPR requirements in their strategies and activities (providing goods and services in EU). Any company is concerned by the GDPR since it stores personal data (name, address, date of birth, location, IP, etc.).

Therefore, companies must comply with the GDPR because data breaches will result in higher penalties: up to 4% of annual turnover or 20 million euros [14]. View the exponential volume of unstructured data that companies handle every day, the implementation of this regulation is not an easy task.

According to the regulation, the identification of personal data must be carried out by an automated extraction process. In this context, companies must develop their compliance culture and update their technology solutions. In order to guarantee compliance

Table 2. Company's responsibilities under the GDPR

Individuals rights		Company's role
Right to access	Request access to personal data Know how data is used	Provide a copy of the personal data (free of charge and in electronic format if requested)
Right to be forgotten	They are no longer customers They withdraw the use of their personal data	Delete personal data
Right to data portability	Transfer data from one service provider to another	Do that in a commonly used and machine-readable format
Right to be informed	Personal data collection	Inform individual before data is gathered
Right to have information corrected	Out of date, incomplete or incorrect	Update personal data
Right to restrict processing	Request that data cannot be used for processing	Remain in place their record without being used A separate basis must be provided for processing special category data
Tight to object	The right to stop the processing of data for direct marketing	Stop personal data processing as soon as the request is received Made it clear at the start of any communication
Right to be notified	Right to be informed in case of the data breach	Inform individual within 72 h of first having become aware of the breach

with the GDPR, cognitive computing which understands data types (structured and unstructured) can assist map personal information.

2.3 Cognitive Technology and Personal Data Protection

The GDPR requirements arose out of global developments with regard to data protection regulation in order to enhance privacy regulation and to prescribe data protection practices. Under GDPR it is important to eliminate the possibility of personal data usage in unjustifiable and intrusive ways. In accordance with GDPR articles, companies should ensure that all personal data is identified, this requires a system able to manage data security and ensure the protection of sensitive data. As such, companies can use cognitive computing to adhere to the regulation.

Cognitive computing is the simulation within a computer model of the human thought system (see [18] and [19]). The advent of the cognitive computing era is driven by the exponential growth in data, specifically unstructured data. This technology is based on machine learning systems using data mining, pattern recognition and the processing of natural language to replicate how the human brain works [20].

The best-known cognitive systems are Apple Siri, Amazon Echo, IBM Watson, and others that combine deep learning, natural language processing (NLP) and machine learning (ML) algorithms to process information [21].

Such systems use algorithms of Machine Learning. Cognitive computing systems gain understanding from the data they collect and process on an ongoing basis. The system refines the way it looks for patterns and how it processes data so that new problems can be anticipated and possible solutions can be modeled. What makes it different is the fact that this technology is dynamic, which means that cognitive computing is built to change and will continue to change dependent on the ingestion of more data and the capability to identify patterns and linkages between elements [22].

This technology can be of paramount importance for companies. Its most promising feature lies in its ability to manage large quantities of data [23]. This technology can boost companies' decision-making processes. Cognitive computing can assist companies to map GDPR using capacities such as cognitive metadata harvesting, personal reporting, data integration, implementation of policies, and lineage tracking [24].

Cognitive computing can process smartly and automatically unstructured content, and continuously analyzing the company's data flow [25]. It identifies, categorizes and can even anonymize/pseudonymize the personal data. Cognitive systems can also help in generating specific reports allowing managers to quickly take corrective actions to the existing processes. This analysis step is crucial in the process of processing personal data and therefore for compliance with GDPR.

To support GDPR compliance, cognitive computing supports data protection with accurate and instant reporting as the regulation recommends. This technology offers to the company:

- An automatic extraction, categorization and anonymization/pseudonymization of a different type of personal data
- A simple personalizing that facilitates extracting target data
- The optimization of the quality of the extracted results
- A scalable system regarding the size of data flows and data warehouses
- Interactive interface, etc.

Companies are therefore committed to protect personal data (customers, employees) against losses, alteration, dissemination or unauthorized access. Compliance with the European regulation is above all a matter of process and organization and requires the use of powerful tools. According to the 2017 GDPR Compliance Report [26], significant concerns to EU companies are: data protection by design and by default (55%), the security of processing (53%) and data to be forgotten and to erasure (51%). Therefore, it means important to redesign the data management system and invest in data protection checks and processes [26].

Companies must take into consideration the distinct criteria of the regulation to recognize and address confidentiality and privacy risks in a cognitive computing setting. According to the 2018 GDPR Compliance Report [27], 71%t of companies stated that making a user data inventory and mapping data in their GDPR compliance measures to protected GDPR policies is a priority initiative.

This motivates introducing cognitive computing techniques into data processing as a technology that can help companies to ensure personal data protection to comply with the GDPR. We noticed that researchers have paid attention to this technology, and we selected some relevant related work that we can present in the following section.

3 Related Work

The idea to bring rights to users, under GDPR, and give them control on their personal data, and require compliance from companies, appears as the most distinct initiative. This idea is addressed by several researchers and mainly discussed in the business context.

However, some studies have addressed the topic related to the development of a framework designed for personal data protection by integrating cognitive solutions, mainly because the GDPR has been implemented since one year only. But, the following researches remain useful and insightful and have played a significant role to develop the framework for the current study.

In his proposal Hoepman in [28] derived eight privacy design approaches to assist IT architects promote privacy by design early during concept creation and analysis in the life cycle of software development. The research was elaborated when the regulation was only a proposal. This work offers essential patterns and Privacy Enhancing Technologies (PETs).

A technique based on a Socio-Technical Security approach was proposed in [15] to gather and check the social aspects of GDPR and to promote the design of systems that comply with GDPR. The proposed approach consists of a modeling language and a reasoning framework (STS-ml). A meta-model to illustrate key relationships between entities defined in the GDPR is proposed in [29]. The meta-model is intended to be used by the designers of e-services for the development of adequate Privacy Level Agreements (PLAs) that demonstrate compliance to the GDPR.

In addition, in [30], Furey and Blue gave speculation on privacy issues related to the capacity of Voice Command Devices (VCDs) to collect information related to an individual's emotional state. Their research was conducted with consideration for the GDPR.

The authors in [31] identified the impact of the PET adoption after the Personal Data Protection Act (PDPA) enforcement on employee work performance, introduced in Malaysia in 2010 and which aims to regulate commercial usage of personal data. They suggest that a holistic evaluation of business process compliance to privacy regulations would include techniques to measure PET adoption among employees and compliance to restructured business processes.

It is also essential to take into consideration studies that focus on the design of information systems with regard to compliance with regulations that are not related to the protection of sensitive data. In this context, a meta-design technique has been implemented by [4], which integrates regulations in the design and information systems implementation. This technique offers a set of high-level guidelines for the selection of suitable regulatory compliance measures and the handling of security concepts.

Furthermore, authors in [32] have suggested a generic framework for diverging cognitive computing methods of deep learning into Cyber Forensics without concentrating on GDPR.

It should be noticed also that, a web application has been developed by [33], which provides an overview of the strength of data protection regulations over the world. This overview categorizes regions in four categories according to the data protection description: heavy, robust, moderate and limited.

In the above relevant mentioned works, none of them has focused on the development of a framework meant for personal data protection and based on cognitive computing techniques under GDPR. For this, the current study aims to propose a sustainable approach to protect sensitive data by adopting a cognitive solution to ensure GDPR compliance. Therefore, the next sections convey the 'what' or the requirements and instruments, as well as the 'how' or personal data protection design under GDPR.

4   Framework Design and Methodology

This section will be primarily focused on the systematic review and provide an overview of existing literature related to the current study. Then, it describes the proposed framework, using a structured scheme, containing a summary of phases and shows the capabilities that cognitive computing can bring to guarantee conformity.

4.1   Systematic Review

As mentioned before, the semantic review and the meta-analysis carried out, allow us to gather the best practice related to the current study. The literature review, as described above, provided a theoretical foundation for a deeper understanding of GDPR, cognitive computing, and personal data. The initial search criteria to identify and select relevant literature was deliberately diverse and with a broad scope.

Cognitive computing for GDPR compliance as a new generation technology has limited research available; therefore the literature reviewed was not assessed or dismissed on the basis of quality or academic focus. The first stage in the study method was the choice of samples. The Web of Science is recommended as the preferred database site because it offers the most valuable and high-impact collection of papers [34].

We then selected all key collection database indexes including Science Core Collection Web, Current Content Connect, KCI-Korean Journal Database, etc. It should be noticed that the literature search was carried out in June 2019 with the following keywords according to the above literature review: "GDPR", "regulation compliance" and "data security". The visualization of GDPR literature is shown in Table 3.

Among them, the publications were maximal respectively in the field of Computer Science, Government Law, and Business Economics. It is worth noting that GDPR has attracted less attention in some fields such as: Legal Medicine, Information science, Health Sciences, etc.

It should be mentioned that the above review of the literature shows a lack of a methodology framework or cognitive solutions able to guide the companies and support their personal data protection process, under GDPR. This paper proposes a framework

Table 3. Distribution of GDPR literature by research areas

Research area	Nbr
Computer Science	34
Mathematical Computational Biology	3
Government Law	20
Healthcare Sciences	3
Communication	3
Business Economics	10
Engineering	9
Legal Medicine and Medical Ethics	4
Information Science, Library science	3

based on the cognitive system to ensure such compliance, achieve the various objectives and to meet the desired goal of GDPR.

This, therefore, has led the authors to think about a diverging approach introducing cognitive computing techniques as a tool to help companies comply. We aim to derive the framework from existing data protection laws and privacy frameworks. We, therefore, think that this framework is useful not only in the design of sensitive data protection schemes but also in the assessment of the effect of IT systems on privacy.

4.2 Framework: Description and Design

The main GDPR requirements, the most significant shift during the last two decades data privacy legislation as per [35] is that individuals need to be informed about many of the elements listed in Table 2. We, briefly summarize those here.

- Data that is collected about them.
- Explain the company's rights to collect data.
- Justify exactly why the company needs to collect such data [36].
- Information about the lawful rights of companies and how personal data will be processed [37].
- How long data is retained [38].
- Provide, in the policy, who can be contacted to remove or produce personal data [39]. This is to say, that clients must be informed who the Data Protection Officers (controllers) are, and how to contact them.
- Provide a timescale indicating to clients how the company will handle access requests by subject [37].
- Indicate and communicate all documentation of privacy information in concise, easy to understand and clear language.

So, we have taken into consideration all these requirements, to build a framework. This framework introduces a cognitive process to understand and frame the human-machine interactions with respect to these aspects of GDPR in terms of data protection and processing. But, the most important thing is to know where to start.

From our point of view, this solution, that aims to help companies ensuring compliance, must take into account data protection and design by default, the security of processing, the right to be forgotten (*article 17*), the responsibility of the controller, and data protection impact assessment, while the system is under creation. These may help companies to support the assessment of PETs that allow them to comply and to satisfy GDPR requirements. Hence, the elaboration of the proposed framework, which is illustrated in Fig. 1, contains the main following phases:

Phase 1: Organization and Preparation. The proposed framework starts with the organization and the determination of the current state of the company regarding data management and security. This phase is essential both to carry out an inventory of fixtures and to determine a trajectory. It helps to visualize the possible gaps, to define risks, to determine the effectiveness of the existing information system, etc. During this phase, data collection and storage, as well as data identification and classification, must be updated to allow the preparation and the classification of the collected data as suggested by GDPR requirements.

Phase 2: Privacy and Processing. When it comes to the "privacy and processing" phase, companies must think about the methods that they must adopt to (i) derive an overview about the definition of personal data (sensitive or not), (ii) where they will be stored, (iii) for how long, (iv) how they will be processed and for which end; and (v) how ensure appropriate security for these data to fulfill the GDPR. It should be mentioned, therefore, that data requires a categorization scheme to be updated and the company must reclassify some data types to include GDPR-compliant personal data.

Furthermore, the records of processing steps require that each controller be responsible for maintaining a record of processing operations. These records include, for example, the processing purposes and a description of the data subject categories and personal data categories (*Article 30*). Regarding controllers' responsibilities, we notice the following implications:

- Focus on the principle (data protection by design and default).
- Ensure by technical and organizational measures that only necessary personal data are processed (how, when and where it is processed).
- Report breaches within 72 h to the authority in order to inform the data subject (how to act when a data breach occurs, the legal basis, security measures, and the subject's rights).

Phase 3: Compliance Evaluation. The compliance evaluation phase focuses on the actions to be undertaken and that requires multiple skills. It is, therefore, important to:

- Assess the complexity of the compliance process with regard to the company and the information system, as well as analyzing the consequences of the regulation.

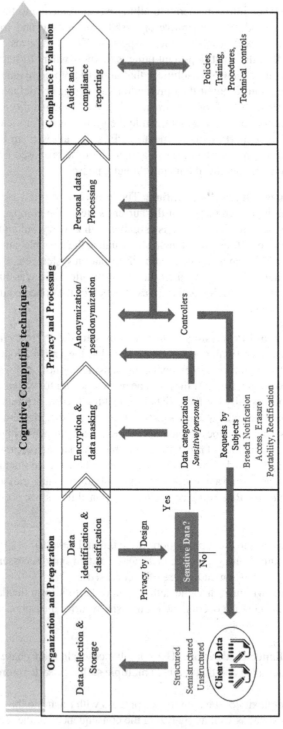

Fig. 1. The proposed framework

- Measure the GDPR compliance various axes such as the control of the life cycle of the personal data and their treatments, the support for change, the appropriation of the policy and the control of its application, etc.
- Identify risks and priorities and establish a trajectory based on the estimation of the risks and priorities.
- Build a process able to monitor and maintain GDPR compliance.

Therefore, we state six key elements (or steps) in the proposed framework that companies need to consider:

- *Data collection and storage:* Companies that are required to comply with the GDPR need to maintain digital records of how they collect and store personal data. In all instances, irrespective of how personal data are stored or collected, the protection requirements of GDPR are met. Under GDPR, only for particular reasons, companies obtain personal data. It became important to indicate the type of data collected as well as the reason why such data is collected in the company's privacy policy in order to remain transparent with the data subjects. Therefore, consent must be freely given.
- *Data identification and classification:* Companies have to collect and store a minimum amount of data and keep them up to date: the concept of "Privacy by Design". The data must also be kept for the shortest possible time. So it becomes important to ask the following question: What personal data companies need to properly deliver their product or service? Identification and classification of personal data, therefore, needs the abilities of semantic analysis.
- *Anonymization/pseudonymization:* This means that the processing of personal data or sensitive data must be carried out in such a way that it cannot be connected to a particular data subject without using any additional data that must be separately protected and stored.
- *Encryption and data masking:* It is necessary to maintain a repository containing the mapping of the sensitive attributes associated with their processing of anonymization or pseudonymization.
- *Personal data processing:* The regulation provides the data subject the right to request portability or erasure of personal information (Article 17) and instructs data collecting firms to keep privacy and data protection in mind in every step along the processing of personal data [2]. This is to say that, only personal data that are necessary for each function of the processing are processed. The personal data collected and stored requires specific analysis and processing tools [40].
- *Audit and compliance reporting:* To comply with the GDPR, companies must think about the appropriate skills of employees. Appropriate trainings are very important especially in data management, data security and work procedure. It is, therefore, important that all employees adapt to the new work procedures. Also, companies must take into consideration the shortcomings in the policy and instructions that need to be resolved and adjusted. In addition, it must schedule periodic compliance audits.

For each phase and step a company must identify essential functions in the process phase as well as in the compliance trajectory phase. Each of these functions can then be supported or accelerated by the implementation of a technological solution (cognitive computing).

5   Discussion: The Role of Cognitive Computing

GDPR compliance involves personal data and its protection (*article 4*) by any company that uses personal data by conducting business in EU member states. The company must identify personal data from the unstructured data (text, images, etc.) collected so that GDPR can be applied to it.

Authors in [2] stated that GDPR's main objectives are (i) strength online privacy rights, and (ii) boost the European digital economy. The specific objectives of GDPR are, therefore, to introduce compulsory security treatment through the implementation of appropriate technical and organizational measures (*Article 32*) and the duty to notify an individual breach to the supervisory authority (*Article 33*) and to the data subject (*Article 34*).

Therefore, ensure the security of EU residents' personal data is one of the key requirements of GDPR (*article 32*), and identifying personal data is a challenge itself.

The challenge lies in the amount of unstructured data that every company collects and which contain sensitive data that must be identified differently from any other pattern or structure while in free texts.

Companies need a smart solution that is self-learning and can adapt to changing of data nature and types, to ensure compliance and apply GDPR requirements.

This smart solution is made up of various types of processes, able to identify this personal and sensitive data. Identifying personal data can be made by using cognitive computing techniques such as Artificial Intelligence (AI), Natural Language Processing, Machine Learning techniques, etc. Cognitive computing contains many capabilities that can be applied to various contexts.

For example, if the data is a photo (unstructured data) of a client, which is stored as an object in the databases, the company needs to identify first where this object is stored before identifying its characters. Then cognitive computing techniques will analyze this object and categorize it as personal information, and then defining the process in which this object will be analyzed, apply GDPR requirements (encryption, etc.) on it, and manage the GDPR problem. This example is more detailed in Fig. 2.

Every request must be taken into account (respond to different requests) as well as check if the request is served.

The learning aspect of cognitive computing presents the most important aspect since it allows the company to learn over time, get more efficient, which results in more accurate usage and therefore more efficient tasks. Using cognitive computing will help the company to manage a large amount of unstructured data, map personal data, and get better control of different types of data to be in compliance with GDPR.

What can be most interesting to the company lies in the fact that every user, integrated into the system, will contribute to the learning process and improve its efficiency. Cognitive computing can assist the GDPR compliance process, and the different implications and methods are shown in Table 4.

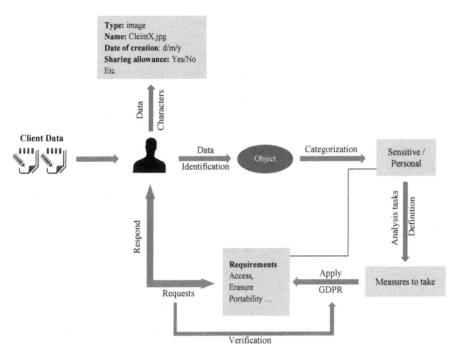

Fig. 2. GDPR compliance using cognitive computing: example

Table 4. How cognitive computing help to comply with GDPR?

Phase	Steps	Role of cognitive solutions	How?
Phase 1 Organization & Preparation	*Data collection & storage*	Growing the capabilities of collect, index and store content Allow collecting more personal data in accordance with GDPR (consent)	Installing some technology (MongoDB, HBase, Cassandra, blockchain, etc.) Capturing sufficient relevant data to teach a particular field or sector in cognitive computing systems and define it in taxonomies for example (required data and in the correct format)
	Data identification & classification	Facilitates the identifications of personal data regarding its self-learning capabilities The company can identify what kind of information is collected, how it is collected and how it is stored	Using *semantic analysis*, for example, to identify, extract and anonymize sensitive data generated in an unstructured format Extracting personal data from structured and unstructured content using NLP methods

(*continued*)

Table 4. (*continued*)

Phase	Steps	Role of cognitive solutions	How?
	Encryption & data masking	Providing capabilities for data encryption which help to protect data from unauthorized access Identify the data that are needed for processing (data minimization) and preserve it Ensure data security and protection (against breaches) and safeguard data from misuse	Using *natural language processing, classification, data mining*, etc. because of the big data volume, they are able to analyze and detect more reliable responses in various tasks
Phase 2 Privacy & Processing	*Anonymization/ pseudonymization*	Data cannot be identified without additional information Allow the company to store separately additional information and protect them	Detect non-compliant occurrences in real-time, such as using technology-based NLP approaches to evaluate and identify data such as Apache Spark or ElasticSearch Solving cybersecurity problems using computerized analytical procedures that meet GDPR's requirements
	Personal data Processing	Identify the purposes of data processing and what is permitted to do with it Control of every process that contains personal data Legally and fairly assist in the transparent processing of personal data with regard to the data subject	NLP solutions can be used to interpret regulation and evaluate the content of the document and what changes to the regulation that can affect privacy and who the stakeholders concerned are, etc
Phase 3 Compliance evaluation	*Audit & compliance reporting*	Connects compliance auditors, IT staff, and business perspectives for a clear picture of identities and their access, controlling access, and helping to ensure user access audit readiness	Use of machine learning methods and NLP to determine the sort of activity and guarantee it falls within the GDPR regulations

Businesses can use NLP, Named Entity Recognition (NER) or any other techniques, to identify automatically personal data (name, ID number, etc.). In this case, the solution can use machine learning algorithms to classify automatically data (sensitive or not) according to GDPR regulation.

Businesses can use NLP, Named Entity Recognition (NER) or any other techniques, to identify automatically personal data (name, ID number, etc.). In this case, the solution can use machine learning algorithms to classify automatically data (sensitive or not) according to GDPR regulation.

In addition to the security aspects and the speed of automated data protection and assessment methods, cognitive computing makes the data gathered to be crossed with different sources such as social networks, enabling more thorough controls to be carried out. This would not only reduce the risk of customer identification but also concentrate on compliance controllers' jobs on greater value-added tasks. So, the implementation of a cognitive solution compliance process helps to handle large amounts of data while allowing human resources to concentrate on more complicated problems.

For example, in the banking sector, the GDPR provides a broad definition of the data to be considered as personal and sensitive (identity, address, credit card number, IP address, etc.) while the banking institutions have larger amounts of such important data. The regulation also needs all private data that are considered unnecessary to be erased.

The challenge in complying with such regulation is, therefore, the quantity of data processed and the dispersal of data between departments and systems. In fact, the manual and accurate inventory of personal data require too much staffing in the face of terabytes of data. To this end, cognitive computing-based solutions aimed at refining the categorization of stored personal data and thus allowing banks to have a global map of the data they hold, subject to control or usage restriction. As a consequence, these solutions make it possible to manage sensitive data more rigorously and quickly.

When personal data are processed, cognitive computing goes further. Indeed, the software that embeds such technology makes it possible to automatically anonymize personal data, prohibit the entry of forbidden characters, prohibit specific data extraction, etc. The implementation of this solution in the personal data processing would therefore not only enable their simple organization but deeper treatment more accurate, more secure and more compliant with the current regulation.

6   Conclusion, Limitation and Future Research

With the current trends in innovative technologies, there will always be a need for new ways and methods to address various challenges. GDPR has created a new approach to handle personal data. In many fields, cognitive computing has been used, hence the need to integrate it into GDPR compliance. Cognitive computing has the ability to tackle challenges related to the security and processing of personal data. This technology can boost effectiveness, reducing workload, saving time, and reducing costs.

In this article, we reviewed the most recent studies especially in those related to the GDPR requirements. This review showed that most studies did not build cognitive computing-based frameworks.

In this article, the authors addressed cognitive computing approaches and their roles in maintaining compliance with GDPR. By building a framework outlined in Sect. 4, the authors interpreted this significance. This framework is split into three main phases: *Organization and Preparation*, *Privacy and Processing*, and *Compliance evaluation*. Steps of each phase are then discussed. This framework also illustrates how it is possible to use cognitive computing to solve GDPR compliance challenges. It demonstrates that by applying cognitive computing methods to data management systems, compliance can be realized.

This framework can assist companies greatly and provide a secure, low-cost compliance process for GDPR. It introduces some significant new concepts related to personal data processing; pseudonymization, transparency, data minimization, etc. However, in many companies, both in the private and public sectors as well as in small and medium enterprises (SMEs), the proposed framework must be assessed and evaluated. It must be supported and approved by the company's GDPR experts as well. Obtaining many evaluations for different companies, as a proof of concept of our proposed framework is one of the most important directions of our further research.

Once a company agrees to use this framework, the phases and steps could be more detailed or more collapsed in order to allow the automatization using AI and ML techniques, according to the company's specific and budget allocated for cognitive computing.

More studies are also needed to enhance the proposed framework as well as spark further debate on the role and the importance of cognitive computing techniques and show how they can enable companies to comply.

Acknowledgement. This research was realized under the "Eugen Ionescu" fellowship program, supported by "Agence Universitaire de Francophonie" (AUF) in Romania. The AUF team played no role in the writing of this article, or the decision to submit it for MDIS 2019 conference.

Conflict of Interest. The authors declare no conflict of interest.

References

1. Storr, C., Storr, P.: Internet of things: right to data from a European perspective. In: Corrales, M., Fenwick, M., Forgó, N. (eds.) New Technology, Big Data and the Law. PLBI, pp. 65–96. Springer, Singapore (2017). https://doi.org/10.1007/978-981-10-5038-1_4
2. Tikkinen-Piri, C., Rohunen, A., Markula, J.: EU general data protection regulation: changes and implications for personal data collecting companies. Comput. Law Secur. Rev. **34**(1), 134–153 (2018)
3. Voigt, P., von dem Bussche, A.: The EU General Data Protection Regulation (GDPR). Springer, Cham (2017). https://doi.org/10.1007/978-3-319-57959-7
4. Becker, J., Knackstedt, R., Braeuer, S., Heddier, M.: Integrating regulatory requirements into information systems design and implementation. In: 35th International Conference on Information Systems "Building a Better World Through Information Systems", ICIS 2014 (2014)
5. Sedkaoui, S., Gottinger, H-W.: The internet, data analytics and big data Chap. 8. In: Gottinger, H.W. (eds.) Internet Economics: Models, Mechanisms and Management, pp. 144–166. eBook Bentham Science Publishers, Sharjah (2017)
6. Mayer-Schonberger, V., Cukier, K.: Big Data: A Revolution That Will Transform How We Live, Work and Think. Houghton Mifflin Harcourt, Boston (2013)
7. Malatras, A., Aanchez, I., Beslay, L., et al.: Pan-European personal data breaches: mapping of current practices and recommendations to facilitate cooperation among data protection authorities. Comput. Law Secur. Rev. **33**, 458–469 (2017)
8. Tankard, C.: What the GDPR means for businesses. Netw. Secur. **6**, 5–8 (2016)
9. Auwermeulen, B.V.: How to attribute the right to data probability in the Europe: a comparative analysis of legislations. Comput. Law Secur. Rev. **33**(1), 57–72 (2017)
10. Data Protection Working Party, Article 29: Opinion 8/2014 on the on Recent Developments on the Internet of Things, WP 223, 16 September 2014
11. Mitrou, L.: Data Protection, Artificial Intelligence and Cognitive Services: Is the general data protection regulation (GDPR) "artificial intelligence-proof"? (2019). https://query.prod.cms.rt.microsoft.com/cms/api/am/binary/RE2PdYu

12. Rizkallah, J.: The Big (Unstructured) Data Problem (2017). https://www.forbes.com/sites/forbestechcouncil/2017/06/05/the-big-unstructured-data-problem/#16ddb612493a
13. Sedkaoui, S.: Data Analytics and Big Data. ISTE-Wiley, London (2018)
14. General Data Protection Regulation (EU) (2016). http://data.consilium.europa.eu/doc/document/ST-5419-2016-INIT/en/pdf
15. Robol, M., Salnitri, M., Giorgini, P.: Toward GDPR-compliant socio-technical systems: modeling language and reasoning framework. In: Poels, G., Gailly, F., Serral Asensio, E., Snoeck, M. (eds.) PoEM 2017. LNBIP, vol. 305, pp. 236–250. Springer, Cham (2017). https://doi.org/10.1007/978-3-319-70241-4_16
16. Schwartz, P., Solove, D.: Reconciling personal information in the United States and European Union. Calif. Law Rev. **102**, 877–916 (2014)
17. Zerlang, J.: GDPR: a milestone in convergence for cybersecurity and compliance. Netw. Secur. **6**, 8–11 (2017)
18. Earley, S.: Executive roundtable series: machine learning and cognitive computing. IT Prof. **17**(4), 56–60 (2015)
19. TechTarget: Cognitive Computing (2017). http://whatis.techtarget.com/definition/cognitive-computing
20. Watson, H.: The cognitive decision-support generation. Bus. Intell. J. **22**(2), 5–14 (2017)
21. Demirkan, H., Earley, S., Harmon, R.: Cognitive computing. IT professional **19**(4), 16–20 (2017)
22. Hurwitz, J., Kaufman, M., Bowles, A.: Cognitive Computing and Big Data Analytics. Wiley, Hoboken (2015)
23. Coccoli, M., Maresca, P.: Adopting cognitive computing solutions in healthcare. J. e-Learn. Knowl. Soc. **14**(1) (2018)
24. Williams, H.: IBM pushes cognitive computing & data-driven solutions ahead of GDPR (2017). https://www.cbronline.com/internet-of-things/cognitive-computing/ibm-pushes-cognitive-computing-data-driven-solutions-ahead-gdpr/
25. Gupta, S., Kumar, A.K., Baabdullah, A., Al-Khowaiter, W.A.A.: Big data with cognitive computing: a review for the future. Int. J. Inf. Manage. **42**, 78–89 (2018)
26. Alert Logic Report: GDPR Compliance in the EU (2017). https://www.alertlogic.com/assets/industry-reports/EU_GDPR_Alert_Logic.pdf
27. Alert Logic Report: GDPR Compliance Report (2018). https://www.alertlogic.com/assets/industry-reports/2018_GDPR_Compliance_Report.pdf
28. Hoepman, J.-H.: Privacy design strategies. In: Cuppens-Boulahia, N., Cuppens, F., Jajodia, S., Abou El Kalam, A., Sans, T. (eds.) SEC 2014. IAICT, vol. 428, pp. 446–459. Springer, Heidelberg (2014). https://doi.org/10.1007/978-3-642-55415-5_38
29. Angelopoulos, K., Diamantopoulou, V., Mouratidis, H., Pavlidis, M.: A metamodel for GDPR-based privacy level agreements. In: ER Forum/Demos (2017)
30. Furey, E., Blue, J.: Alexa, emotions, privacy and GDPR. In: Proceedings of the 32nd International BCS Human Computer Interaction Conference (HCI 2018), Belfast, UK (2018)
31. Gan, M.F., Chua, H.N., Wong, S.F.: Personal data protection act enforcement with PETs adoption: an exploratory study on employees' working process change. In: Kim, K.J., Kim, H., Baek, N. (eds.) ICITS 2017. LNEE, vol. 450, pp. 193–202. Springer, Singapore (2018). https://doi.org/10.1007/978-981-10-6454-8_25
32. Karie, N.-M., Kebande, V.-R., Venter, H.S.: Diverging deep learning cognitive computing techniques into cyber forensics. Forensic Sci. Int. Synerg. **1**, 61–67 (2019)
33. DLA Piper Data Protection. https://www.dlapiperdataprotection.com/
34. Falagas, M.E., Pitsouni, E.I., Malietzis, G.A., Pappas, G.: Comparison of PubMed, Scopus, web of science, and Google scholar: strengths and weaknesses. FASEB J. **22**(2), 338–342 (2008). Official Publication of the Federation of American Societies for Experimental Biology

35. EU Parliament: Home Page of EU GDPR (2017). https://www.eugdpr.org/
36. Cormack, A.: GDPR: What's your justification? (2017). https://community.jisc.ac.uk/blogs/regulatory-developments/article/gdpr-whats-your-justification
37. Information Commissioner's Office: Preparing for the General Data Protection Regulation (GDPR): 12 Steps to Take Now (2018). https://ico.org.uk/media/1624219/preparing-for-the-gdpr-12-steps.pdf
38. Data Protection Network: GDPR Data Retention Quick Guide (2017). https://www.dpnetwork.org.uk/gdpr-data-retention-guide/
39. Gantner, J., Demetz, L., Maier, R.: All you need is trust: an analysis of trust measures communicated by cloud providers. In: Debruyne, C., et al. (eds.) OTM 2015. LNCS, pp. 557–574. Springer, Cham (2015). https://doi.org/10.1007/978-3-319-26148-5_38
40. Sedkaoui, S., Khelfaoui, M.: Understand, develop and enhance the learning process with big data. Inf. Discov. Deliv. **47**(1), 2–16 (2019)

Machine Learning

Prediction of Greenhouse Series Evolution. A Case Study

Maria-Alexandra Badea, Cristina-Cleopatra Bacauanu, and Alina Barbulescu[✉]

Ovidius University of Constanta, Constanța, Romania
alinadumitriu@yahoo.com

Abstract. One of the major global concerns nowadays is definitely the pollution. The effects are more and more visible as time passes, our daily activities affecting the environment more than they should. Pollution has effects on air, water and soil. According to the European Economic Area (EEA), air pollution is the main cause of premature death in 41 European nations. Their studies found high levels of air pollutants in Poland that came second on the list, topped by Turkey. Therefore, in this article we aim to determine a model for greenhouse gas (GHG) emissions and atmospheric pollutants in Poland based on a set of data retrieved from a European statistics website.

Keywords: Pollution · Modeling · Environment · Prediction

1 Introduction

Although pollution is a seemingly unobservable phenomenon, the consequences are extremely serious and difficult to overcome. The air we breathe contains 79% nitrogen, 20% oxygen and the remaining 1% carbon dioxide, hydrogen, methane, helium, and others. When these toxic gases increase in proportion in the atmospheric air, pollution occurs, and the effects are severe. This phenomenon can appear due to natural causes, as volcanic eruptions, dust storms or even mist, or due to anthropogenic activities [1, 3–8, 14].

The artificial sources of pollution are those created by humans, i.e.: the burning of fossil fuels that throw large quantities of carbon dioxide into the atmosphere, the industrial processes and the use of solvents in the chemical industry, agriculture, after which many particles of used substances are dispersed in the air, etc.

Pollution falls into three categories depending on its source:

- Physical pollution, which includes noise pollution, created by land and air transport, construction sites, industrial platforms, and radioactive pollution, due to the emission and propagation of electromagnetic waves, the processing of radioactive minerals, nuclear fuels and others;
- Chemical pollution, which occurs when carbon oxides, sulphur compounds, or nitrogen compounds (all of which come mostly from fuel combustion) are released into the atmosphere in immense quantities;

© Springer Nature Switzerland AG 2020
D. Simian and L. F. Stoica (Eds.): MDIS 2019, CCIS 1126, pp. 133–145, 2020.
https://doi.org/10.1007/978-3-030-39237-6_9

- Biological pollution, which occurs as a result of the spread of microbial germs in the atmosphere.

To combat these issues globally, many countries have agreed to pass laws that would reduce certain types of pollution by introducing green energy from solar panels, wind forests, or dams – instead of chemical plants, investing in the development of electric motors for cars, or establishing jurisdictions for discouraging the waste from plants and factories [1].

There are several websites where real-time data on pollution levels are displayed for many cities around the world [11]. Analysing those data, it can be seen that in Asia the air quality index sometimes reaches alarming levels of over 500, while in Europe it generally does not exceed 130.

From the industrial revolution to the present days, the society has experienced an exponential increase of the industry and implicitly of the environmental pollution. Although the side effects have started to be visible relatively recently, the society still does not take seriously how severe the situation is.

The gas emissions that create the greenhouse effect, the carbon dioxide, sulphates, and all the elements eliminated in the atmosphere through various industrial procedures lead slowly to the climate and health problems we are facing today, although they could be avoided with the development of green energy technologies [1].

Throughout the 1960s, northern Europe experienced one of the largest deforestation and transformation of the region into human residences, factories and especially mining areas. This fact has altered the environment by extracting ores and releasing toxic gases into the atmosphere through industrialization [14].

Poland, the country studied in this article, experienced an accelerated development of the industry after the World War II, today being one of the most polluted countries in Europe [8]. Until the 1990s, carbon dioxide emissions reached alarming levels; however they began to decline, due to the environmental protection rules implemented and imposed by the governments of northern European countries, Germany, the Czech Republic and Poland [20].

In the Polish power plants, 80% of the burnt fossil fuel is coal, which led to serious diseases and premature death [19]. Another factor that determines the high level of pollution in Poland is the infrastructure that allows people to use poor quality coal or garbage to supply their heating systems in winters instead of using an electric heating system which is more environmentally friendly [1].

At this moment, the policy of the Warsaw government is aimed at protecting the mining industry in the coal sector, which has a large impact on the labour market in the country. According to World Health Organization (WHO), the inhabitants of Poland breathe air containing almost 30 times more carcinogenic particles than ten years ago, and, consequently every year in Poland about 50,000 people die prematurely from poor air quality [14, 19, 21]. Moreover, 36 of the 50 most polluted towns and cities in Europe are in Poland [20], mostly from the mining areas of Silesia, and the southern areas affected by deforestation. For locals in Krakow, for example, diseases such as asthma and heart or circulatory system disorders are commonly encountered due to exposure to high levels of air pollution [19].

2 Study Region and Data Acquisition

In this paper we aim to determine a model capable of making predictions for greenhouse gas (GHG) emissions in Poland. Data were collected from the website of Eurostat, the statistical office of the European Union [12].

The study series, together with a parabolic trend are presented in Fig. 1. One can remark a high variability of the study series, so no deterministic model can be fitted to this series.

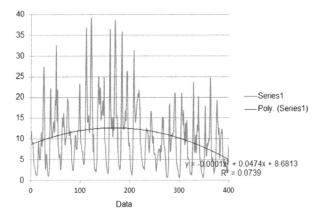

Fig. 1. Data series and a parabolic trend

3 Mathematical Modeling

3.1 Data Series Statistical Analysis

The first stage of the study was to perform the statistical analysis of the data series, as the computation of the basic statistics, testing data normality, homokedasticity and autocorrelation.

Data normality was tested using the Shapiro-Wilk test [2]. The homokedasticity was assessed by the Levene test, and autocorrelation was studied by using the autocorrelation function [2].

3.2 Change Points Detection

We define a break as a change of the probability low at a certain moment [17, 18]. The break tests permit to detect a change in a time series mean. The methods used to detect a breakpoint utilized in this study are: the "U"- Buishand test [9, 10], and the segmentation procedure of Hubert [16].

The null hypothesis that must be tested is: H_0: There is no breakpoint in the series $(X_i)_{i \in \overline{1,N}}$ and the alternative one is: There is at least a breakpoint in the series.

The "U" Buishand test is a Bayesian procedure applied in the hypothesis that the studied series is normal. The break absence represents the null hypothesis, H_0 [9, 10]. The test is based on the following model that supposes a change in the series mean:

$$X_i = \begin{cases} \mu + \varepsilon_i, i = 1, \ldots, m \\ \mu + \varepsilon_i + \delta, i = m+1, \ldots, N \end{cases} \tag{1}$$

where ε_i are independent and normal distributed random variables, with null expectancy and a constant unknown variance, σ^2. The break point, m, and the parameters μ and δ are not known.

An alternative to finding break points is the application of the Hubert test, and the validation of these points is done with the help of Scheffe's test at a significance level equal to 1%. The principle is to divide our series in n segments ($n > 1$) such that the calculated means of the neighbours sub-series significantly differ. To limit the segmentation, the means of two contiguous segments must be different [16].

3.3 Series Stationarity

The third step was to determine the series stationarity in level and trend by using the KPSS test (Kwiatkowski–Phillips–Schmidt–Shin) [2].

In the KPSS test, the series (level – or trend-) stationarity is assumed under the null hypothesis. Considering the model:

$$X_t = \beta' D_t + \mu_t + u_t, \mu_t = \mu_{t-1} + \varepsilon_t \tag{2}$$

where ε_t is a white noise, D_t is the deterministic component, u_t is a stationary process, the test statistic is:

$$KPSS = T^{-2}\hat{\lambda}^{-2} \sum_{t=1}^{T} \hat{S}_t^2 \tag{3}$$

where $\hat{S}_j = \sum_{j=1}^{t} \hat{u}_j$ is the residual of a regression of X_j on D_j and $\hat{\lambda}^2$ is a consistent estimate of the long-run variance of using $\hat{u}_j$.

The null hypothesis is rejected if the p-value is less than 0.05.

3.4 Additive/Multiplicative Seasonal Decomposition

The next stage was the modelling of the evolution in time of the series, using additive/multiplicative seasonal decomposition.

The seasonal decomposition consists of dividing the series into a seasonal component, a combined trend-cycle component and a residual component [2]. The decomposition can be done using an additive or multiplicative scheme, as follows.

In the additive model, the decomposition can be written as:

$$y_t = Y_t + S_t + \varepsilon_t, \tag{4}$$

where: Y_t is the trend, S_t is the seasonal compound and ε_t is the random variable, while in the multiplicative decomposition, the addition is replaced by multiplication.

Performing tests for different season lengths, one must obtain a value as small as possible for the mean standard deviation. This parameter indicates how well the data set was estimated.

3.5   Series Evolution Forecast

The fifth stage was to determine a prediction of the series evolution using:

- Moving average;
- Simple exponential smoothing method;
- Double exponential smoothing;
- Holt-Winters method.

These methods generate smoothed values, attenuating arbitrary fluctuations in the data series.

The moving average method is applied when the phenomenon has oscillations (seasonal, cyclical, etc.). Basically, the method consists of calculating moving averages of k terms of the chronological series.

This method is currently the most widely used method for measuring seasonal variations. Because the variations have, by definition, a periodicity of 12 months, we calculate 12-month moving averages.

The simple exponential smoothing method is based on the following formula:

$$\hat{y}_{t+1} = \hat{y}_t + \alpha(y_t - \hat{y}_t), \tag{5}$$

where y_t is the value recorded at time t, $\hat{y}_t$ and $\hat{y}_{t+1}$ are the values estimated at times t, respectively $t + 1$. $0 < \alpha < 1$ is the smoothing parameter. The closer α is to 0, the greater the smoothing effect is [13].

For fitting a given data series, the mean standard deviation (MSD) and Mean Absolute Deviation (MAD) should be as small as possible.

The double exponential smoothing method is based on the following model:

$$\begin{cases} S_t = \alpha \cdot y_t + (1 - \alpha) \cdot (S_{t-1} + b_{t-1}), \ 0 < \alpha < 1 \\ b_t = \gamma \cdot (S_t - S_{t-1}) + (1 - \gamma) \cdot b_{t-1}, \ 0 < \gamma < 1 \end{cases}, \tag{6}$$

where $S_t =$ the level at time t, $b_t =$ the trend at time t, $y_t =$ the value recorded at time t.

Unlike the simple exponential smoothing method, the double one uses two parameters: one for level and one for trend, expressed by α and γ, respectively. Therefore, this model is better at handling trends than the previous one [13].

The Holt-Winters seasonal method includes the forecast equation and three smoothing equations – one for level, one for trend, and one for the seasonal component, with corresponding smoothing parameters, α, γ and β:

$$\begin{aligned} S_t &= \alpha \cdot \frac{y_t}{I_{t-L}} + (1 - \alpha) \cdot (S_{t-1} + b_{t-1}) \\ b_t &= \gamma \cdot (S_t - S_{t-1}) + (1 - \gamma) \cdot b_{t-1} \\ I_t &= \beta \cdot \frac{y_t}{S_t} + (1 - \beta) \cdot I_{t-L} \\ F_{t+m} &= (S_t + m \cdot b_t) \cdot I_{t-L+m} \end{aligned} \tag{7}$$

where $m =$ the number of seasons in a year, $y_t =$ the value recorded at time t, $S_t =$ the level at time t, $b_t =$ the trend at time t, $I_t =$ the index of seasonality at time t, $F_{t+m} =$ forecast at m periods from t [13].

We performed tests for different α, γ α, γ and β values to minimize the MSD, in a similar way to the previous exponential smoothing methods.

3.6 AR(p)

Our final step was to determine an autoregressive model (AR) and performing the prediction using the determined model.

Autoregressive processes are memory processes, because each value is correlated with the previous. In the case of a moving average process, each value is determined according to the value of the current shock and one or more shocks. The order of the moving average indicates the number of previous shocks.

The autoregressive model of order p, AR(p), is a linear process $(X_t; t \in \mathbb{Z})$ defined by the following formula:

$$X_t = \sum_{i=1}^{p} \varphi_i \cdot X_{t-i} + \varepsilon_t, \forall \varphi_q \neq 0, t \in \mathbb{Z}, \tag{8}$$

where $(\varepsilon_t, , t \in \mathbb{Z})$ is a white noise with the dispersion σ^2.

For the model validation, we performed the residual analysis using:

- the Kolmogorov-Smirnov test for normality;
- the Durbin-Watson test for autocorrelation;
- the Levene test and F-test (Fisher-Snedecor) for homoskedasticity.
- the Box-Pierce test for white noise.

For detail on ARIMA and hybrid models, one can see [2, 15, 22].

4 Results

4.1 Statistical Analysis

The normality test showed that the series is not normally distributed, but after a Box-Cox transformation with a parameter 0.48, it becomes Gaussian. Therefore, the Buishand test could be performed.

The results of the Levene test performed by dividing the initial series in four groups are displayed in Fig. 2. The dispersion of the data belonging to Group 2 is quite different

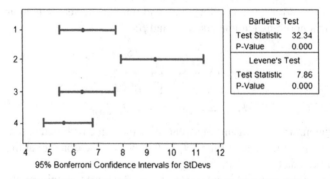

Fig. 2. The result of the Levene test on the initial data series

compared to those of the other groups. The p-value associated to the Levene test is almost zero, so less than 0.05, so the homoskedasticity hypothesis can be rejected.

The correlogram built to study the data autocorrelation (Fig. 3) shows high data autocorrelation at different lags [5]. Remark the autocorrelations at the lags 1, 2, and 3 (vertical bars representing the autocorrelation values, intersect the dashed curved representing the limits of the confidence intervals).

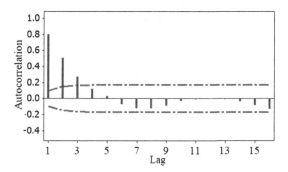

Fig. 3. The correlogram of the data series

4.2 Break Points Detection

The control ellipse of Bois, in the Buishand test is displayed in Fig. 4. One can remark the existence of break points since there are many values of the data series above the Bois' ellipse at all the confidence levels (90%, 95%, 99%).

By performing Hubert's segmentation procedure with Scheffe's validation test at a significance level equal to 1%, many break points have been found (Table 1). This difference between the two results is given because of the break points estimation procedure – the first one based on the statistical distribution of the data, the second one based on segmentation.

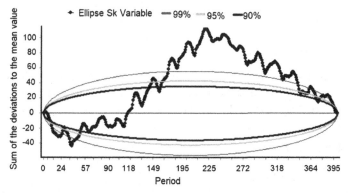

Fig. 4. The control ellipse of Bois, in the Buishand test performed at different confidence levels (90%, 95%, 99%)

Table 1. Results of the Hubert segmentation procedure. Beginning and end represent the moments when the subseries detected begin and start. Mean and standard deviation of the subseries are displayed in the third and fourth columns.

Beginning	End	Mean	Standard deviation
1	110	9.785	6.195
111	125	21.973	9.261
126	134	4.633	2.935
135	149	18.673	3.489
150	158	4.744	3.02
159	196	16.963	9.448
197	206	5.23	3.309
207	220	19.529	4.216
221	400	8.32	5.291

Therefore, for modelling purposes, the series should be divided in sub-series. But, for forecast the future values, this is not a good idea because the pattern of the series evolution is not entirely captured.

4.3 KPSS Test

The results of the KPSS test are the following:

- KPSS test for stationarity in level: test statistics = 0.3802, p-value = 0.08569,
- KPSS test for stationarity in trend: test statistics = 0.14787, p-value = 0.04844.

Therefore, the results show that the series is stationary in level, but not stationary in trend, at the significance level of 5%. This result confirms the visual examination of series chart (Fig. 1). However, for a lower level of significance below 4%, the hypothesis of stationarity in trend could not be rejected.

4.4 Seasonal Decomposition

After performing tests for several season lengths, the seasonal decomposition didn't give satisfactory results. The best result obtained using an additive model, for k = 12 seasons, can be seen in Fig. 5. However, the value for MSD is 41.184, which is quite high.

4.5 Smoothing Methods

Applying the Moving Average method to the study series, with 12 terms, no improvement has been notice, in terms of MSD or MAD. Diminishing the terms considered

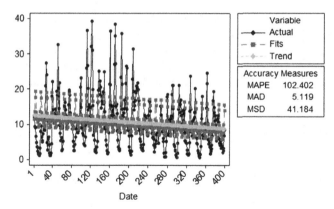

Fig. 5. Seasonal decomposition

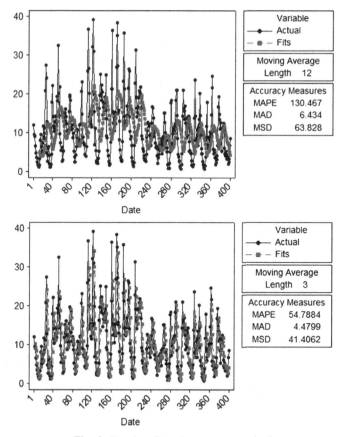

Fig. 6. Results of moving average method

in computing the moving average, a small improvement is noticed. In Fig. 6 comparative results for moving average with lengths 12 and 3 are displayed. For the last case, MSD = 41.4062 and MAD of 4.4799.

Performing the Simple Exponential Smoothing using the MINITAB trial version a better result has been obtained and is presented in Fig. 7. In this case, the MSD value was 20.8037 and MAD = 2.9497 for $\alpha = 0.29305$. Although the result is acceptable, we applied the other smoothing methods as well, searching for a better fit.

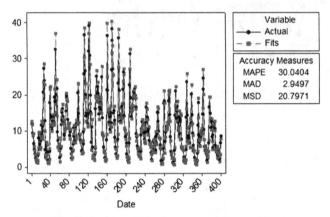

Fig. 7. Results of simple exponential smoothing

Using the Double Exponential Smoothing for different level of the parameters, the MSD corresponding to the best fitting was 22.705, with a MAD of 3.086, so no improvement comparing to Simple Exponential Smoothing.

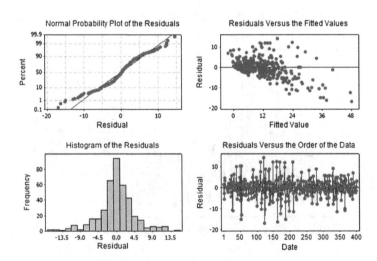

Fig. 8. Results of Holt-Winters method

Applying the Holt-Winters Method, for m = 12 months, $\alpha = 0.99$, $\gamma = 0.3$ and δ = 0.99 we obtained the most satisfying MSD value, 19.7428, with MAD = 2.9760 and MAPE = 30.8553 (greater than in the previous model). The residual plot corresponding to this last model is presented in Fig. 8.

The residuals values vary in between -19 and 12, the majority being between -10 and 10. Their dispersion about the mean is not constant, their distribution is almost symmetric (see the histogram) and they are not Gaussian (see the Normal Probability Plot). Therefore, this smoothing method is not good enough. Thus, we looked for a better model, presented in the following section.

4.6 AR Model

To select the best ARIMA model, BIC and Schwarz criteria have been used. The best one was obtained after taking logarithms of the data. It has the equation:

$$Y_t = 1.31288 - 0.51294 \cdot Y_{t-1} + 0.18063 \cdot Y_{t-2} + \varepsilon_t, t \geq 3 \qquad (9)$$

where Y_t is the variable at the moment t and ε_t is a white noise.

The results of the residuals' validation are presented in Figs. 9, 10 and 11.

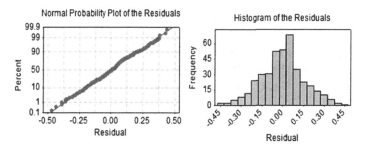

Fig. 9. Normal probability plot and histogram of residuals in AR(2) model

From Fig. 9 it results that the residuals are symmetrical distributed and Gaussian. The residuals' correlogram (Fig. 10) shows that the residual are not correlated, all the values of the autocorrelation function being inside the confidence interval [1, 2].

The Bartlett and Levene test of homoskedasticity (Fig. 11) prove that the hypothesis of the residuals' homoskedasticity cannot be rejected since the p-values associated to these tests are greater than 0.05 [1, 2].

Following the Box-Pierce test, it results that the residual series form a white noise. Therefore, the AR(2) model proposed is correct point of view of statistics.

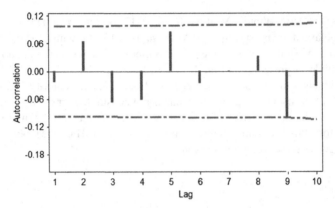

Fig. 10. Residuals' correlogram

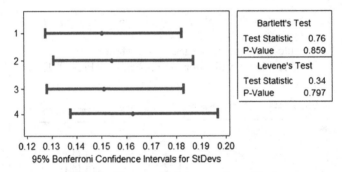

Fig. 11. Homoscedasticity tests for residual

5 Conclusion

The study emphasized different methods for modelling the pollutants' evolution in Poland. It was shown that detecting a model in the presence of change points in a data series is a very difficult task. After performing several tests and analysing the presented models, we determined that the model that suited best our data set is of AR (2) type. It was validated by statistical methods, so it can be used for forecast. In similar condition, the model gives good forecasts for the pollution in the study region.

Do to the high variability of the pollution phenomena and the increasing trend observed nowadays, it is important to know to model and predict the evolution of associated data series. Other methods can be attempted, using, for instance, artificial intelligence, such as deep learning, neural networks or genetic algorithms [4, 20].

References

1. Atkinson, R.W., Ross Anderson, H., et al.: Acute effects of particulate air pollution on respiratory admissions: results from APHEA 2 project. Air Pollut. Healndth **164**, 1860–1866 (2001)

2. Bărbulescu, A.: Studies on Time Series. Applications in Environmental Sciences. Springer, Heidelberg (2016). https://doi.org/10.1007/978-3-319-30436-6
3. Bărbulescu, A., Barbes, L.: Models for the pollutants correlation in the Romanian Littoral. Rom. Rep. Phys. **66**(4), 1189–1199 (2014)
4. Bărbulescu, A., Barbes, L.: Mathematical modelling of sulfur dioxide concentration in the western part of Romania. J. Environ. Manag. **204**(Part 3), 825–830 (2017)
5. Bărbulescu, A., Barbes, L.: Modeling the carbon monoxide dissipation in Timisoara Romania. J. Environ. Manag. **204**(Part 3), 831–838 (2017)
6. Bărbulescu, A., Barbes, L., Nazzal, Y.: New model for inorganic pollutants dissipation on the northern part of the Romanian Black Sea coast. Rom. J. Phys. **63**(5–6), 806 (2018)
7. Bărbulescu, A., Nazzal, Y.: Statistical analysis of the dust storms in the United Arab Emirates. Atmos. Res. **231**, 104669 (2000)
8. Binkowski, L.J., et al.: Relationship between air pollution and metal levels in cancerous and non-cancerous lung tissues. J. Environ. Sci. Health. Part A **51**(14), 1303–1308 (2016)
9. Buishand, T.: A: Some methods for testing the homogeneity of rainfall records. J. Hydrol. **58**, 11–27 (1982)
10. Buishand, T.A.: Tests for detecting a shift in the mean of hydrological time series. J. Hydrol. **58**, 51–69 (1984)
11. European Environment Agency, Air quality in Europe – 2018. https://www.eea.europa.eu/publications/air-quality-in-europe-2018. Accessed 20 July 2019
12. Europa.eu. Database – Eurostat. https://ec.europa.eu/eurostat/data/database. Accessed 20 July 2019
13. Gardner, E.S.: Exponential smoothing: the state of the art - Part II. Int. J. Forecast. **22**(4), 637–666 (2006)
14. Górski, J., Dragon, K., Kaczmarek, P.M.J.: Nitrate pollution in the Warta River (Poland) between 1958 and 2016: trends and causes. Environ. Sci. Pollut. Res. **26**(3), 2038–2046 (2019)
15. Hillmer, S.C., Tiao, G.C.: An ARIMA model-based approach to seasonal adjustment. J. Am. Stat. Assoc. **77**(377), 63–70 (1982)
16. Hubert, P., Carbonnel, J.P.: Segmentation des séries annuelles de débits de grands fleuves africains. Bulletin de liaison du CIEH **92**, 3–10 (1993)
17. Kehagias, A.: A hidden Markov model segmentation procedure for hydrological and environmental time series. Stoch. Env. Res. Risk Assess. **18**(2), 117–130 (2004)
18. Lee, A.F.S., Heghinian, S.M.: A shift of the mean level in a sequence of independent normal random variables - a bayesian approach. Technometrics **19**(4), 503–506 (1977)
19. Parascandola, M.: Ambient air pollution and lung cancer in Poland: research findings and gaps. J. Health Inequalities **4**(1), 3–8 (2018)
20. reddit (2011). https://www.reddit.com/r/europe/comments/8i4ia3/36_out_of_50_most_polluted_cities_in_the_eu_are/. Accessed 10 Sept 2019
21. The World Air Quality Index project. World's Air Pollution: Real-time Air Quality Index (2019). http://waqi.info/. Accessed 20 July 2019
22. Zhang, G.P.: Time series forecasting using a hybrid ARIMA and neural network model. Neurocomputing **50**, 159–175 (2003)

Analysing Facial Features Using CNNs and Computer Vision

Diana Borza[1]([✉]), Razvan Itu[1], Radu Danescu[1], and Ioana Barbantan[2]

[1] Technical University of Cluj-Napoca, Memorandumului Street 28,
400114 Cluj-Napoca, Romania
diana.borza@cs.utcluj.ro

[2] Tapptitude, 31-33 Gheorghe Doja Street, 400068 Cluj-Napoca, Romania

Abstract. This paper presents an automatic facial analysis system which is able to perform gender detection, hair segmentation and geometry detection, color attributes extraction (hair, skin, eyebrows, eyes and lips), accessories (eyeglasses) analysis from facial images. For the more complex tasks (gender detection, hair segmentation, eyeglasses detection) we used state of the art convolutional neural networks, and for the other tasks we used classical image processing algorithms based on geometry and appearance models. When data was available, the proposed system was evaluated on public datasets. An acceptance study was also performed to assess the performance on the system in real life scenarios.

Keywords: Facial attributes analysis · Gender detection · Hair segmentation · Convolutional neural networks · Color analysis

1 Introduction

Facial attributes analysis has received considerable attention in the last decade due to its numerous implications in real-world applications, including video surveillance systems, soft biometrics analysis, fashion and visagisme and face image synthesis.

Video surveillance has been used to improve safety and security, especially in crowded spaces such as airports or more recently in schools, universities and even concert venues. Analyzing faces is useful for identifying potentially blacklisted persons. On a similar note, with the rise of online shopping a new field in the fashion industry was developed - visagisme - which helps people select the accessories which best fit their appearance in the comfort of their home. One important module of any visagisme system is the automatic analysis of facial attributes: gender, hair color, hair hairstyle, skin and eye colors etc.

The remainder of this work is organized as follows: in Sect. 2 we briefly describe other state of the art works which tackle the problem of facial attribute analysis. In Sect. 3 we present the outline of the proposed solution, and we detail all the modules in Sects. 4 and 5. The conducted experiments are described in Sect. 6 and, finally, the conclusions are presented in Sect. 7.

© Springer Nature Switzerland AG 2020
D. Simian and L. F. Stoica (Eds.): MDIS 2019, CCIS 1126, pp. 146–157, 2020.
https://doi.org/10.1007/978-3-030-39237-6_10

2   State of the Art

The eyes are one of the most prominent and expressive features of the human face, giving information about the person's identity (iris biometrics), state of mind, attention, fatigue level etc. Therefore, eye/iris tracking is perhaps one of the most studied problems in the field of computer vision. Numerous eye tracking benchmarks and survey papers that exhaustively present the new advances and future challenges in this field, are available today [5]. However, to the best of our knowledge, the problem of eye color analysis has not been explored yet. In [2], the authors investigated the reliability of eye colors as a soft biometric trait; in this sense they developed an eye color recognition system (with four classes: black, brown, green, blue), based on color analysis using Gaussian mixture models.

Most of the research regarding skin analysis has focused on skin detection but scarcely on skin tone analysis. In the field of dermatology, the Fitzpatrick scale differentiates between six skin tones, ranging from I to VI, and it is used to estimate the skin response to ultraviolet light. In [9], the skin tone is coarsely differentiated between light and dark using simple thresholding in the RGB colorspace. Other methods described in [6,20] proposed more complex classification scales (with 16 skin tones), but they require the use of a color calibration pattern for skin tone matching.

Although automatic analysis of internal facial features was extensively studied by the scientific community, little work was done for hair analysis. In [19] the hair region is extracted from frontal face images using color feature and region growing. In [17] the hair is segmented by the intersection of two image masks: one based on color features, and the other computed based on frequency analysis. In [16] the hair pixels are determined using a two step approach. First, a rough hair probability map is constructed from local image patches computed by convolutional neural networks; next, based on this probability map, a support vector machine classifier performs hair classification at pixel level using local ternary patterns. The problem of hair segmentation for caricature synthesis is addressed in [18]. In the training phase, the priors for hair's position and color are estimated from a labeled dataset of images. In the test phase, the hair pixels are determined through graph-cuts and k-means clustering.

3   Proposed Solution for a Facial Analysis System

We present an automatic facial analysis system which is able to extract demographical, shape and color attributes from facial images captured in unconstrained environments. The proposed system combines both classical image processing methods, as well as deep learning algorithms.

The outline of the proposed solution is depicted in Fig. 1.

From a high level perspective the system can be split into two main types of modules: the localization modules (which are responsible for the precise estimation of the facial features) and the attribute recognition modules (which are further used to analyze and classify the previously detected regions). In Fig. 1 the

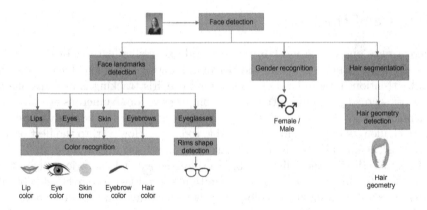

Fig. 1. Solution outline. The localization modules are displayed in red, while the attribute analysis modules are displayed in blue. (Color figure online)

localization modules are red, while the recognition modules are blue. First, we use an off-the-shelf face machine learning library [12] to localize the face region and extract 68 points around the most prominent features of the face, referred to in the following as landmarks.

Next, based on the position of these landmarks we devised several modules to localize and analyze the color of the lips, eyes, hair, skin and eyebrows. Due to the complexity of the problem we use fully convolutional neural networks to segment the hair pixels. Following this step, the obtained segmentation masks were matched against some predefined hair templates to determine the geometry of the hair. A lightweight convolutional neural network was used to extract the gender information from face images. Finally, a separate module determined the presence of eyeglasses and their shape.

We defined two categories of tasks based on the technology we employed: learning based tasks and image processing based tasks. The learning based tasks include the tasks where we made use of either machine learning classifiers such as decision trees and support vector machines and various convolutional neural networks. The image processing based tasks were implemented employing pattern matching strategies and probabilistic algorithms. There were also tasks that required an ensemble of technologies, which we will include in the learning based tasks category.

4   Learning-Based Facial Features Detection

4.1   Gender Detection

Due to the complexity of the problem, the gender detection task was tackled by employing convolutional neural networks. We opted for a lightweight network - MobileNet [8], which replaces all the classical convolutional layers with depthwise convolutions and therefore it is suitable for fast classification even on mobile devices. The network was trained on 60.000 images from the CelebA [13] dataset, using stochastic gradient descent optimizer and a batch size of 128 images.

4.2   Face Detection and Face Landmark Localization

We used an off-the-shelf detector - *dlib* machine learning library [12] - to locate the face and the 68 facial landmarks in the input image. The face detector uses Histogram of Oriented Gradients (HOG) and support vector machines (SVMs) for localization. Next, an ensemble of regression trees which operates on a sparse representation of the input image, are employed to locate the 68 landmarks within the previously detected face region [11].

The position of the face and of these landmarks are used as a starting point by all the feature localization modules of the proposed system.

4.3   Hair Segmentation and Hair Geometry Estimation

Hair segmentation is more complex than the localization of other facial features: first of all, the hair region cannot be easily estimated as modern hairstyles have different geometries (short, asymmetrical, curly, braided etc.). Second, the color distribution of natural hair tones is not uniform.

Our system uses a modified version of the *vgg-16* neural network architecture as in [14]. The segmentation network comprises 5 convolutional layers each one followed by max-pooling layers. It uses ReLU as activation functions, followed by three fully connected layers. At the end, a de-convolutional layer is added. The network was pre-trained on the Pascal VOC dataset [4].

The network was trained on facial images of size 224×224. Each image, both for training and for inference, undergoes the following pre-processing steps. First, the image is cropped based on the face rectangle; the face region is enlarged by a factor of 3.5 so that it comprises the hair area and only this enlarged face area will be processed by the network. Next, the pixels intensities from this cropped image are scaled as described in [14].

The network was trained to distinguish between two classes of pixels: hair and non-hair, and we used Intersection over Union (IoU) as loss function: This metric is a scale invariant, and it calculates the similarity between two finite sets, by dividing the size of the intersection by the size of the union:

$$IoU(A, B) = \frac{|A \cap B|}{|A| \cup |B|}. \tag{1}$$

The network was trained on images from the Part Labels Database database [10]. Some examples of hair segmentation masks are depicted in Fig. 2.

The next step is to estimate the hair geometry based on the segmentation masks computed by the network. We created two sets of predefined hair templates: one for female haircuts $Hair_F$ and the other one for male haircuts $Hair_M$, as depicted in Fig. 3. All the template images have a width equal to $MW = 200$ pixels and contain only the hair area (with no extra padding). The template

Fig. 2. Hair segmentation samples - in each image the detected hair area is overlayed with red. (Color figure online)

matching process takes into account the gender information: the segmentation mask is compared only with the hair templates form $Hair_F$ if the gender recognition network gave a positive female prediction, and only with the templates from $Hair_M$ otherwise.

(a) Female   (b) Male

Fig. 3. Examples of hair templates used for hair shape estimation

Prior to matching a mask with the predefined templates, it undergoes the following transformations: first, all the pixels that segmented as hair pixels and lie within the face area (determined by the *dlib* landmarks) are suppressed (marked as non-hair). Then, the hair mask is cropped to the bounding rectangle of the largest detected hair area. This cropped image is scaled so that its width is equal to MWS and the height dimension is scaled accordingly such that the aspect ratio of the mask is preserved.

Finally, the processed hair mask is compared to the templates from the adequate set ($Hair_M$ or $Hair_F$) using the IoU (Eq. 1) metric. The template which gave the highest IoU is given as output by the hair geometry analysis module.

To determine the hair color, we use the method described in Sect. 5.2.

4.4   Eyeglasses Detection and Shape Estimation

The proposed system also determines the presence (detection) and shape of the eyeglasses. For the detection part we trained a neural network using images from the CelebA [13] dataset. We used a CNN classifier and not classical image processing methods based on edge/gradient related features, because we noticed that the gradient magnitude is quite small in the case of rimless eyeglasses.

If the network detects the presence of eyeglasses, we use a two stage algorithm to determine the shape of the rims. We apply the same algorithm twice, symmetrically, for the left and the right rim. The image and facial landmarks used in this module are rotated such that the roll angle is zero. The first step is to determine the geometry of the eyeglasses rims: their center and their size. We crop the image to a region around the eyes and we perform a Canny edge detection on this region. The edges corresponding to the eye are filtered out (this edges can be easily determined from *dlib* facial landmarks). Next, we project the Canny edge map both vertically and horizontally, and we compute the bounding box of the rim based on the local maxima of these projections. After the region of the eyeglasses is established, we apply Distance Transformation on the Canny edge map.

Finally, we use a Distance Transform matching to select the shape of the eyeglasses from a predefined dataset of eyeglasses contours. Each eyeglasses template shape is superimposed over the Distance Transform map and the matching score is computed as the average of all pixels Distance Map which lie underneath the template. Prior to the matching step, the contours from the predefined dataset are scaled (by preserving the aspect ratio), such that the width of the bounding rectangle of the contour is equal to the bounding rectangle of the detected eyeglasses.

5   Image Processing-Based Facial Features Detection

5.1   Skin Segmentation

The skin segmentation module uses both geometry and appearance information to determine the skin pixels.

First, based on the position of the facial landmarks we estimate a region of interest around the cheeks and the nose where only skin pixels should be present. We select this region of interest as other regions on the face such as the chin, forehead or cheeks are more likely to be covered by facial hair. Next, we convert the image to HSV color-space and we use histogram back-projection to compute a mask of the skin pixels: $mask\_backproj$.

To ensure that we don't take any information outside the face area, we compute the intersection of $mask\_backproj$ with a mask which describes the geometry: $mask\_geom$. This mask is generated from the position of the facial landmarks. The entire process process in illustrated in Fig. 4.

Fig. 4. Skin pixels detection module. (a) ROI around the nose and cheeks used for histogram back-projection. (b). Mask obtained from histogram back-projection. (c). Skin mask determined from the *dlib* landmarks positions. (d). Skin mask.

5.2 Skin Color Extraction

The proposed system analyses the color of the following facial features: the eyes, the eyebrows, the lips, the skin and the hair. One of the most challenging problems in color analysis is its sensitivity towards illumination changes.

We devised a statistical method to ensure stability towards illumination changes. We computed a target brightness value for the skin pixels using images from the Chicago face database [15]. The database contains high-resolution facial images captured in highly controlled environments of subjects belonging to different ethnicities. In order to make sure the persons in these images to belong to different ethnicities, we manually selected a subset of 300 images from this database. We extracted the skin pixels (as described in Sect. 5.1), converted them to HSV color space and we computed the average value of the *Value* channel: AVG_h.

For each test image, we converted it to HSV color space, we set the value channel to the precomputed target value, AVG_h, and we converted the image back to the RGB color-space. This way we ensure that our method is robust to brightness changes. The color analysis operates on this transformed RGB image. To detect the dominant color from a region we compute a 3D histogram from all the pixels within the region of interest and we select the center of the maximal sub-cube (the sub-cube that contains the highest density of pixels) as the prominent color of that region.

5.3 Eyebrow Detection

For the eyebrow segmentation part we started from the eyebrow points detected by the *dlib* framework [8] and we established a rectangular region of interest, thus approximating their position.

Next, we applied Otsu thresholding on this area to find an optimal threshold which would highlight the eyebrow pixels (it is fair to assume the histogram of this area has a bimodal distribution, as there are only skin and eyebrow pixels). However, we noticed that in images captured in challenging brightness conditions, some skin pixels fall within the "darker" class using Otsu thresholding.

Therefore, we defined a maximal shape and location for the eyebrow pixels based on the landmarks detected by dlib. In the final step, only the pixels from the "darker" class, which fall under this ideal eyebrow mask are considered to be eyebrow pixels. Some results of this step are illustrated in Fig. 5.

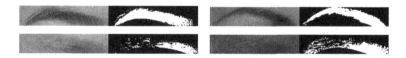

Fig. 5. Eyebrow segmentation samples. In each cell, the first image represents the region of interest for the eyebrow localization module, while the second is the segmented eyebrow mask.

The color of the eyebrows is determined as described in Sect. 5.2.

5.4 Iris Localization and Color Recognition

The landmarks detected by the *dlib* machine learning library only include the contour of the eyes but not the position of the iris center. To locate the iris center we used the approach presented in [1]: we search for objects with high circularity within the inner contour of the eyes determined by the facial landmarks. The iris radius is estimated as 0.42 of the eye width, as dictated by anthropometric proportions.

However, to estimate the colors of the eyes we need to remove the pupil pixels as these should not be taken into account when computing the iris color. We make the assumption that the pupil and iris are concentric and that the maximum pupil dilation [7] (ratio between pupil and iris radius) is 0.25. To implement this, we generate a binary pupil mask *mask_geom* which contains a central circle of radius *iris_radius* × 0.25 and is black for all other locations.

Next, the pupil area is determined using appearance methods. Based on the histogram of the iris region, we compute a threshold *th* for the pupil pixels: this threshold is set as the gray-level which "contains" approximately 30% of the iris pixels. We apply a binary thresholding operation with *th*, and obtain another *mask_appearance*. Finally, the pupil area is computed as the intersection between the two masks:

$$mask\_pupil = mask\_geom \cap \neg mask\_appearance \qquad (2)$$

Next, we analyse the iris pixels and classify them into one of the following classes: *blue*, *green*, *black* and *brown*. We use a simple, statistical approach in the HSV color space. First, if the Value channel is below a threshold TH_{bl} the *black* eye color class is set to *black*. Otherwise, we analyse the Hue channel to distinguish between the other eye color classes. We manually selected 30 images (10 for each of the remaining classes; 60 irises) and we computed each eye color's Hue interval based on these images. At test time, we use a simple voting mechanism to determine the eye color based on these pre-computed hue intervals.

6   Experimental Results

To evaluate the proposed solution for facial analysis we used images from several publicly available datasets: Adience [3], Chicago Face database and CelebA. The images we used for evaluations have not been used for training, and we used 29000 test images. The majority of images from these databases (Adience and CelebA) were captures in unconstrained environments, so they cover large pose variations, illumination conditions and background clutter.

6.1   Train and Test Datasets

CelebA is a large image database comprised of more than 200.000 facial images captured in unconstrained scenarios. The dataset provides rich annotations: each image is labeled with the position of 5 facial locations, 40 attributes and the identity of the person. The binary attributes include various information regarding the person: gender, hair color, face shape, hair shape (bangs, bald etc.) and about the accessories the person is wearing (glasses, hat etc.).

The Chicago face database [15] contains high-resolution, standardized image of subjects with different ethnicities with an age span between 17 and 65 years. Each image is labeled with the subject's gender, ethnicity, emotion (neutral, smiling, angry etc.), as well as with subjective information (for example, attractiveness). This database was mainly used to compute the target skin tone distribution, which was employed in the proposed solution to ensure its stability towards illumination changes.

Adience face database [3] was created by gathering images from Flickr albums assembled by automatic upload from iPhone devices; the dataset was mainly designed for the problems of automatic age and gender recognition problems. Adience comprises more than 26000 images, with more than 2200 subjects.

In the remainder of this section we report the performance of each module we employed using real data where available and defining an acceptance study where a human evaluation was necessary. The performance of the gender recognition module is reported in Table 1. From our tests, the gender recognition module made only one confusion between female-male class, on an image captured at night-time.

Table 1. Gender recognition performance.

Class	Precision	Recall	F1-Score	Support
Female	0.97	0.95	0.96	13246
Male	0.96	0.97	0.97	16364
Average	0.96	0.96	0.96	29610

The hair segmentation task was evaluated on images from Part Labels Database (PLD) (images which have not been used at training time) and from images from Figaro-1k database. The latter database comprises of approximately 1000 hair images, each annotated with the hairstyle and with a segmentation mask. However, the face is not visible in all the images, so we selected only the samples in which the face was detected (171 images). The performance of our system is reported in Table 2.

Table 2. Hair segmentation performance of Label Parts Database and Figaro1k

Metric	LPD	Figaro 1K
mIoU	0.8709	0.8279
pixelAcc	0.9701	0.9115

In Table 2, $mIoU$ stands for mean Intersection over Union, while $pixelAcc$ stands for pixel accuracy:

$$pixelAcc = \sum_i n_{ii} / \sum_i t_i, \tag{3}$$

$$mIoU = \frac{1}{n_{cl}} \sum_i \frac{n_{ii}}{t_i + \sum_j n_{ij} - n_{ii}}. \tag{4}$$

In Eq. 3, above, n_{cl} represents the total number segmentation classes, n_{ij} is the number of pixels of class i predicted to be in class j, and t_i the total number of pixels in ground truth segmentation of class i.

To evaluate the eyeglasses detection task, we randomly selected 5000 images from the CelebA dataset (2500 with persons wearing glasses and 2500 without glasses), which were not seen by the network at the training phase. The network attained 99.4% classification accuracy. During our evaluation, the eyeglasses detection module gave no false positives.

To the best of our knowledge, for all the other image processing based tasks (color analysis) no public data is available. Therefore, we also performed an acceptance study to see how the proposed system behaves on real world data. We developed a mobile application, which takes a picture using the front camera of the device and extracts the facial attributes using the proposed system.

The system was tested by more than 15 subjects in different scenarios: indoor, outdoor, in the car, day-time, night-time etc. In total, we evaluated the system on more than 250 images. The skin and hair color extracted were good approximates for the actual skin and hair color. However, in the case of eye color analysis we noticed the following: in poor lighting conditions (outdoor-nighttime images or indoor images with low light), the proposed system outputs *black* or *brown* eye colors, even if the person depicted in the images had blue or green eyes. However, for these degraded images, one might argue that even the human performance for determining the eye color is low.

Another issue we observed was that if the person is wearing glasses and strong reflections are present on the eyeglasses lens, our eye color extraction module is biased towards the *blue* class. We plan to fix this issue in a future version, by also taking into account the eyeglasses information when analyzing the eye color.

7   Conclusions and Future Work

This paper presented an all in one system for facial attributes analysis and accessories detection; the proposed method is able to detect gender, eye, hair and skin color, hair shape, eyebrow shape. The proposed system uses deep learning methods for the recognition and segmentation of complex features, such as gender information and hair segmentation. The other features (eyes, lips, eyebrows, eyeglasses) are localized and analyzed using classical image processing methods. When possible (if data were available), the system was evaluated on publicly available databases. For all the other tasks, we performed an acceptance study (all the observations are presented in Sect. 6).

The proposed system has implications into a variety of domains, such as soft biometrics analysis, fashion (accessories recommendation based on a person's appearance), human computer interaction (automatic avatar generation) etc.

As a future work we plan to extend the system, so that it will be able to detect other facial features, such as the presence and shape of the facial hair, hairstyle classification and emotion estimation.

Acknowledgements. This work was made possible with the support of the "Institute of Research, Development and Education in Computer Vision" (Asociația Institutul de Cercetare, Dezvoltare și Educație în Viziune Artificială, http://icvcluj.eu/), Cluj-Napoca, Romania, and Tapptitude (https://tapptitude.com/), a product development agency, where the first iteration of the algorithm was built.

References

1. Borza, D., Itu, R., Danescu, R.: In the eye of the deceiver: analyzing eye movements as a cue to deception. J. Imaging **4**(10), 120 (2018)
2. Dantcheva, A., Erdogmus, N., Dugelay, J.L.: On the reliability of eye color classification as a soft biometrics trait. In: Proceedings of WACV (2011, to appear)
3. Eidinger, E., Enbar, R., Hassner, T.: Age and gender estimation of unfiltered faces. IEEE Trans. Inf. Forensics Secur. **9**(12), 2170–2179 (2014)
4. Everingham, M., Gool, L., Williams, C.K., Winn, J., Zisserman, A.: The Pascal visual object classes (VOC) challenge. Int. J. Comput. Vision **88**(2), 303–338 (2010)
5. Hansen, D.W., Ji, Q.: In the eye of the beholder: a survey of models for eyes and gaze. IEEE Trans. Pattern Anal. Mach. Intell. **32**(3), 478–500 (2010)
6. Harville, M., Baker, H., Bhatti, N., Susstrunk, S.: Consistent image-based measurement and classification of skin color. In: IEEE International Conference on Image Processing 2005, vol. 2, pp. II–374. IEEE (2005)
7. Hollingsworth, K.P., Bowyer, K.W., Flynn, P.J.: The importance of small pupils: a study of how pupil dilation affects iris biometrics. In: 2008 IEEE Conference on Biometrics: Theory, Applications and Systems. pp. 1–6. IEEE (2008)

8. Howard, A.G., et al.: MobileNets: efficient convolutional neural networks for mobile vision applications. arXiv preprint arXiv:1704.04861 (2017)
9. Jmal, M., Mseddi, W.S., Attia, R., Youssef, A.: Classification of human skin color and its application to face recognition. In: The Sixth International Conferences on Advances in Multimedia, MMEDIA. Citeseer (2014)
10. Kae, A., Sohn, K., Lee, H., Learned-Miller, E.: Augmenting CRFs with Boltzmann machine shape priors for image labeling (2013)
11. Kazemi, V., Sullivan, J.: One millisecond face alignment with an ensemble of regression trees. In: Proceedings of the IEEE Conference on Computer Vision and Pattern Recognition, pp. 1867–1874 (2014)
12. King, D.E.: Dlib-ml: a machine learning toolkit. J. Mach. Learn. Res. **10**, 1755–1758 (2009)
13. Liu, Z., Luo, P., Wang, X., Tang, X.: Large-scale CelebFaces attributes (CelebA) dataset (2018). Accessed 15 Aug 2018
14. Long, J., Shelhamer, E., Darrell, T.: Fully convolutional networks for semantic segmentation. In: Proceedings of the IEEE Conference on Computer Vision and Pattern Recognition, pp. 3431–3440 (2015)
15. Ma, D.S., Correll, J., Wittenbrink, B.: The Chicago face database: a free stimulus set of faces and norming data. Behav. Res. Methods **47**(4), 1122–1135 (2015)
16. Muhammad, U.R., Svanera, M., Leonardi, R., Benini, S.: Hair detection, segmentation, and hairstyle classification in the wild. Image Vis. Comput. **71**, 25–37 (2018)
17. Rousset, C., Coulon, P.Y.: Frequential and color analysis for hair mask segmentation. In: 15th IEEE International Conference on Image Processing, ICIP 2008, pp. 2276–2279. IEEE (2008)
18. Shen, Y., Peng, Z., Zhang, Y.: Image based hair segmentation algorithm for the application of automatic facial caricature synthesis. Sci. World J. **2014** (2014)
19. Yacoob, Y., Davis, L.: Detection, analysis and matching of hair. In: Tenth IEEE International Conference on Computer Vision, ICCV 2005, vol. 1, pp. 741–748. IEEE (2005)
20. Yoon, S., Harville, M., Baker, H., Bhatii, N.: Automatic skin pixel selection and skin color classification. In: 2006 International Conference on Image Processing, pp. 941–944. IEEE (2006)

Composite SVR Based Modelling
of an Industrial Furnace

Daniel Santos[1], Luís Rato[1], Teresa Gonçalves[1(✉)], Miguel Barão[1],
Sérgio Costa[2,4], Isabel Malico[2,4], and Paulo Canhoto[2,3]

[1] Computer Science Department, University of Évora, Évora, Portugal
{dfsantos,lmr,tcg,mjsb}@uevora.pt
[2] Physics Department, University of Évora, Évora, Portugal
{smcac,imbm,canhoto}@uevora.pt
[3] ICT Institute of Earth Sciences, University of Évora, Évora, Portugal
[4] LAETA, IDMEC, University of Lisbon, Lisbon, Portugal

Abstract. Industrial furnaces consume a large amount of energy and
their operating points have a major influence on the quality of the final
product. Designing a tool that analyzes the combustion process, fluid
mechanics and heat transfer and assists the work done during energy
audits is then of the most importance.

This work proposes a hybrid model for such a tool, having as its base
two white-box models, namely a detailed Computational Fluid Dynamics (CFD) model and a simplified Reduced-Order (RO) model, and a
black-box model developed using Machine Learning (ML) techniques.

The preliminary results presented in the paper show that this composite model is able to improve the accuracy of the RO model without
having the high computational load of the CFD model.

Keywords: Energy efficiency · Industrial furnaces · CFD · Reduced
order model · Support vector regression · Hybrid model

1 Introduction

Industrial furnaces are important heating equipment used in many industries.
Their correct operation has a major influence on the quality of the final products
but they also consume large amounts of energy.

The objective of this work is to develop a tool that analyzes the combustion
process, fluid mechanics and heat transfer and assists the work done by energy
auditors in the data analysis and in the definition of measures for improving
energy efficiency. This tool should have a high degree of accuracy without a high
computational cost and be able to be applied to a variety of furnace geometries.

The work presented in this paper was carried out under the "Audit Furnace"
project, and is part of the prototype development of such a tool. Primarily,
two physics based models were built up for a specific billet heating furnace [3]: a

D. Simian and L. F. Stoica (Eds.): MDIS 2019, CCIS 1126, pp. 158–170, 2020.
https://doi.org/10.1007/978-3-030-39237-6_11

detailed Computational Fluid Dynamics (CFD) model and a simplified Reduced-Order (RO) model. These two white-box models constitute the base of a black-box model developed using Machine Learning (ML) techniques. The goal of such a hybrid model is to further improve the accuracy of the Reduced-Order model; on the other hand, the data generated by the CFD model is used for the training phase of the ML model.

The rest of this paper is organised as follows: Sect. 2 presents the white, black and grey model approaches and Sect. 3 introduces the different models built to model a billet heating furnace, namely the CFD, RO and ML models. Section 4 details the designed experiments and presents and discusses the results obtained. Finally, in Sect. 5 conclusions and future work are presented.

2   White, Black and Grey Model Approaches

Mathematical modelling of physical systems is usually tackled using two main approaches: white-box and black-box models [10–12]. White-box approaches model a physical system entirely using physical laws and principles. On the other hand, black-box approaches model a system entirely based on data, such as input-output measurements. These models are usually constructed under statistical approaches, such as estimation of auto-regressive models, or machine learning methods such as neural networks and support vector machines.

It is very common to have models that mix white- and black-box approaches but they remain essentially in one of the two categories. Nevertheless, some hybrid and composite approaches of mathematical modelling deeply combine both, generating what is known as grey-box approaches. Slate-Grey, Smoke-Grey, and Steel-Grey modelling [11] are examples of such approaches.

In this work we propose a hybrid grey-box approach, where a simplified white-box model, based on physical laws, is connected to a black-box model based on machine learning techniques.

Black box approaches have been extensively used to model physical systems [2,4,7,9,13–16]. These approaches require large amounts of rich data for the training phase; by rich data we mean data which is representative of all relevant situations of the system. In industrial plants, however, acquiring such rich data is difficult and sometimes impossible because of practical constraints such as safety, or the economic impact of changing the operating points of the system. In order to overcome this difficulty, for the training step of the machine learning model we'll use a dataset generated by a white-box detailed model.

Thus, for the proposed approach we aim at:

- higher accuracy when compared to RO model;
- faster response times (lower computational load) when compared to CFD;
- lower dependence from real experimental data for the ML training phase.

3   Modelling a Billet Heating Furnace

Industrial furnaces are often large-scale complex systems with many different functions; as far as mathematical modelling is concerned, each of these complex systems has its own challenges. As already mentioned, this paper presents a study of an industrial billet heating furnace. The next subsections introduce the furnace and describe the models developed, namely the Computational Fluid Dynamics model, the Reduced-Order model and the proposed Machine Learning model.

3.1 The Furnace

The studied furnace is a linear propane furnace used to heat metal parts, known as billets, to a temperature of approximately 1030 K to 1060 K [17], and thus preparing them for extrusion. The billets are produced in a melting furnace, have a variable composition and are in the shape of a cylinder (see Fig. 1).

Fig. 1. Geometrical model of the billet heating furnace (the walls of the furnace are represented in grey and the billets are copper-coloured).

The furnace is composed of two preheating zones, where heat is transferred to the billet (HE1 and HE2), one fresh air pre-heater (HE3) and nine combustion zones. Billet circulate from the left to the right entering at ambient temperature of around 35 °C and is heated to 745 °C before getting out of the furnace to be extruded. Along the 9 combustion zones, there are 312 burners distributed radially in groups of 4. Figure 2 presents a scheme of the furnace.

Immediately after entering the furnace, the billets are preheated by the combustion gases that flow in counter-current to the billets in their way out of the furnace.

The temperature of each sub-zone is controlled automatically according to a set point imposed manually (in the sub-zone) and is a function of the material that is being heated.

3.2 Computational Fluid Dynamics Model

Large industrial process heating furnaces are complex systems designed to deliver heat to loads for many distinct processes. They are critical for the final product quality and should run efficiently so that energy usage and operation costs are kept the lowest possible.

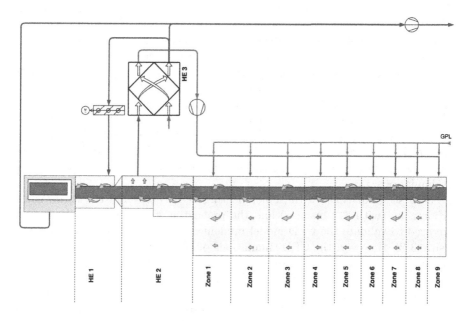

Fig. 2. Scheme of the furnace.

Although using Computational Fluid Dynamics models to simulate furnaces is the approach that provides the most detailed information, this includes complex tasks, such as constructing a spatial discretization grid and dealing with reactive turbulent flow, or with two-phase flow. Additionally, due to the diversity of processes and raw materials processed, the types of furnaces are numerous. Therefore, there is no universal model and the CFD model must be adapted to each furnace so that it can well represent the physical and chemical phenomena that take place inside the furnace.

Generically, a CFD simulation of industrial furnaces consists of the numerical solution of the transport equations of mass (Eq. 1), momentum (Eq. 2), energy (Eq. 3), and species (Eq. 4) supported by a suitable spatial discretization of the furnace.

$$\frac{\partial \rho}{\partial t} + \nabla \cdot (\rho \boldsymbol{u}) = 0 \tag{1}$$

$$\frac{\partial \rho \boldsymbol{u}}{\partial t} + \nabla \cdot (\rho \boldsymbol{u} \otimes \boldsymbol{u}) = -\nabla p + \nabla \cdot \tau + S_F \tag{2}$$

$$\frac{\partial \rho e}{\partial t} + \nabla \cdot (\rho \boldsymbol{u} e) = -p \nabla \boldsymbol{u} + \nabla \cdot (k \nabla T) + S_e \tag{3}$$

$$\frac{\partial \rho Y_i}{\partial t} + \nabla \cdot (\rho \boldsymbol{u} Y_i) = \nabla \cdot (\rho D_i \nabla Y_i) + \dot{\omega}_i + S_i \tag{4}$$

In these equations, ρ stands for density, t for time, $\boldsymbol{u}$ is the velocity vector, p the pressure, τ the shear stress, e the specific energy and k the thermal conductivity. Furthermore, Y_i is the mass fraction of the ith chemical species, D_i the diffusivity coefficient of the ith chemical species in the mixture, $\dot{\omega}$ the reaction rate and S_F, S_e, and S_i are the source terms for the equations of momentum, energy and mass of the ith chemical species.

In this study, the three-dimensional, steady transport equations were solved, following the Reynolds-averaged Navier-Stokes (RANS) approach and using the two equations realizable k-ϵ model for turbulence closure. Combustion was treated as an irreversible reaction and radiation was also taken into account in the simulations.

The first simulations of the billet heating furnace covered the entire combustion zone (with 312 burners) and the preheating zone that precedes it and were used to validate the CFD model implemented against real data measured on site [3,8]. However, the CFD simulations of the long furnace took too much time (around 300 h each) and proved to be inadequate for the generation of the large training dataset needed by the machine learning model. As a consequence, a smaller, simplified geometrical model of the real furnace was built. The model is composed of a line of burners (4 burners) instead of the 78 lines of burners ($4 \times 78 = 312$ burners). Although, much shorter, it is a representation of a generic section of the combustion zone of the furnace and retains the basic phenomena that occur inside the furnace.

For the simulations, the commercial software Fluent 19.0 was used [1]. Further description of the model development can be found in [3,8].

3.3   Reduced-Order Model

Reduced-Order models, based on physical principles and laws, are simplified models usually with extremely light computational load when compared with CFD ones. This gives them much faster response times, the models being, also, simpler to build. RO models do not consider all the details and complexity of the physical phenomena involved while keeping an acceptable accuracy regarding the overall energy and mass balances.

In this work the developed RO model is based on the division of the furnace into a relatively small number of zones and on solving energy and mass balances for each of these zones. The combustion process is modelled considering the complete combustion of the fuel in a single step reaction, which allows determining the energy released in each zone of the furnace and the composition and temperature of the combustion gases according to the stoichiometry of the reaction and taking into account the excess air present. The dependence of the gas properties with temperature is also considered. The heat transfer by convection between the combustion gases and the processed material (billets) is modelled using existing correlations in the literature for simple geometries, while the heat transfer by thermal radiation inside the furnace is modelled using the solution of the radiative transfer equation for a simplified geometry that encloses a volume (annular region) filled with a participating medium (combustion gases).

The solution of the resulting system of non-linear equations allows obtaining the mean inlet and outlet temperatures of the combustion gases and billets, mass flow rates and heat transfer in each zone as a function of the operating conditions of the furnace.

The RO model does not produce detailed information on the fluid flow and heat transfer inside the furnace and its accuracy is expected to be lower when compared to CFD output. Thus, RO models compromise accuracy by building less complex models, which leads to a reduced computational cost (while also increasing the versatility of computational tools based on such models to adapt to different furnace configurations). As a consequence, if the drawback of accuracy loss is acceptable to some extent, RO models become a potentially useful tool in the context of energy audits of industrial furnaces.

3.4 Machine Learning Model

The proposed Machine Learning model approach uses data from the RO and CFD models for training to further increase RO model accuracy, making the new model closer to the CFD one. Thus, it can be seen as a composite model of black-box and white-box models, consisting of the RO model generated output along with an adjustment generated by the ML model. This grey-box model aims at being a trade-off between the high complexity/more accurate CFD model and the much simpler/less accurate RO model.

The training phase of machine learning approaches may require large amounts of data. This data must be representative of all relevant situations of the system operation. As such, it should include a diversity of operating regimes as well as furnace characteristics. As already mentioned, we propose to use the data generated by the detailed CFD model as the training dataset in order to overcome the difficulty of obtaining real data from industrial furnaces covering all the relevant situations (operation regimes and furnaces characteristics).

Figure 3 presents this grey-box model composed by the RO and ML models along with the CFD and RO only model.

4   Experiments and Results

This section details the designed experiments. It introduces the SVR algorithm, describes the dataset and introduces the experiments and corresponding setup; finally it presents and discusses the results obtained.

4.1   Support Vector Regression

Support Vector Machines (SVM) [5] is a machine learning algorithm mostly used in classification tasks. It is numerically efficient and has a low computational cost, because of the use of the so-called kernel 'trick'. The kernel is a function that allows the computation of the dot product between two vectors in a high dimensional feature space without the need to work on that space. Besides

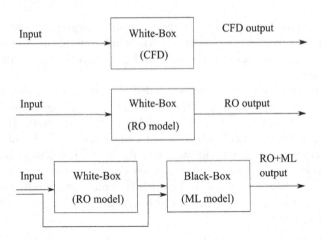

Fig. 3. CFD model, RO model and grey-box model composed by the RO and ML models.

classification problems, this idea can also be used for regression problems where it is referred as Support Vector Regression (SVR) [6].

This algorithm has a set of hyper-parameters, the most important ones being:

- *kernel:* the function that transforms the data from the original space into a high dimension feature space. It can be linear, polynomial, sigmoid or radial basis (RBF) functions, among others;
- *C:* the penalty parameter. It controls the trade-off between overfitting (low training error) and generalization (low testing error);
- *epsilon:* Determines the level of accuracy of the approximated function;
- *degree:* polynomial kernel parameter;
- *gamma:* RBF kernel parameter.

4.2   Dataset

As previously mentioned, and since it was not possible to get enough furnace working points real data, we used the results of the CFD model of a section of an industrial furnace for heating metal billets that uses liquefied propane gas as fuel.

First, an analysis of all the available variables (from the CFD and RO models) was made to decide which would be the input (able to be measured during the operation of the furnace) and the output variables for the machine learning model development.

The exhaust combustion gas temperature downstream, known as *TGO*, one of the eight CFD continuous variables was considered the dependent variable that the ML model will estimate (also known as output variable). The other seven CFD variables behave as inputs to the model. The RO model generates new five continuous variables (beside the exhaust combustion gas temperature estimated output) that are also considered input variables. This totals thirteen continuous input variables plus the output one.

Then, the correlation between all pairs of variables was calculated and a heatmap produced. The heatmap can be seen in Fig. 4.

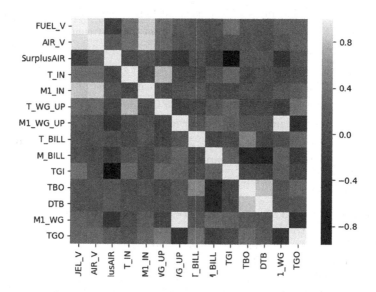

Fig. 4. Heatmap of the thirteen variables

We found a high correlation between *SurplusAir* and *TGI* (−0.961) and between *M1_WG* and *M1_WG_UP* (0.996), and, as such, *TGI* and *M1_WP_UP* were dropped. Thus, the generated data set includes eleven input continuous variables plus the variable to be predicted − *TGO*. The input variables are presented in Table 1. Since the variables have different scales, they were normalised to the interval [0, 1].

A total of 100 cases corresponding to different furnace working settings were generated by the CFD model, and the input values of the RO model were adjusted to the CFD inputs in order for both outputs to be comparable.

The high computational complexity of this task is essentially related to the CFD simulations; running the RO model has a negligible computational load.

4.3   Experiments

The proposed method was tested according to 2 different architectures:

1. *RO+SVR:* the estimated exhaust combustion gas temperature from the RO model is added to the SVR output;
2. *RO2SVR:* the estimated exhaust combustion gas temperature from the RO model is used as an input variable to the SVR.

Table 1. Continuous variables used as input for the ML model.

Name	Meaning	Source
SurplusAir	Excess air	CFD
T_IN	Temperature of fuel and air at burner inlets	CFD
M1_IN	Mass flow rate of fuel plus air at burner inlets	CFD
T_WG_UP	Flue gas temperature entering from the upstream section	CFD
T_BILL	Billet inlet temperature	CFD
DTB	Variation of billet temperature	CFD
M1_WG	Flue gas mass flow rate – downstream (outlet of furnace)	CFD
FUEL_V	Inlet volume flow rate of fuel in the burners	RO
AIR_V	Inlet volume flow rate of air in the burners	RO
M_BILL	Billet mass flow rate	RO
TBO	Output billet temperature	RO

In the first proposed architecture, *RO+SVR*, the SVR aims at predicting the difference between the RO model output and the CFD output (the RO model prediction error). This difference enables the adjustment of the RO model output to a value closer to the CFD output.

In the second case, *RO2SVR*, the SVR receives, as input, the estimated exhaust combustion gas temperature (*TGO*) from the RO model, besides the remaining fourteen attributes and directly aims at predicting the TGO value given by the CFD model.

4.4   Experimental Setup

To tune the SVR, a grid search algorithm was used to find the best combination of hyper-parameters. The chosen kernel was RBF and the considered range for the parameters was:

- $C \in \{0.1, 1, 100, 1000\}$
- $epsilon \in \{0.0001, 0.0005, 0.001, 0.05, 0.01, 0.05, 0.1, 0.5, 1, 5, 10\}$
- $gamma \in \{0.0001, 0.001, 0.01, 0.1, 1, 3, 5\}$

Using 80% of the dataset and a 10 fold cross-validation procedure, the optimal combination of hyper-parameters was found to be $C = 100$, $gamma = 1$ for both architectures and $epsilon = 0.0005$ and $epsilon = 0.01$ for *RO+SVR* and *RO2SVR*, respectively.

Having set the parameters, a 10-fold cross validation was used to evaluate the performance of the built model. To evaluate the SVR prediction power two measures were used: the root mean square error (*RMSE*) and the mean absolute percentage error (*MAPE*), that can be calculated by Eqs. 5 and 6, respectively. In the equations, n is the number of examples, Y_i is the real value and $\hat{Y}_i$ is the predicted one.

$$RMSE = \sqrt{\frac{1}{n} \sum_{n=1}^{n} \left(Y_i - \hat{Y}_i\right)^2} \tag{5}$$

$$MAPE = \frac{100\%}{n} \sum_{n=1}^{n} \left| \frac{Y_i - \hat{Y}_i}{Y_i} \right| \tag{6}$$

4.5   Results

Table 2 presents the results obtained for the two evaluation measures (*RMSE* and *MAPE*) and two proposed architectures (*RO+SVR* and *RO2SVR*); the last column presented the results given by the Reduced-Order model. Note that while *MSE* and *RMSE* are calculated over absolute differences, *MAPE* is a normalised measure.

Table 2. Results of the *RO model* and *RO+SVR* and *RO2SVR* architectures.

	RMSE	MAPE (%)
RO model	144.73	12.24
RO+SVR	36.54	3.24
RO2SVR	42.53	3.52

As we can see, the proposed approach (using any of the proposed architectures) significantly reduces the error to around one third in *RMSE* and *MAPE* when compared to the results from the RO model. On the other hand, the errors obtained with the *RO+SVR* and RO2SVR architectures are very similar.

Figure 5 presents, for each test example, the *RO+SVR* model data points: the *TGO* predicted vs. actual values (CFD output).

On the other hand, Fig. 6 presents, again for each test example, the *RO2SVR* model data points: *TGO* predicted vs. actual values (CFD output).

Looking at Fig. 5 one can argue that, of the 20 test operating points only four have a difference higher than $50K$, and nine have a difference less than $25K$. On the other hand, looking at Fig. 6 the number of predicted points having a difference higher than $50K$ is three, with nine having a difference less than $25K$. Nonetheless, given the size of the dataset these differences don't seem to be significant (as also can be seen from Table 2).

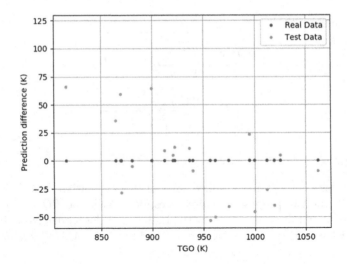

Fig. 5. *RO+SVR*: TGO predicted vs. actual values for the test set.

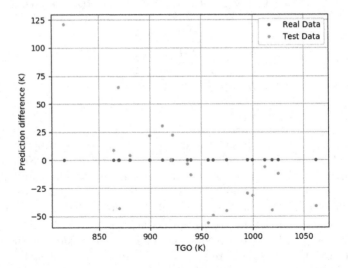

Fig. 6. *RO2SVR*: TGO predicted vs. actual values for the test set.

5   Conclusions and Future Work

The results presented in this work show that the Machine Learning proposed approach is adequate to help building mathematical models to use in energy audits. The proposed approach demonstrates that physically based Reduced-Order models complemented with black-box models generate a hybrid composite grey-box model with increased accuracy while keeping a low computational load to run.

These hybrid Machine Learning based models depend on having a training set for model development. As such, the generation, by detailed CFD simulation, of adequate, large and sufficiently rich datasets can be seen as the main obstacle to the implementation of such methods.

Although the presented work is still a work in progress, these experiments demonstrate the effectiveness of this approach considering a dataset of 100 CFD generated data points. The minimum necessary amount of data depends on the ML techniques used; nevertheless, this preliminary results show that this approach to increase the RO model accuracy is feasible. Moreover, the CFD dataset generated is an initial step that can scale up as a function of the computer power put in the task. We should note that this strategy helps to overcome the difficulty of obtaining rich experimental data from industrial furnaces.

In order to support these conclusions, we intend, as future work, to test this approach using a bigger number of CFD simulations for the same furnace but also test the approach on other furnaces. We also plan to use genetic algorithms to better fine tune the SVR model and try other ML algorithms, such as artificial neural networks.

Moreover, the proposed model will be incorporated into a computer tool, which will allow a rapid analysis of furnaces in the scope of energy efficiency audits.

Acknowledgements. This study was funded by the Alentejo 2020, Portugal 2020 program (Contract nr: 2017/017980) and by FCT – Fundação para a Ciência e Tecnologia (project UID/EMS/50022/2013).

References

1. ANSYS: FLUENT software. https://www.ansys.com/products/fluids/ansys-fluent. Accessed 02 Aug 2019
2. Bernieri, A., D'Apuzzo, M., Sansone, L., Savastano, M.: A neural network approach for identification and fault diagnosis on dynamic systems. IEEE Trans. Instrum. Meas. **43**(6), 867–873 (1994). https://doi.org/10.1109/19.368083
3. Cavaleiro Costa, S., et al.: Simulation of a billet heating furnace. In: V Congreso Ibero-Americano de Emprendimiento, Energía, Ambiente y Tecnología (CIEEMAT 2019), vol. 1, September 2019
4. Chon, K.H., Cohen, R.J.: Linear and nonlinear ARMA model parameter estimation using an artificial neural network. IEEE Trans. Biomed. Eng. **44**(3), 168–174 (1997). https://doi.org/10.1109/10.554763
5. Cortes, C., Vapnik, V.: Support-vector networks. Mach. Learn. **20**(3), 273–297 (1995). https://doi.org/10.1023/A:1022627411411
6. Drucker, H., Burges, C.J.C., Kaufman, L., Smola, A.J., Vapnik, V.: Support vector regression machines. In: Mozer, M.C., Jordan, M.I., Petsche, T. (eds.) Advances in Neural Information Processing Systems, vol. 9, pp. 155–161. MIT Press, Cambridge (1997). http://papers.nips.cc/paper/1238-support-vector-regression-machines.pdf
7. Hachino, T., Takata, H.: Identification in nonlinear systems by using an automatic choosing function and a genetic algorithm. Electr. Eng. Jpn. **125**(4), 43–51 (1999)
8. IPS, UEv: Simulações CFD. Descrição de Resultados. Deliverable 3.3. Audit Furnace Project (2019)

9. Liao, Y., Wu, M., She, J.: Modeling of reheating-furnace dynamics using neural network based on improved sequential-learning algorithm. In: 2006 IEEE Conference on Computer Aided Control System Design, 2006 IEEE International Conference on Control Applications, and 2006 IEEE International Symposium on Intelligent Control, pp. 3175–3181, October 2006. https://doi.org/10.1109/CACSD-CCA-ISIC.2006.4777146

10. Ljung, L. (ed.): System Identification: Theory for the User, 2nd edn. Prentice Hall, Upper Saddle River (1999)

11. Ljung, L.: Perspectives on system identification. IFAC Proc. Vol. **41**(2), 7172–7184 (2008). https://doi.org/10.3182/20080706-5-KR-1001.01215. 17th IFAC World Congress

12. Ljung, L.: Approaches to identification of nonlinear systems. In: Proceedings of 29th Chinese Control Conference, Beijing, China, July 2010

13. Narendra, K.S., Parthasarathy, K.: Identification and control of dynamical systems using neural networks. IEEE Trans. Neural Netw. **1**(1), 4–27 (1990). https://doi.org/10.1109/72.80202

14. Narendra, K.S., Parthasarathy, K.: Neural networks and dynamical systems. Int. J. Approximate Reasoning **6**(2), 109–131 (1992). https://doi.org/10.1016/0888-613X(92)90014-Q

15. Patra, J.C., Modanese, C., Acciarri, M.: Artificial neural network-based modelling of compensated multi-crystalline solar-grade silicon under wide temperature variations. IET Renew. Power Gener. **10**(7), 1010–1016 (2016). https://doi.org/10.1049/iet-rpg.2015.0375

16. Rajesh, N., Khare, M., Pabi, S.: Application of Ann modelling techniques in blast furnace iron making. Int. J. Model. Simul. **30**(3), 340–344 (2010). https://doi.org/10.1080/02286203.2010.11442589

17. Trinks, W., Mawhinney, M., Shannon, R.A., Reed, R.J., Garvey, J.R.: Industrial Furnaces. Wiley, New York (2004)

A Conceptual Framework for Software Fault Prediction Using Neural Networks

Camelia Serban$^{(\boxtimes)}$ and Florentin Bota$^{(\boxtimes)}$

Babes-Bolyai University, Cluj-Napoca, Romania
{camelia,botaflorentin}@cs.ubbcluj.ro

Abstract. Software testing is a very expensive and critical activity in the software systems' life-cycle. Finding software faults or bugs is also time-consuming, requiring good planning and a lot of resources. Therefore, predicting software faults is an important step in the testing process to significantly increase efficiency of time, effort and cost usage.

In this study we investigate the problem of Software Faults Prediction (SFP) based on Neural Network. The main contribution is to empirically establish the combination of Chidamber and Kemer software metrics that offer the best accuracy for faults prediction with numeric estimations by using feature selection. We also proposed a conceptual framework that integrates the model for fault prediction.

Keywords: Software faults · Software metrics · Machine learning

1 Introduction

Object oriented technology through its mechanisms like inheritance, abstraction, data encapsulation, and polymorphism, can provide a comprehensive description of software's internal structure and nature. It is well known that, as in chess, only knowing the rules, here the mechanisms of object orientation, are not enough to achieve high quality design [17]. Therefore, we need principles and strategies that need to be applied when designing an object oriented system.

Four internal characteristics are linked to object orientation: coupling, cohesion, complexity and data abstraction. These aspects define the main principles of good object design. Thus, a software system design having *low coupling, high cohesion, manageable complexity* and *proper data abstraction*, aims to achieve quality attributes such as reliability, maintainability, extensibility, scalability and reusability. In this respect, we can assess the internal characteristics of a software system design in order to predict its external behaviour.

Software metrics are powerful means to quantify those aspects of a software system design that are relevant for its assessment. Their values can be used in order to predict other software attributes that are correlated with them. In this respect, several studies reveal Chidamber and Kemerer (CK) [4] metrics having a strong impact on software quality and particularly on software reliability by predicting fault prone classes [1,3,12,15].

© Springer Nature Switzerland AG 2020
D. Simian and L. F. Stoica (Eds.): MDIS 2019, CCIS 1126, pp. 171–186, 2020.
https://doi.org/10.1007/978-3-030-39237-6_12

Software faults prediction deals with developing models that can be used in the early phases of software development life cycle for detecting software components that contain faults (bugs). Software testing is a time-consuming activity, requiring also good planning and a lot of resources. Therefore, predicting software faults is an utmost important process prior to testing activity to significantly increase efficiency of time, effort and cost usage.

The contribution of this paper is twofold: firstly, we aim to approach the problem of software fault prediction, defining a conceptual framework that incorporates components such as: the object oriented design model, metrics, and methods used for prediction. Secondly, the paper aims to empirically establish a combination of CK software metrics that offers the best accuracy for fault prediction.

The reminder of the paper is organized as follows. In Sect. 2 we briefly describe the main components of the proposed framework, the object oriented design model, metrics, and neural network as a method for prediction. The formal statement of the proposed approach and the research questions are defined in Sect. 3 whereas Sect. 4 reviews related work on software fault prediction. Section 5 describes our proposed model for fault detection based on neural metrics and CK metrics. We conclude our paper and give suggestions for extending the approach in Sect. 6.

2   Setting the Context

The following sections briefly introduce the components which define our proposed framework for software faults detection: the object oriented design model, metrics used to quantify the internal structure of the software system and neural network - the method used for fault prediction.

2.1   Object Oriented Design Model

One of our objectives for this research is to define a contextual framework for software faults prediction problem regarding an object oriented system. In this respect, we recall here the object oriented design model as it was introduced by Marinescu [17], and then formalized and detailed in [21].

An *object oriented design model* for a software system S is defined as a 3-tuple, $M(S) = (E, Prop(E), Rel(E))$, where:

- E represents the *design entities* set of S, an element from E can be a package, a class, a method from a class, an attribute from a class, a parameter from a method, a local variable declared in the implementation of a method or a global variable;
- $Prop(E)$ defines the *properties* of the elements from E, i.e abstraction, visibility, reusability, kind, instantiation ...
- $Rel(E)$ represents the *relations* between the design entities of E set, i.e inheritance relations between classes, method invocation relation, attributes reference relation.

An example of an object oriented design model is also presented in [21]. The above mentioned model for object oriented design offers support for metrics definition. The values of metrics act as features for instances used in software fault prediction model.

2.2 Metrics Used

Software metrics plays an important role in understanding, controlling and improving software quality. They are more and more used in Software Engineering domain. A lot of object oriented metrics has been proposed so far and new metrics continue to appear in the literature regularly. Chidamber and Kemerer proposed in their work [4] six new object oriented metrics. This suite is one of the most popular and highly cited suites for measuring object oriented design. In this approach we selected the CK metrics suite due to the following reasons:

- These metrics measure four *internal characteristics* that are essential to object-orientation, i.e. coupling, inheritance, cohesion and structural complexity [17].
- Several studies have been conducted to validate CK's metrics. Basili et al. [3] presented an empirical validation of CK's metrics. Their results suggest that five of the six CK's metrics are useful quality indicators for predicting fault-prone classes. Tang et al. [22] validated CK's metrics using real-time systems and the results suggested that WMC can be a good indicator for faulty classes. Li [14] theoretically validated CK's metrics using a metric-evaluation framework proposed by Kitchenham et al. [12].

In what follows we briefly present the six CK metrics [4]:

- *Depth of Inheritance Tree* (DIT) is defined as the length of the longest path of inheritance from a given class to the root of the tree;
- *Weighted Methods per Class* (WMC) metric defined as the sum of the complexity of all methods of a given class. The complexity of a method is the cyclomatic complexity;
- *Coupling Between Objects* (CBO) for a class c is the number of other classes that are coupled to the class c, namely that Two classes are coupled when methods declared in one class use methods or instance variables defined by the other class;
- *Response for a Class* (RFC) metric is defined as the total number of methods that can be invoked from that class;
- *Lack of Cohesion in Methods* (LCOM) is defined by the difference between the number of method pairs using common instance variables and the number of method pairs that do not use any common variables.
- *Number of children of a class (NOC)* is defined as the number of all direct sub-classes of a given class.

2.3   Neural Networks

An artificial neural network [19] consists of multiple nodes or neurons with links between them. There are some nodes that are used to supply the network with values from outside and they are named *input nodes*. Also, there are some nodes that are used to send to the outside values and they are named *output nodes*. Each link between two neurons has a *weight* associated with it. Actually, the learning take place by updating the weights such that difference between the values sent to the outside by the network and the expected values converges to zero. A layered feed-forward neural network (LFFNN) is a neural network that has one input layer, one output layer and multiple hidden layers between them. Each layer can have as many nodes as it is necessary. Nodes in a LFFNN have the property that they can be linked only with the nodes in the next layer. Figure 1 represents a layered feed-forward neural network with 6 nodes in input layer, multiple hidden layers and one output node.

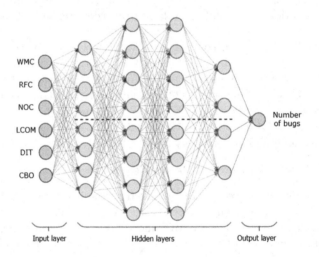

Fig. 1. Feed-forward Neural Network.

The learning happens in the following way: for a given input, the network computes the output and compares it with the expected output. The error is computed by taking the difference between the expected output and the actual output of the network. If the error is acceptable (i.e. less than a previously defined value), nothing happens and the learning process is terminated. Otherwise, the computed error is used to adjust every weight from the network. Back-propagation algorithm uses gradient descendent to determine how to adjust each weight such that the next error to be smaller.

3 Problem Statement

The current research defines the problem of Software Fault Prediction as a regression problem, the goal being to predict the number of faults (bugs) found for a given software component.

Supervised machine learning algorithms are commonly used to solve classification problems. They work as follows. As input, a set of instances are given, each instance having a vector of features as independent variables. As output, the algorithm predicts the value of a given feature, named dependent variable. In our case, instances are object oriented design entities that are classes, their features being the values of CK metrics, and the predicted value is the number of bugs of the specified class. We chose classes as design entities for fault prediction due to the fact that classes are the building blocks for an object oriented design system, being self-contained elements from the point of view of design and implementation.

Initially, a set of instances together with the values for the dependent and independent variable are given, defining the training set. The act of generating a classification model from the training set is referred to as learning. Learning algorithms extract features from a given instance, and try to learn from the training set the relation between the features of an instance and its class. A key to the success of machine learning algorithms is the selection of features considered for prediction. Many possible features were proposed in the literature for software fault prediction. In this approach, the features are selected from the CK [4] software metrics set, defined in Sect. 2.2.

3.1 Formal Statement of SFP Problem

The problem of Software Faults Prediction can be formally defined as follows. Being given:

- A set of design entities $C \subset E$ that represent classes from an object oriented design model, $M(S) = (E, Prop(E), Rel(E))$, corresponding to a software system S;
- The CK set of metrics $Metrics = \{m_1, m_2, ..., m_6\}$ described in Sect. 2.2;
- Each class $c \in C$ has a vector of features, $c = (m_{1c}, m_{2c}, ..., m_{nc})$, representing the metrics values from $Metrics$, i.e the set as *dependent variables* in our prediction model;
- Each class $c \in C$ has a number of faults, i.e the *independent variable* in the prediction model;

Our goal is to predict, using a neural network model, the number of faults (bugs) that a new class could be affected by.

3.2 Objectives and Research Questions

In this paper, we seek to investigate and validate the following two high level research questions.

RQ1: Does a subset of the CK metrics performs better than all metrics for the task of predicting the number of bugs found in a class?

RQ2: Does the NN based prediction model performs better using a data set defined by one single project than considering the dataset obtained by reunion of all projects?

4   Software Fault Prediction – Related Work

Considerable research has been performed on software fault prediction based on machine learning, so far, and there still is a highly interesting research in this subject. Several systematic literature reviews [8–10,16] reveal more than two hundreds of papers carried out on software fault prediction subject. Most of these researches approach software fault prediction as a classification problem. Given a software component, the goal is to determine its class – healthy or faulty. Also, the dataset used is preponderate Promise [20] repository or others similar ones that the only information they have for a software component are the values of its features and its class – healthy or faulty. However, most projects these days use a version control system (Git) and an issue tracking system (Bugzilla) enable tracking which modifications to the source were done in order to fix a specific bug. Thus, for a given software component we can find all the bugs that affect that component, revealing the degree to which that component is faulty.

In relation to existing approaches, ours investigates how we can use CK metrics to predict software faults using a dataset that extract information from a version control system and an issue tracking system, defining a general and scalable framework for software fault prediction. In this respect, we used the dataset described in [5]. Therefore, the following paragraphs briefly review some papers related to our approach, considering the above mentioned aspects and which use machine learning based methods.

Zimmermann et al. approached the problem of cross-project defect prediction. They defined prediction models from a project and applied it on a different one [24]. Their experiments revealed that using models from projects in the same domain or with the same process does not lead to accurate predictions. In this respect, our approach uses a dataset having five types of project with different characteristics: UI, Framework, Indexing and search technology, Plug-in management and Task management.

Michele Lanza et al. [5] presented a publicly available benchmark for defect prediction, consisting of several software systems, and provide an extensive comparison of the explanatory and predictive power of well-known bug prediction approaches. They discussed the performance and stability of the approaches with respect to their benchmark and deduced a number of insights on bug prediction models. Our proposed approach uses the same dataset, integrating some relevant aspects in the proposed framework.

Elmishali et al. [6] introduced a novel paradigm for incorporating Artificial Intelligence in the modern software troubleshooting process. The paradigm, integrated three AI technologies: (1) machine learning: learning from source-code structure, revision history and past failures, which software components are more likely to contain bugs, (2) automated diagnosis: identifying the software components that need to be modified in order to fix an observed bug, and (3) automated planning: planning additional tests when such are needed to improve diagnostic accuracy. In relation with this approach, ours defines a framework that could incorporate all the elements of the paper we compare with, also we investigate what combination of metrics perform better for defect prediction, and uses a similar kind of dataset.

Kumar et al. [13] build an effective fault prediction tool by identifying the predictive power of several most used software metrics for fault prediction. They build the fault prediction model using Least Squares Support Vector Machine learning method associated with linear, polynomial and radial basis function kernel functions.

5 Proposed Model and Experiments

5.1 Benchmark Dataset

The data set used for this research, named "Bug prediction dataset" [5], is collected from the last version of five different software systems. These projects are:

- JDT (Java development tool) - Eclipse, an incremental Java compiler, code analysis and index-based search infrastructure used for refactoring, code assistant;
- PDE (Plug-in Development Environment), a tool providing a solution for developing, testing, debugging and deploying Eclipse plug-ins;
- Equinox, an implementation of the OSGi R6 framework;
- Lucene, a tool for indexing and search technology as well as code analysis and spell checking;
- Mylyn, a task management tool for developers.

This data contain CK metrics, historical data, such as versions, fixes and authors and number of bugs for a period of six months after release, categorized (with severity and priority) for each class of the system as follows: bugs considered to be priority, bugs being non trivial, bugs having a major importance and bugs considered to be critical. Because the reliability value was missing from database, it is computed based on number of bugs and/or historical data, for a time interval of six months.

More information about the number of classes in each project and number of bugs may be visualized in Table 1 (#C=number of total classes with no bugs, #CB=number of classes with bugs, #B=number of bugs, #BNT=number of bugs Non Trivial, #BM=number of bugs Major, #BC=number of bugs Critical, #BHP=number of bugs High Priority), and #Bugs - number of bugs that were not categorized.

Table 1. Datasets information

Projects	#C	#CB	#B	#BNT	#BM	#BC	#BHP	#Bugs
JDT	44	997	11605	10119	1135	432	459	—-
PDE	426	1497	5803	4191	362	100	96	—-
Equinox	120	324	1496	1393	156	71	14	—-
Lucene	197	691	1714	1714	0	0	0	—-
Mylyn	701	1862	14577	6806	592	235	8004	—-

5.2   Data Preprocessing

Data Normalization

Our dataset has different ranges for each input metric, which can be observed in
Table 2. This problem is often encountered in machine learning [7] and has a high
potential to negatively affect the performance of our model. To solve this issue,
data normalization, also called *feature scaling or standardization* is performed
to the raw values, as described conceptually in Fig. 2.

$$s = \sqrt{\frac{1}{N-1} \sum_{i=1}^{N}(x_i - \overline{x})^2} \tag{1}$$

We used the sample standard deviation from 1 and the formula from 2 to
normalize our data. As you can see, we used *z-score* normalization because it
works better for outliers, meaning we actually standardized the data (reduced
the standard deviation to 1), as opposed to normalization, which rescales data
to 1 and 0 range.

$$z_i = \frac{x - \overline{x}}{s} \tag{2}$$

Table 2. Statistics from the JDT (Eclipse) training dataset

Metric	Count	Mean	Std	Min	25%	50%	75%	Max
WMC	1016	105.62	221.86	0	11.75	33	104	1680
DIT	1016	2.64	1.65	1	1.00	2	4	8
RFC	1016	144.50	318.40	0	15.00	45	130	2603
NOC	1016	0.78	2.08	0	0.00	0	1	26
CBO	1016	17.87	24.17	0	4.00	9	21	156
LCOM	1016	842.42	5563.92	0	10.00	45	171	81003

In Table 2, the *count* column represents the number of valid observations (i.e
the number of classes containing all the required metrics values, not null/NA),

mean is the average of the distribution and *std* is the standard deviation of the observations. The *min, max, 25%, 50%, 75%* columns are alternative to perspectives regarding the *kurtosis* of the distribution and their values show us the dispersion(spread) of the records.

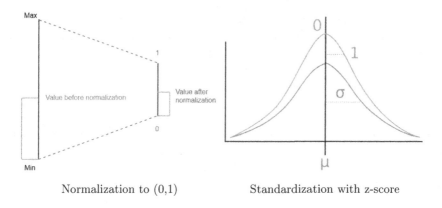

Normalization to (0,1)   Standardization with z-score

Fig. 2. Normalization methods

Imbalanced Data

Another issue we found in this project was that the classes featuring bugs were a minority in our data source. For example, in the *Eclipse* dataset, only 20.66% of the classes had at least one bug, so a *naive* model which always predicts *0 bugs* would perform with ≈80% accuracy.

There are several solutions for this problem, and we experimented in our case with one of them, specifically *upsampling*. Upsampling means replicating records from the minority class and resample the set of data to increase its cardinality. We oversampled our data after the split between training and testing sets so we would have a balanced set of information. A random sampling algorithm was used with a pseudo-random fixed seed and we experimented with several orders of magnitude over the majority class (data with no bugs).

Another common solution is *undersampling* which consists in resampling the majority class and keep only a part of the records. Of particular interest is also the *SMOTE* (Synthetic Minority Over-sampling Technique) method, which creates synthetic data based on the minority records. *SMOTE* synthesizes new instances of minority data between the existing ones in order to shrink the imbalance.

5.3   Neural Network Prediction Model Description

In order to predict the number of bugs for a given class, a feed-forward neural network with back-propagation learning is used, with the following structure (see Fig. 1): six nodes on the input layer, one node on the output layer and four hidden layers, each of them having between 64 and 500 nodes. Each node uses the ReLU activation function [18].

The CK metrics mentioned above are chosen to be the input vector of the neural network. The number of bugs for a class is computed as the sum of all types of bugs found in that class (see Table 1), being the expected output vector.

The termination condition of training is either no improvement of the cross-validation data loss over *100* epochs, or the number of epochs to be at most *1200*. After training this neural network, we obtained a neural network prediction model for the number of bugs in a class.

5.4   Experiments Description

Our conducted investigation used *4* experiments, with the five projects/datasets. In each experiment, we trained a neural network-based prediction model using 65% of random sampled data and we used the rest for model validation, a method called *holdout*, the simplest version of cross-validation.

In machine learning, validation represents the process of evaluation on a testing data set (a separate portion of the information set), which measures the generalization ability of a trained model [2].

Table 3. Input sample from the JDT (Eclipse) training dataset

wmc	dit	rfc	noc	cbo	lcom
115.0	2	174.0	0	23	820
3.0	3	5.0	1	4	6
10.0	2	14.0	0	8	15
93.0	3	125.0	0	12	78
1.0	2	2.0	0	2	0
...	...	...	...	...	...
57.0	3	85.0	0	7	105
49.0	5	73.0	0	13	10
100.0	2	105.0	0	8	780

In Table 3 we can see a sample of the input for our neural network after the normalization process.

For this project we used the Google Colaboratory as a cloud-based machine learning environment. We created several notebooks for each experiment, where we used python as a programming language and Keras on top of Tensorflow as a machine learning framework. The virtual machines presented 12.72 GB of RAM and 24 GB of GPU GDDR5 memory. The training times were usually fast, as our model is quite simple.

First Experiment

The first experiment was our baseline system check, where we used the default parameters and variables, without any data cleanup or optimization, from the Eclipse data set. We used only two hidden layers with 64 nodes each and the optimizer was *RMSProp*(Root Mean Square Propagation) with a learning rate of *0.001. Learning rate* or *step size* is a *hyperparameter*, which controls the rate at which the model adapts to the new values during training. A high value might get the model to jump over optimum values, while a too small value might take long to train and can get stuck in a local minima. We started with a small number of layers to test if the model can offer reliable results by using fewer resources.

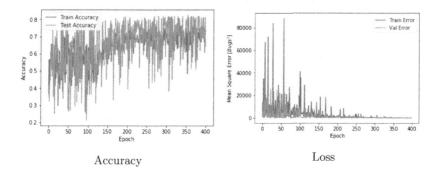

Accuracy   Loss

Fig. 3. Results of the first experiment

We ran the training for 400 epochs and the predictions were not very good, with a volatile accuracy of the model. We used *mean square error* for our loss function(one of the standard regression measures of the quality of an estimator [23]), and the results can be seen in Fig. 3. The accuracy is normally calculated as the fraction between the amount of correct predictions and the total number of predictions.

Second Experiment

A second experiment was conducted to improve the results of our model and check if the estimation proposed can be obtained using neural networks. In the first experiment we used 2 hidden layers and the results were not the expected ones, so we increased the number of layers to 4 in order to allow the network to determine more complex patterns, with better accuracy. We processed the data as described in Sect. 5.2 and added two more hidden layers in our model. The learning rate was updated to *0.00001* and the optimizer was replaced with *Adam*(Adapted Moment Estimation). Adam [11] is an adaptive learning rate method, developed specifically for deep neural networks(it computes different learning rates for different parameters) and is one of the most used optimizers.

The results seen in Fig. 4 are visibly better, and the Adam optimizer outperforms the previous one (it also outperforms SGD - Standard Gradient Descent

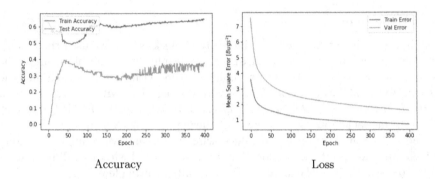

Accuracy   Loss

Fig. 4. Results of the second experiment

for our data). There still are issues with the accuracy of the validation data, but we can fix them mainly in the preprocessing phase. The final version of the second experiment results can be seen in Fig. 5. They were obtained by increasing the number of epochs to 1200, oversampling the minority data by a factor of 20 and changing the *holdout* percentage to 60%.

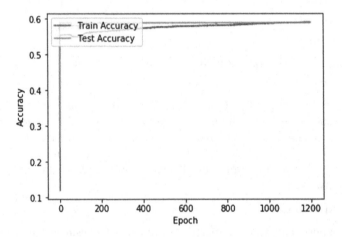

Fig. 5. Accuracy in the second experiment

Third Experiment

In the third experiment we discovered a correlation between several metrics and decided to perform the training using *feature selection*. The framework was fitted with a subset selection component and we used an exhaustive search approach.

All the combinations of three metrics were generated (20 sets of data) and we trained then tested the network on each of them separately. The results can be seen in Table 4. For comparison we also ran the model over all the metrics and the results are shown in Table 5. The accuracy and prediction error are highlighted in Fig. 6.

Table 4. Prediction statistics of the model using combinations of three metrics

Features	MEA (bugs)	Accuracy	Loss
WMC DIT LCOM	1.24	0.5	5.27
WMC RFC LCOM	1.3	0.5	5.02
DIT CBO LCOM	1.57	0.5	7.79
NOC CBO LCOM	1.66	0.5	7.89
WMC NOC LCOM	1.56	0.49	7.9
RFC CBO LCOM	1.51	0.49	6.09
WMC DIT CBO	1.33	0.48	4.56
WMC RFC CBO	1.46	0.48	5.3
WMC CBO LCOM	1.64	0.48	8.24
DIT RFC NOC	1.36	0.48	6.42
DIT RFC CBO	1.52	0.48	7.3
WMC RFC NOC	1.62	0.46	7.91
WMC NOC CBO	1.76	0.46	8.68
WMC DIT NOC	1.49	0.45	8.24
DIT NOC CBO	1.59	0.44	7.41
DIT RFC LCOM	1.47	0.43	6.13
RFC NOC CBO	1.53	0.42	5.71
WMC DIT RFC	1.49	0.41	6.24
RFC NOC LCOM	1.5	0.4	6.73
DIT NOC LCOM	1.56	0.35	7.55

We can observe two high-performing combinations: *(WMC, DIT, LCOM) and (WMC, RFC, LCOM)* which have a better accuracy than most of their counterparts and even better than the results of all the metrics combined.

One of the worst performing combinations was *(DIT, NOC, LCOM)* and it can be explained by the fact that these metrics are related to only two characteristics of object orientation: inheritance and cohesion, whereas those combinations that perform better, are related to more aspects of design internal structure: coupling, cohesion, complexity etc.

Fourth Experiment

For our final experiment we used all the projects in the data source as training and validation data. The results and differences between a single project and complete usage can be seen in Table 5.

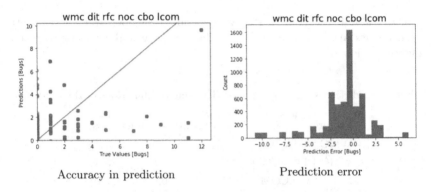

| Accuracy in prediction | Prediction error |

Fig. 6. Results of the third experiment, with all CK metrics

Table 5. Prediction statistics of the model using combinations of all CK metrics

Projects (All metrics)	MEA (bugs)	Accuracy	Loss
JDT (Eclipse)	1.39	0.41	5.21
JDT PDE EQUINOX LUCENE MYLYN	2.45	0.22	9.36

Random Forests model (RF - collection of random decision trees) was trained on our dataset, using all the metrics, with 200 estimators, for comparison reasons. The results in our case show that neural networks performed better, RF prediction presenting MAE: 1.49, MSE: 6.25, RMSE 2.50 and rounded accuracy of 0.27.

5.5   Results and Validation

In the first experiment the predictions were very volatile and there were significant deviations (up to 62.5% decrease, ranging from 0.8 accuracy to 0.3), which offered us unreliable results. We used this knowledge to increase the precision for the second experiment, where the differences between training and testing data were negligible.

In the third experiment we determined a 42.86% increase in accuracy between the low performing and high performing CK combinations. The difference can be seen in Table 4, where (DIT, NOC, LCOM) have 0.35 accuracy, versus (WMC, DIT, LCOM) which present 0.5 accuracy.

Each prediction model was validated using evaluation over the separated testing data. We found that there are combinations of metrics *((WMC, DIT, LCOM) and (WMC, RFC, LCOM))* which outperform all the metrics at predicting the number of bugs found in a class. We determined that there is a 21.95% increase in precision by using a high-performing combination of metrics instead of using all the CK metrics. The high performing CK metrics presented a 0.5 precision in our tests, while using all the metrics delivered a 0.41 accuracy. This answers our first research question from Sect. 3.2.

An interesting answer for the second question was that when using all the projects from the dataset the predictions performed worse than by using a single project. In our experiments the accuracy was worse by 46.34%, from 0.41 accuracy for the JTD (Eclipse) project to 0.22 for all the projects (see Table 5).

6   Conclusions and Future Work

In this study, we proposed an integrated framework for software fault prediction, defining a neural network based model to empirically establish a combination of CK software metrics that enhance the accuracy for faults prediction. The experimental results showed that there is a 21.95% increase in precision by using a high-performing combination of metrics instead of using all the CK metrics and that a combination of all the projects performed worse in prediction than a single project.

As a future research, we plan to extend our experimental evaluation by considering additional case studies based on real software systems together with corresponding datasets. We also aim to use other machine learning methods for learning or a combination of them, assuming that a hybrid model could be better. Other improvements will be to use other metrics for model validation and different solutions for the problem of imbalanced data.

References

1. e Abreu, F.B., Melo, W.L.: Evaluating the impact of object-oriented design on software quality. In: 3rd IEEE International Software Metrics Symposium (METRICS 1996), From Measurement to Empirical Results, March 25–26, 1996, Berlin, Germany, pp. 90–99 (1996)
2. Alpaydin, E.: Introduction to Machine Learning. MIT Press, Cambridge (2014)
3. Basili, V., Briand, L., Melo, W.: A validation of object-oriented design metrics as quality indicators. IEEE Trans. Software Eng. **20**(10), 751–761 (1996)
4. Chidamber, S., Kemerer, C.: A metric suite for object-oriented design. IEEE Trans. Software Eng. **20**(6), 476–493 (1994)
5. D'Ambros, M., Lanza, M., Robbes, R.: An extensive comparison of bug prediction approaches. In: Proceedings of MSR 2010 (7th IEEE Working Conference on Mining Software Repositories), pp. 31–41. IEEE CS Press (2010)
6. Elmishali, A., Stern, R., Kalech, M.: An artificial intelligence paradigm for troubleshooting software bugs. Eng. Appl. AI **69**, 147–156 (2018)
7. Gao, J.: Machine learning applications for data center optimization. Technical report, Google (2014)
8. Hall, T., Beecham, S., Bowes, D., Gray, D., Counsell, S.: A systematic literature review on fault prediction performance in software engineering. IEEE Trans. Software Eng. **38**(6), 1276–1304 (2012)
9. Isong, B., Ekabua, O.O.: A systematic review of the empirical validation of object-oriented metrics towards fault-proneness prediction. Int. J. Software Eng. Knowl. Eng. **23**(10), 1513 (2013)
10. Isong, B., Ekabua, O.O.: State-of-the-art in empirical validation of software metrics for fault proneness prediction: Systematic review. CoRR abs/1601.01447 (2016)

11. Kingma, D.P., Ba, J.: Adam: A method for stochastic optimization. arXiv preprint arXiv:1412.6980 (2014)
12. Kitchenham, B.A., Pfleeger, S.L., Fenton, N.E.: Towards a framework for software measurement validation. IEEE Trans. Software Eng. **21**(12), 929–943 (1995)
13. Kumar, L., Sripada, S., Sureka, A., Rath, S.K.: Effective fault prediction model developed using least square support vector machine (LSSVM). J. Syst. Softw. **137**, 686–712 (2017)
14. Li, W.: Another metric suite for object-oriented programming. J. Syst. Softw. **44**(2), 155–162 (1998)
15. Li, W., Henry, S.M.: Object-oriented metrics that predict maintainability. J. Syst. Softw. **23**(2), 111–122 (1993)
16. Malhotra, R.: A systematic review of machine learning techniques for software fault prediction. Appl. Soft Comput. **27**, 504–518 (2015)
17. Marinescu, R.: Measurement and Quality in Object Oriented Design. Ph.D. thesis, Faculty of Automatics and Computer Science, University of Timisoara (2002)
18. Nair, V., Hinton, G.E.: Rectified linear units improve restricted boltzmann machines. In: Proceedings of the 27th International Conference on Machine Learning (ICML 2010), pp. 807–814 (2010)
19. Russell, S.J., Norvig, P.: Artificial Intelligence: A Modern Approach. Prentice Hall, Upper Saddle River (1995)
20. Sayyad Shirabad, J., Menzies, T.: The PROMISE Repository of Software Engineering Databases. School of Information Technology and Engineering, University of Ottawa, Canada (2005). http://promise.site.uottawa.ca/SERepository
21. Serban, C.: Metrics in Software Assessment. Ph.D. thesis, Faculty of Mathematics and Computer Science, Babes-Bolyai University (2012)
22. Tanh, M., Kao, M., Chen, M.: An empirical study on object-oriented metrics. In: 6th IEEE International Software Metrics Symposium (METRICS 1999), 4–6 November 1999, Boca Raton, FL, USA. pp. 242–249 (1999)
23. Wang, Z., Bovik, A.C.: Mean squared error: love it or leave it? A new look at signal fidelity measures. IEEE Signal Process. Mag. **26**(1), 98–117 (2009)
24. Zimmermann, T., Nagappan, N., Gall, H.C., Giger, E., Murphy, B.: Cross-project defect prediction: a large scale experiment on data vs. domain vs. process. In: Proceedings of the 7th joint meeting of the European Software Engineering Conference and the ACM SIGSOFT International Symposium on Foundations of Software Engineering, 2009, Amsterdam, The Netherlands, August 24–28, 2009, pp. 91–100 (2009)

Support Vector Machine Optimized by Fireworks Algorithm for Handwritten Digit Recognition

Eva Tuba[1], Romana Capor Hrosik[2], Adis Alihodzic[3], Raka Jovanovic[4], and Milan Tuba[1($\boxtimes$)]

[1] Singidunum University, Belgrade, Serbia
{etuba,tuba}@ieee.org
[2] Maritime Department, University of Dubrovnik, Dubrovnik, Croatia
romana.capor@unidu.hr
[3] Faculty of Science, University of Sarajevo, Sarajevo, Bosnia and Herzegovina
adis.alihodzic@pmf.unsa.ba
[4] Qatar Environment and Energy Research Institute (QEERI),
Hamad bin Khalifa University, Doha, Qatar
rjovanovic@hbku.edu.qa

Abstract. Handwritten digit recognition is an important subarea in the object recognition research area. Support vector machines represent a very successful recent binary classifier. Basic support vector machines have to be improved in order to deal with real-world problems. The introduction of soft margin for outliers and misclassified samples as well as kernel function for non linearly separably data leads to the hard optimization problem of selecting parameters for these two modifications. Grid search which is often used is rather inefficient. In this paper we propose the use of one of the latest swarm intelligence algorithms, the fireworks algorithm, for the support vector machine parameters tuning. We tested our approach on standard MNIST base of handwritten images and with selected set of simple features we obtained better results compared to other approaches from literature.

Keywords: Handwritten digit recognition · Machine learning · Support vector machine · Optimization · Swarm intelligence · Fireworks algorithm

1 Introduction

Digital images become a part of almost every field in life and science, mostly because digital image processing techniques facilitate applications unforeseeable while only analog images were used. Numerous applications that use digital images include object recognition, thus it represents a significant research area and it deals with recognition of specific objects in digital images. One of the object the recognition subareas is optical character recognition (OCR) which can

© Springer Nature Switzerland AG 2020
D. Simian and L. F. Stoica (Eds.): MDIS 2019, CCIS 1126, pp. 187–199, 2020.
https://doi.org/10.1007/978-3-030-39237-6_13

be further divided into typed and handwritten character recognition. Recognition of the typed characters is easier because characters are regular and uniform in shape and the differences are only in the angle of view, color, font size, etc. On the other hand, one handwritten character can vary a lot for different handwriting styles. Moreover, one character written several times by the same person can be significantly different.

Since OCR represents an important task in computer vision, artificial intelligence and computer science in general, it was divided into subfields and one subfield is digit recognition. The same division as the one for OCR can be transferred to digit recognition: typed and handwritten digit recognition. Typed or printed digit recognition is used in applications such as license plate recognition, street numbers recognition, etc. while handwritten digit recognition applications include reading bank checks, mail sorting in post offices and others.

Digit recognition is an active research area. One of the first methods for object recognition is template matching. The idea is to recognize an unknown object from an image by comparing it with numerous images from the template database. The unknown object should be the same or very similar to at least one image from the database. It is a simple technique but it is not suitable for handwritten digit recognition since for one digit a large number of templates is needed and it is impossible to cover all possible handwriting styles, angles, pencil thicknesses, etc. Nowadays, algorithms for handwritten digit recognition usually contain three major parts: preprocessing, feature extraction and classification.

The preprocessing step is used to remove irrelevant elements from digit images such as background artifacts and noise and to prepare it for feature extraction. Preprocessing usually includes binarization, pixelization, normalization, centering, denoising, etc.

After the preprocessing step, some features that describe the digit in the image are selected and extracted. Chosen features need to describe the similarity of the same digits and dissimilarity of different digits. Numerous features were proposed in literature such as projections histograms, geometric moments, affine invariant moments, Legendre moments, Zernike moments, Hu moments, DCT coefficients and others [1]. Projection histograms are usually used only for typed digit recognition [2].

The third step is classification. Classification model based on the features is built to differentiate digits. For classification various techniques were proposed such as k-nearest neighbor [3], neural networks [4], support vector machine (SVM) [5] and others and most of them were applied to handwritten digit recognition applications. In [6] a method for handwritten digit recognition based on deep learning neural networks was proposed. Another neural network based approach was presented in [7] where spiking deep belief neural network was used. In [8] classification was done by deep convolutional extreme learning machine.

In this paper we propose using SVM optimized by the latest GFWA swarm intelligence algorithm for handwritten digit recognition intentionally using weak features with which other approaches would not give good results. Our proposed algorithm was tested on standard MNIST dataset for handwritten digit recognition and performance was better than other approaches from literature [9–11].

The rest of the paper is organized as follows. In Sect. 2 several methods for handwritten digit recognition from literature are described. Guided fireworks algorithm that is used for SVM optimization is described in Sect. 3. Our proposed algorithm is presented in Sect. 4 and experimental results are described in Sect. 5. At the end conclusion is given in Sect. 6.

2   Literature Review

Handwritten digit recognition was intensively studied in the past and numerous methods were proposed in literature. In general, these methods contain three parts where feature extraction and classification are the main parts of the method while preprocessing, even though important, usually is not a crucial part of the method.

Feature extraction technique based on recursive subdivisions of the character image was proposed in [12]. Division of the handwritten digit image was done so that the resulting sub-images at each iteration had approximately equal number of digit pixels. For recognition a two-stage classification based on the granularity level of the feature extraction method was used.

Histogram of oriented gradients was proposed as feature for handwritten digits in [13]. It has been shown that this histogram was stable on illumination variation since it is a gradient based descriptor. Linear SVM was used for classification.

In [14] a two-stage process for handwritten digit recognition was proposed. The first stage was based on adaptive resonance theory and it was used to find the initial solution. At the second stage a fine tuning was done for generating the best prototypes. The classification was performed by the k-nearest neighbor classifier.

Biologically inspired model for handwritten digit recognition was proposed in [15]. Feature space was determined by the proposed biologically inspired model and it was represented as binary code that was used as input vector for a linear classifier. Competitive accuracy was achieved when compared to other linear classifiers from literature.

3   Guided Fireworks Algorithm

Guided fireworks algorithm (GFWA) represents the latest version of the fireworks algorithm (FWA) and it was proposed by Li, Zheng and Tan in 2016 [16]. Original fireworks algorithm was proposed in 2010 by Tan and Zhu [17] and the idea was to simulate fireworks explosion with two different types of fireworks. The first type is well manufactured firework which produces many sparks centralized around explosion point (exploitation, intensification) while the second type is badly manufactured firework which produces several sparks scattered in the space (exploration, diversification) [17].

Fireworks algorithm was successfully used in various applications for solving hard optimization problems such as SVM parameters tuning [18], medical image processing [19,20] and multi-objective RFID network planing problem [21].

Fireworks algorithm has been constantly improved during the last years and the result is existence of several versions. The second version of the FWA was proposed in 2013 and it was named enhanced FWA (EFWA). In that version five modification to the initial fireworks algorithm were introduced [22]. Cooperative FWA (CoFWA) was proposed as the third version of the FWA in [23]. In CoFWA the exploitation and exploration abilities were improved. Exploitation was enhanced by introducing independent selection operator, while exploration capacity was increased by implementing crowdedness-avoiding cooperative strategy. Additional improvements of exploration were added in the fourth version of the FWA that was presented in [24]. In the fourth version dynamic adjustment of the number of sparks based on the fitness function results and the search results was proposed. The latest version that was used in this paper is guided FWA (GFWA) and it will be briefly described.

In each generation guided fireworks algorithm generates n fireworks and their corresponding sparks. Fireworks and their sparks are represented as points in d-dimensional space, where d is the dimension of the problem. In each generation and for each firework x_i the number of the sparks is determined by the following equation:

$$\lambda_i = \hat{\lambda} \frac{y_{max} - f(x_i)}{\sum_{j=1}^{n}(y_{max} - f(x_j))}, \tag{1}$$

where $\hat{\lambda}$ is algorithm's parameters that controls the number of sparks in one generation while $y_{max} = \max(f(x_i), \ i = 1, 2, ..., n)$ is the worst solution in the population.

Positions of the sparks are calculated based on fireworks explosion amplitude that is defined by following equation:

$$A_i = \hat{A} \frac{f(x_i) - y_{min}}{\sum_{j=1}^{n}(f(x_j) - y_{min})}, \tag{2}$$

where $\hat{A}$ represents the highest value of the explosion amplitude and $y_{min} = \min(f(x_i), \ i = 1, 2, ..., n)$ is the best solution in one generation of n fireworks, named core firework (CF). For the CF, explosion amplitude is calculated differently according to the following equation [16]:

$$A_{CF}(t) = \begin{cases} A_{CF}(1) & \text{if } t = 1, \\ C_r A_{CF}(t-1) & \text{if } f(X_{CF}(t)) = f(X_{CF}(t-1)), \\ C_a A_{CF}(t-1) & \text{if } f(X_{CF}(t)) < f(X_{CF}(t-1)) \end{cases} \tag{3}$$

where t is the number of the current generation and $C_a > 1$ and $C_r < 1$ are constants, parameters of the algorithm.

In the GFWA, a guiding spark (GS) is generated for each firework. The GS is obtained by adding a guiding vector (GV) to the firework's position. The position of the guiding spark G_i for firework X_i is defined by the following algorithm [16]:

Algorithm 1. Generating the Guiding Spark for X_i [16]

Require: X_i, s_{ij}, λ_i and σ

Sort the sparks by their fitness values $f(s_{ij})$ in ascending order.

$\Delta_i \leftarrow \frac{1}{\sigma\lambda_i}(\sum_{j=1}^{\sigma\lambda_i} s_{ij} - \sum_{j=\lambda_i-\sigma\lambda_i+1}^{\lambda_i} s_{ij})$

$G_i \leftarrow X_i + \Delta_i$

return G_i

In Algorithm 1 guiding vector Δ_i represents the mean of $\sigma\lambda_i$ vectors which is defined by the following equation:

$$\Delta_i = \frac{1}{\sigma\lambda_i} \sum_{j=1}^{\sigma\lambda_i} (s_{ij} - s_{i,\lambda_i-j+1}) \qquad (4)$$

Guided fireworks algorithm is summarized in Algorithm 2.

Algorithm 2. Guided fireworks algorithm [16]

Randomly initialize μ fireworks in the potential space.

Evaluate the fireworks' fitness.

repeat

    Calculate λ_i according to the Eq. 1

    Calculate A_i according to the Eq. 2 and Eq. 3

    For each firework, generate λ_i sparks within the amplitude A_i

    For each firework, generate guiding sparks according to previous algorithm.

    Evaluate all the sparks' fitness.

    Keep the best individual as a firework.

    Randomly choose other $\mu - 1$ fireworks among the rest of individuals.

until termination criteria is met.

return the position and the fitness of the best individual.

---

4   The Proposed Algorithm

We propose using SVM optimized by the guided fireworks algorithm for handwritten digit recognition using intentionally weak features with which other approaches would not give good results.

4.1   Feature Extraction

In this paper projection histograms were used as the feature set for handwritten digits. These features were usually used for typed digit recognition and even then not as the only features but in combination with some others. We intentionally selected this weak set of features to test our proposed optimized SVM classifier. Projection histograms for different digits on x-axis are shown in Fig. 1.

Fig. 1. Projection histograms on x-axis $(y = 0)$

Because of various writing styles and other mentioned problems, projection histograms can be significantly different for one digit while they can be similar for different digits. Figure 2 shows examples of histograms for digits 0, 3 and 8 where projection histograms on x axis are similar for digit 8 and 3, while histograms on y axis are similar for 0 and 8. On the other hand, projection histograms on x axis for 0 and 8 are clearly different, similarly 8 and 3 can be differentiated from projection histograms on y axis.

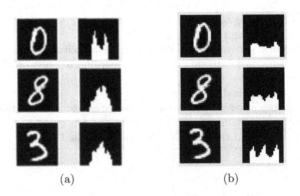

Fig. 2. Example of histograms for digits 0, 8 and 3 on (a) x-axis and (b) y-axis

In order to differentiate digits, projection histograms on 4 different axis were used, x, y, lines $y = x$ and $y = -x$. Examples of four histograms for five samples of digit 3 are shown in Figs. 3 and 4. Since last two projections are on the diagonals, their histograms contain more points.

(a)   (b)

Fig. 3. Digit 3 histograms on (a) x and (b) y axis

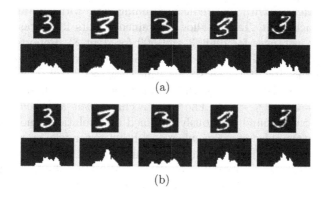

(a)

(b)

Fig. 4. Digit 3 histograms on (a) $y = x$ and (b) $y = -x$

4.2 Classification

We used support vector machine as a classifier, where the described four histograms were used as features i.e. input vector. Handwritten digit recognition is a multi-classification problem and SVM is a binary classifier. Two well know techniques are used for performing multi-classification by binary classifier. The first is *one-against-all* that makes one model for each class where one class is differentiated from all others and the second method is *one-against-one* where $\frac{n(n-1)}{2}$ models need to be made (n is the number of classes). In *one-against-one* method for each pair of classes one model is built. After obtaining the results from all models, final decision can be made by voting. Both of these techniques have good and bad characteristics, thus we proposed combination of them for handwritten digit recognition. Our proposed classifier uses two stage classification where in the first phase classes were determined by 10 different models (*one-against-all*). In the second phase, if the class was not determined uniquely in the first phase, *one-against-one* technique was used.

SVM parameters C and γ need to be tuned in order to achieve better classification accuracy. As it was mentioned before, one of the simplest methods to select these parameters is grid search. Grid search is time consuming and moreover it performs rather rough search. For both parameters search range and step size need to be set. Usually, grid search is performed in several iteration. The first iteration has larger search range and larger step and in each next iteration both are reduced. In order to achieve satisfying accuracy, in some cases step need to be rather small. Thus, stochastic optimization algorithm is better choice for this problem because of its faster convergence towards better solution and its search space is not discrete.

As a preliminary step, we compared grid search and the proposed GFWA on limited training data. Based on the results from our previous work in [9] it has been established that the biggest problem was to differentiate digit 3 from digit 8. Since that is example where accuracy can be increased, we tested one-against-one model for digits 3 and 8.

We experimented with two reduced training sets, with 500 and with 2000 instances of each digit. Table 1 shows obtained results for dataset with 1000 instances (500 instances for digit 3 and 500 for digit 8). Reported accuracies were obtained by 10-fold cross validation. Grid search was performed in several iterations. In the first iteration search range was set to $[2^{-5}, 2^{15}]$ for C and $[2^{-15}, 2^5]$ for γ. Initially step for the exponent was 2. The best accuracy was 97.1% for $C = 3$ and $\gamma = -1$. The same accuracy was achieved when search range was reduced around previously obtained best solutions and the step was reduced to 1. In the third iteration when search range was even more reduced and step was set to 0.25 accuracy of 97.4% was achieved and in the following iteration that accuracy was not improved. Overall time for finding the best solution was 398 s. The proposed GFWA tuning found the model with the same accuracy for parameters $C = 10.8222$ and $\gamma = -0.2700$ in 545 s. In this case grid search found equivalent accuracy in less time. It should be noticed that the used training set is rather small, thus it was easier to deal with.

Table 1. Grid search and GFWA optimization results on data set with 500 instances for digits 3 and 8

	GS step 2	GS step 1	GS step 0.25	GFWA
Accuracy (%)	97.1	97.1	97.4	97.4
Time (s)	164.2	38.4	94.1	545.4

When small training dataset is used, optimal parameters can be found easily. But in the case of larger dataset, task is more complicated. It has been shown in the next experiment where 2000 instances of both, digit 3 and 8 were used. In Table 1 results for this case are shown, organized as in the previous case. As it can be seen SVM model optimized by the GFWA obtained better accuracy then grid search and moreover it was achieved faster. The best accuracy when GFWA was used was 98.675% while with grid search, even when step was reduced to 0.1, it was 98.624%. Based on this two examples it can be concluded that optimization algorithm has advantage to grid search for larger datasets. For handwritten digit recognition where large training datasets are needed, obviously GFWA is a better choice (Table 2).

Table 2. Grid search and GFWA optimization results on data set with 2000 instances for 3 and 8

	GS step 2	GS step 1	GS step 0.25	GFWA
Accuracy (%)	98.500	98.550	98.625	98.675
Time (s)	2389.3852	841.7378	4021.4713	5401.9947

5   Experimental Results

Our proposed algorithm was implemented in Matlab version R2016b and LIB-SVM (Version 3.21) [25] was used for SVM classification. All experiments were performed on Intel ® Core™ i7-3770K CPU at 4 GHz, 8 GB RAM computer with Windows 10 Professional OS.

The proposed handwritten digit recognition algorithm was tested on standard MNIST dataset [26], available at http://yann.lecun.com/exdb/mnist/. All images in the MNIST dataset are centralized gray scale images that have resolution of 28 * 28. Examples of images in the dataset are shown in Fig. 5.

Fig. 5. Examples of digits from the MNIST dataset

In this paper SVM classifier optimized by the guided fireworks algorithm for handwritten digit recognition was proposed. Rather simple features were used in order to prove the quality of the proposed classifier. Our proposed algorithm was compared with [9] where bat algorithm was used for the SVM optimization using the same features, and with [11] where projection histograms combined with zoning technique were used as features, while multi-layer perception neural network was used as classifier.

In Table 3 confusion matrix obtained by the proposed algorithm is presented. The lowest accuracy was achieved for digit 3 (92%), but it was increased compared to the method proposed in [9] (89%). Improvements were also obtained for digits 2 (from 95% to 98%), 4 (from 98% to 99%), 5 (from 91% to 93%), 7 (from 93% to 95%) and 9 (from 95% to 96%). Accuracy for the rest of the digits, i.e. 0, 1, 6 and 8 was the same.

Comparison results for overall accuracy are presented in Table 4. As it can be seen, guided fireworks algorithm successfully improved accuracy of classification.

SVM optimized by bat algorithm in [9] achieved overall accuracy of 95.60%, while accuracy of the method proposed in this paper was 96.60%. Improvement

Table 3. Accuracy of classification for our proposed method (%)

	0	1	2	3	4	5	6	7	8	9
0	99	0	0	0	0	0	0	0	1	0
1	0	99	0	0	0	0	0	0	1	0
2	0	0	98	0	0	1	0	0	1	0
3	0	1	0	92	0	3	0	0	3	1
4	0	0	0	0	99	0	0	0	0	1
5	0	0	1	5	0	93	0	0	1	0
6	0	0	0	0	0	0	100	0	0	0
7	0	0	0	0	0	0	0	95	0	5
8	0	0	1	1	0	1	1	1	95	0
9	1	0	0	0	2	0	0	1	0	96

Table 4. Accuracy of classification reported in [9,11] and our proposed method

Digit	MLNN	SVM-BAT	SVM-FWA
0	86.45	99.00	99.00
1	94.39	99.00	99.00
2	88.73	97.00	98.00
3	77.02	89.00	92.00
4	76.12	98.00	99.00
5	84.10	91.00	93.00
6	78.81	100.00	100.00
7	77.12	93.00	95.00
8	79.03	95.00	95.00
9	49.64	95.00	96.00
Global	79.14	95.60	**96.60**

was uniform over all digits i.e. accuracy of recognition for each digit was better or same compared to the method proposed in [9]. It has been proven earlier that for handwritten digit recognition SVM with parameters tuned by the GFWA provides better results than grid search. Moreover, in [9] results were compared with results from [11], which are also included in this paper. Method from [9] outperformed the method proposed in [11] and our proposed algorithm outperformed both. The worst accuracy in [9] was for digit 3 which was also the case for our proposed algorithm. In [9] digit 3 was recognized with accuracy of 89% while in this paper it was recognized with accuracy of 92% which is significant improvements. Compared to other digits recognitions accuracy was the same or with 1% improvements which leads to conclusion that GFWA was able to find better parameters for SVM models.

Performance of our proposed method was better than other approaches from literature [9–11]. Based on this results it can be concluded that the proposed SVM based algorithm tuned by GFWA can be successfully used for handwritten digit recognition. Based on the fact that accuracy was improved by creating better classification model, it can be concluded that with different, more complicated features accuracy can be further increased.

6   Conclusion

In this paper we proposed a method for handwritten digit recognition that uses system of support vector machines optimized by recent swarm intelligence guided fireworks algorithm. Simple features known to be insufficient for this classification were intentionally used to prove the quality of the proposed optimized SVM, i.e. that SVM optimized by GFWA can perform high recognition of handwritten digit with features that are usually not sufficient for any acceptable accuracy. Our proposed method outperformed other approaches from literature that also used projection histograms as features. As future work the proposed optimized SVM can be tested using additional features.

Acknowledgment. This research was supported by the Ministry of Education, Science and Technological Development of the Republic of Serbia, Grant No. III-44006.

References

1. Singh, P.K., Sarkar, R., Nasipuri, M.: A study of moment based features on handwritten digit recognition. Appl. Comput. Intell. Soft Comput. **2016**, 1–17 (2016)
2. Jagannathan, J., Sherajdheen, A., Deepak, R., Krishnan, N.: License plate character segmentation using horizontal and vertical projection with dynamic thresholding. In: International Conference on Emerging Trends in Computing, Communication and Nanotechnology (ICE-CCN), pp. 700–705, March 2013
3. Babu, U.R., Venkateswarlu, Y., Chintha, A.K.: Handwritten digit recognition using k-nearest neighbour classifier. In: World Congress on Computing and Communication Technologies (WCCCT), pp. 60–65. IEEE (2014)
4. Desai, A.A.: Gujarati handwritten numeral optical character reorganization through neural network. Pattern Recogn. **43**(7), 2582–2589 (2010)
5. Neves, R.F.P., Zanchettin, C., Filho, A.N.G.L.: An efficient way of combining SVMs for handwritten digit recognition. In: Villa, A.E.P., Duch, W., Érdi, P., Masulli, F., Palm, G. (eds.) ICANN 2012. LNCS, vol. 7553, pp. 229–237. Springer, Heidelberg (2012). https://doi.org/10.1007/978-3-642-33266-1_29
6. Ashiquzzaman, A., Tushar, A.K.: Handwritten Arabic numeral recognition using deep learning neural networks. In: IEEE International Conference on Imaging, Vision & Pattern Recognition, pp. 1–4. IEEE (2017)
7. Stromatias, E., Neil, D., Galluppi, F., Pfeiffer, M., Liu, S.C., Furber, S.: Live demonstration: handwritten digit recognition using spiking deep belief networks on SpiNNaker. In: IEEE International Symposium on Circuits and Systems (ISCAS), p. 1901. IEEE (2015)

8. Pang, S., Yang, X.: Deep convolutional extreme learning machine and its application in handwritten digit classification. Comput. Intell. Neurosci. **2016**, 1–10 (2016). Article ID 3049632
9. Tuba, E., Tuba, M., Simian, D.: Handwritten digit recognition by support vector machine optimized by bat algorithm. In: Computer Science Research Notes CSRN: Papers from the 24th International Conference in Central Europe on Computer Graphics, Visualization and Computer Vision 2602, pp. 369–376 (2016)
10. Tuba, E., Bacanin, N.: An algorithm for handwritten digit recognition using projection histograms and SVM classifier. In: 23rd IEEE Telecommunications Forum TELFOR, pp. 464–467 (2015)
11. Kessab, B.E., Daoui, C., Bouikhalene, B., Fakir, M., Moro, K.: Extraction method of handwritten digit recognition tested on the MNIST database. Int. J. Adv. Sci. Technol. **50**(6), 99–110 (2013)
12. Vamvakas, G., Gatos, B., Perantonis, S.J.: Handwritten character recognition through two-stage foreground sub-sampling. Pattern Recogn. **43**(8), 2807–2816 (2010)
13. Ebrahimzadeh, R., Jampour, M.: Efficient handwritten digit recognition based on histogram of oriented gradients and SVM. Int. J. Comput. Appl. **104**(9), 10–13 (2014)
14. Impedovo, S., Mangini, F.M., Barbuzzi, D.: A novel prototype generation technique for handwriting digit recognition. Pattern Recogn. **47**(3), 1002–1010 (2014)
15. Cardoso, A., Wichert, A.: Handwritten digit recognition using biologically inspired features. Neurocomputing **99**(1), 575–580 (2013)
16. Li, J., Zheng, S., Tan, Y.: The effect of information utilization: introducing a novel guiding spark in the fireworks algorithm. IEEE Trans. Evol. Comput. **21**(1), 153–166 (2017)
17. Tan, Y., Zhu, Y.: Fireworks algorithm for optimization. In: Tan, Y., Shi, Y., Tan, K.C. (eds.) ICSI 2010. LNCS, vol. 6145, pp. 355–364. Springer, Heidelberg (2010). https://doi.org/10.1007/978-3-642-13495-1_44
18. Tuba, E., Tuba, M., Beko, M.: Support vector machine parameters optimization by enhanced fireworks algorithm. In: Tan, Y., Shi, Y., Niu, B. (eds.) ICSI 2016. LNCS, vol. 9712, pp. 526–534. Springer, Cham (2016). https://doi.org/10.1007/978-3-319-41000-5_52
19. Tuba, E., Tuba, M., Dolicanin, E.: Adjusted fireworks algorithm applied to retinal image registration. Stud. Inform. Control **26**(1), 33–42 (2017)
20. Tuba, E., Jovanovic, R., Beko, M., Tallón-Ballesteros, A.J., Tuba, M.: Bare bones fireworks algorithm for medical image compression. In: Yin, H., Camacho, D., Novais, P., Tallón-Ballesteros, A.J. (eds.) IDEAL 2018. LNCS, vol. 11315, pp. 262–270. Springer, Cham (2018). https://doi.org/10.1007/978-3-030-03496-2_29
21. Tuba, M., Bacanin, N., Beko, M.: Fireworks algorithm for RFID network planning problem. In: Proceedings of the 25th International Conference Radioelektronika, pp. 440–444, April 2015
22. Zheng, S., Janecek, A., Tan, Y.: Enhanced fireworks algorithm. In: 2013 IEEE Congress on Evolutionary Computation, pp. 2069–2077, June 2013
23. Zheng, S., Li, J., Janecek, A., Tan, Y.: A cooperative framework for fireworks algorithm. IEEE/ACM Trans. Comput. Biol. Bioinf. **14**(1), 27–41 (2017)
24. Li, J., Tan, Y.: Enhancing interaction in the fireworks algorithm by dynamic resource allocation and fitness-based crowdedness-avoiding strategy. In: IEEE Congress on Evolutionary Computation (CEC), pp. 4015–4021, July 2016

25. Chang, C.C., Lin, C.J.: LIBSVM: a library for support vector machines. ACM Trans. Intell. Syst. Technol. **2**(3), 27:1–27:27 (2011)
26. LeCun, Y., Bottou, L., Bengio, Y., Haffner, P.: Gradient-based learning applied to document recognition. Proc. IEEE **86**(11), 2278–2324 (1998)

Author Index

Printed in the United States
By Bookmasters